MANAGER'S TOUGH QUESTIONS ANSWER BOOK

◆◆◆◆◆◆

Word for Word Responses for the Most Difficult Questions Managers Face

AL GUYANT ◆ SHIRLEY FULTON

PRENTICE HALL
Paramus, New Jersey 07652

Printed in the United States of America

10 9 8 7 6 5 4 3 2 1   10 9 8 7 6 5 4 3 2

ISBN 0-13-226515-X (C)   ISBN 0-13-226507-9 (PBK)

ATTENTION: CORPORATIONS AND SCHOOLS

Prentice Hall books are available at quantity discounts with bulk purchase for educational, business, or sales promotional use. For information, please write to: Prentice Hall Special Sales, 240 Frisch Court, Paramus, New Jersey 07652. Please supply: title of book, ISBN number, quantity, how the book will be used, date needed.

PRENTICE HALL
Paramus, NJ 07652

A Simon & Schuster Company

On the World Wide Web at http://www.phdirect.com

Prentice-Hall International (UK) Limited, *London*
Prentice-Hall of Australia Pty. Limited, *Sydney*
Prentice-Hall Canada Inc., *Toronto*
Prentice-Hall Hispanoamericana, S.A., *Mexico*
Prentice-Hall of India Private Limited, *New Delhi*
Prentice-Hall of Japan, Inc., *Tokyo*
Simon & Schuster Asia Pte. Ltd., *Singapore*
Editora Prentice-Hall do Brasil, Ltda., *Rio de Janeiro*

Dedication

To our spouses and best friends, John and Patti, for their support and love; and to our precious children Amy, Christy, Terri, and Maggie, who patiently tolerated the many months of isolation this book demanded of us.

Acknowledgments

We would like to give special thanks to Donald G. Fulton, who kept us from sinking below the high road and succumbing to negative thinking, confrontation, and contempt, especially when dealing with workplace jerks. After surviving 39 years and numerous bosses for *one company*, his insights and skills in handling difficult questions with finesse and compassion were invaluable. He was our barometer for prudence.

We also owe special gratitude to Susan Hartung, a battle-weary fighter in the trenches of corporate America, whose insightful contributions were numerous and clever.

We're indebted to the superior editing skills of Joseph Ferrare, a master sergeant in the United States Army. And to Don Johanning, Jim McDermott, Jack Hale, Professor Barry Stennett, Roger Shields, Professor Douglas Brown, Jack Teems, Trudy Jeffers, Professor Gary Villereal, D. M. Brown, and the many other human resource and management professionals who, via the Internet, generously reviewed chapters in their areas of expertise. Much of the book's improvement is due to the superb contributions of the aforementioned; however, we remain solely responsible for all errors, remaining flaws, and other embarrassments.

About the Authors

Shirley Fulton and Alan Guyant are partners in Capital Communicators Group, a national management training, communications services, and public relations firm based in Madison, Wisconsin. They are former television and newspaper journalists, managers of information programs for major state agencies, lobbyists, and consumer service and crisis communication managers.

The book is based on their popular seminar, presented to several thousand managers nationwide: *Thinking on Your Feet: Great Responses to Tough Trick and Hostile Questions.*

To learn more about their seminars, or to pose your own tough questions for their comment and analysis, call, write, or e-mail:

Capital Communicators Group, 833 Northland Drive, Madison, WI 53704
voice (608) 274-1638, fax (608) 238-9977

E-mail addresses:
Alan Guyant: aguyant@ix.netcom.com
Shirley Fulton: 75377,1234@compuserve.com
(Contact your Internet host to determine if you need a special prefix for these addresses; i.e., using INTERNET:aguyant@ix.netcom.com)

Introduction

WHAT THIS BOOK WILL DO FOR YOU

Show us one manager who communicates well and we'll show you several thousand who don't. Show us one manager who says the right things to employees, bosses, and clients under the glare of red-hot questions and we'll show you several thousand who burn with embarrassment after inflicting verbal harm and escalating conflict.

Knowing how to conduct yourself in today's fiercely competitive and downsized business environment is often tougher than knowing how to just plain do your job.

How do you react when a colleague intentionally says something wounding in front of others? What do you say to a boss who asks too much of you, without sounding incapable or disloyal? What do you say to an employee who says morale is bad, and you're the reason? What's the fine line between asking for what you rightfully deserve and inadvertently showing a presumptuous sense of entitlement?

Every day we face difficult questions from employees, bosses, clients, customers, and colleagues that can make or break us professionally. Handling tough questions is part of office politics. And all of us are part of our company's political system, whether we like it or not. Part of succeeding at office politics is knowing what to say when you're forced to sit on the hot seat.

Imagine always having an appropriate response. Imagine always knowing the right way to react to people who pose tough, trick, or hostile questions such as these:

❐ The boss demands to know why your projects are always late.

❐ An employee accuses you of favoritism.

❐ An angry client questions whether you'll reprimand a rude employee.

❒ A co-worker intentionally puts you on the hot seat in front of others.

❒ You have to bug people for their work, and they accuse you of harassment.

❒ You're the new boss and your former co-workers accuse you of selling out.

❒ The boss wants to know why you aren't doing a better job of delegating.

❒ You're accused of being politically incorrect.

How many of us can confidently and persuasively answer career-altering questions like these right then and there? Not many. Most of us lie in bed at night replaying over and over the frantic moment, gnashing our teeth at what we should have said. And wondering how we'll undo the damage from what we did say!

The *Manager's Tough Questions Answer Book* is your "thesaurus" of responses to common biting questions you're likely to face as a manager. It also gives you techniques that highly skilled communicators use to conquer questions that seek to damage, control, divide, or defeat. It shows you how to take control of questions and situations.

HOW TO USE THIS BOOK

The best way to use this book is to keep it handy and make it a permanent part of your desk collection. The book is designed so you can refer to it quickly at critical times. If you're like most managers who regularly face verbal challenges from employees, bosses, and customers, you'll probably find yourself referring to it often in the coming months.

Here are some Tips on how to get the most out of the *Manager's Tough Questions Answer Book:*

1. *Keep in mind that the main purpose of this collection is to generate ideas.* It's not designed to put words in your mouth as much as thoughts in your head. Use the answers as a starting point, or a hint on how to construct your own great responses.

2. *Read the book (or at least seriously scan it) from cover to cover.* This will give you some valuable insights on why certain responses are so effective.

It will also acquaint you with the categories of questions so you can refer to them quickly. When you see responses or methods that interest you, look for cross-reference notes that refer you to related comments elsewhere in the book.

     3. *Use the work sheets at the end of each chapter to test yourself often.* Refer to a tough question you might face, scan the recommended responses, and adapt one to fit your situation. Jot it down on the work sheet for future reference.

     4. *Revise answers so they fit your own conversational and managerial styles.* If it sounds foreign or stilted to you, it certainly will sound that way to others. After you get the idea of what a response is trying to convey, use words you are comfortable with. Just make sure you don't revise the "strength" out of the response.

     5. *Be as specific as you can in your practice responses,* but pay special attention to the difference between an answer and a response. As demonstrated in Chapter 1 and frequently throughout this book, **a response gives you something to say without giving yourself away.** That point is an intentional redundancy in parts of the book to help drive the point by showing you the many ways it can—and should—be done.

     6. *Remember that these methods and model responses reflect many years of experience.* As you ponder the suggestions and advice in this book, be aware that they were derived from thousands of experiences by many managers in public and private organizations throughout the United States and Canada. In addition to their own experiences, the authors drew upon the lessons learned by skilled managers the authors have met over the years and via the Internet. The authors are not saying these methods are the "right" ones, but they do say the techniques illustrated in this book have been effective countless times for many thousands of successful managers.

     7. *Contact the authors if you have questions or comments.* The authors want you to be delighted with this book. If you have questions or comments, you may reach us by Internet e-mail, phone, fax, or postal mail. We would be particularly interested in receiving brief summaries of the toughest questions you've faced and what responses you felt worked. Or, tell us about tough questions you may face but for which you haven't found a suitable response. See the Authors' page for details on contacting us.

Contents

PART 1

1

KEY STEPS IN MASTERING TOUGH, TRICK, OR HOSTILE QUESTIONS   3

2

BRIDGING FORMULAS THAT REALLY WORK   19

3

EXPLOITING WEAKNESSES IN TOUGH QUESTIONS   33

4

DON'T THROW FUEL ON THE FIRE:
KEEPING INCENDIARY WORDS OUT OF YOUR RESPONSES   45

8

COLLARING STAFF WHO GO OVER YOUR HEAD   83

9

DEFENDING YOUR DECISION TO PROMOTE YOUNGER WORKERS   95

10

HANDLING DIVERSITY QUESTIONS EFFECTIVELY   103

11

GOOD REASONS WHY YOU DIDN'T DO MORE   115

12

STAYING SAFE WHILE RESPONDING TO AN OVERLY DEMANDING BOSS   123

13

ANSWERING UP WHEN YOUR BOSS FORGETS HIS OWN ORDERS   131

14

DEFENDING YOURSELF DURING AN UNFAIR JOB EVALUATION   139

15

DISCIPLINING A DISGRUNTLED EMPLOYEE WHO DOESN'T MEASURE UP   153

16

FACING DIFFICULT PLEAS WHEN FIRING NEW EMPLOYEES   165

17

SURVIVAL RESPONSES AMID NEPOTISM, CRONYISM, AND FAVORITISM 175

18

HOLDING FIRM WHILE INSISTING ON ALCOHOL/DRUG-ABUSE HELP 183

19

SUCCESSFULLY REBUTTING DRESS-CODE QUERIES   201

20

HANDLING CUSTOMERS WHO GRILL YOU ABOUT EMPLOYEES' MISTAKES   209

21

SERVING WELL EVEN WHEN ACCUSED OF BEING "THE BIG BAD BUREAUCRAT"   217

22

23

24

25

26

REDUCING THE AGONY FROM PAINFUL LAYOFF QUESTIONS   281

27

FORTHRIGHT REPLIES TO CALM DISTRUST AFTER LAYOFFS   291

28

AVOIDING THE DAMAGE OF THE BLAME GAME   299

29

SHIELDING YOURSELF FROM QUESTIONS ON GUILT AND LIES   305

PART 1

1

Key Steps in Mastering Tough, Trick, or Hostile Questions

If you've ever been pinned to the wall by an unexpected attack from a co-worker, boss, or client, you know the gut-wrenching stress that comes from having to defend yourself on the spot. It's an exasperating struggle to find the right words to ease the tension and gain understanding instead of using ridicule or blame.

Most of us simply aren't accustomed to having to defend ourselves with "brief" responses, which is about all we're allowed in today's frenzied business climate. And once out the lips, it's darn hard to take back an unintended comment. More than one career has been made, broken, or stalled because of a poorly handled reply to an unexpected question.

These first four "theory" chapters show you how to minimize or altogether avoid falling victim to tough, trick, or hostile questions. They outline key steps and techniques for gaining control of the momentum of questions so the emphasis is on your positive information. These techniques are demonstrated throughout the book in actual responses to specific questions that managers typically face.

People make a lot of embarrassing comments when responding under the stress of vexing questions. When we're under attack, our defenses kick in and our anxiety pumps urgent messages to the brain recommending "fight or flight." It's a natural human reaction to want to deny, lie, evade, or strike back in return.

Sometimes those actions work, but usually they produce miserable results. This book demonstrates effective alternatives. It demonstrates how the art of mastering tough questions can be learned by anyone.

But don't mistake technique for substance. Don't think that rhetoric alone can succeed under the fire of hostile questions. Don't become one of those managers who foolishly believes that a few tricky techniques will make him or her a silver-tongued executive. These managers fantasize themselves sidestepping verbal bullets like the James Bond character who dances unharmed among machine-gun fire and exploding bombs. In real managerial life, you can't avoid all verbal wounds. Nevertheless, your wounds don't have to be many, or fatal to your career or public standing.

To adequately defend yourself, you ought to have both substantive information and a good grasp of the methods set forth in this book. You intuitively know this already; think of the times you thought of the perfect rejoinder—ten minutes too late. You had the substance at hand but not the technique. Skillful rhetoric combined with substantive responses will make your words powerful.

1.1 TAKING STEPS TO MASTER HOSTILE QUESTIONS

Mastery over hostile questions is not difficult to learn. Once you've done some practicing, it will come naturally, as it does for many people who are widely admired for their skills in communicating during controversy. But they didn't get their skills by luck. Learn the few techniques the excellent communicators you know have mastered, practice them regularly, and you will surprise yourself by how comfortable you feel with your responses.

1.2 UNDERSTANDING TOUGH QUESTIONS LEADS TO MASTERY

To master hostile questions, the first step you must take is to understand them. You must realize that many tough questions are not inquiries at all. They are attacks, plain and simple.

They may attack your

- ❐ Cause, plan, logic
- ❐ record, actions, omissions
- ❐ organization, role, position
- ❐ expertise, credentials, character
- ❐ premise, assumptions, information
- ❐ and anything else in range

Most hostile questioners do not seek information alone, if at all. They usually attempt to damage, divide, embarrass, or defeat either you or your organization. They are more like moves in a chess game than like a discussion. If you treat them as a discussion, you lose. So, if they aren't really questions, how does a manager answer them? (See section 21.1 for related comments.)

1.3 THE ADVANTAGE OF A RESPONSE OVER AN ANSWER

Understanding hostile questions will help you learn why a response is often better than an answer. A response gives you something to say without giving yourself away. In this context, a response includes what *you* want to say, not what you think you are supposed to say (answer). Answers deal only with the literal meaning of the question but a response goes deeper by addressing major concerns surrounding the question. You will leap forward in your command of tough questions when you grasp this point.

Forget what your elementary school teacher said when she told you to "answer the question." You don't have to "answer" anything, unless you choose to do so. This doesn't mean you should never answer. Just remember that you have a CHOICE—answer or respond.

As a manager, you frequently have legitimate reasons for not giving direct answers to hostile questions. Because most hostile questions include attacks, you have legitimate reason to treat them as the threats they are.

Tough questions can be difficult to answer for as many reasons as there are people who throw barbs at you. Perhaps intense or angry feelings prevent you from being as open or as factual as you'd like. There's no way to say "I'm firing you because I just plain don't like you!" or "I'm not finished with the report because it was a stupid request on your part to begin with and not worth my precious time!"

Other times you may not have an immediate answer, but know you should say something. Consequently, you're stuck between the proverbial rock and a hard place. This is where half-truths, lies, exaggerations, and guesses can unwittingly spill from even the most honest among us.

So what's the alternative? You need a response that will change the other person's perception of objective reality (the facts). Don't mistake that for being dishonest or deceptive. Objective reality is the hard facts of a situation, and each of us forms a different perception of a set of facts or objective reality. The perception isn't reality or the "truth." Therefore, leading a person to a new perception is merely asking that person to see reality or the facts from another viewpoint, or perception. The facts don't change, just our opinion of them.

Consider the difference between an answer and a response regarding a delay in one your assignments:

Hostile question: "Why aren't you making more progress?"

Here's what an answer limited to the literal question might sound like:

"Our committee has met three times and hasn't agreed on which solution to implement. Some committee members have offered recommendations that other members strongly oppose. We don't know when we are going to reach agreement."

Now notice how the following response addresses both the cause of delays and the underlying concern of what it will take to make progress, which is really the primary issue.

Response: "These are complex problems, and there aren't any instant cures. The committee members have different backgrounds and have pretty diverse viewpoints. It's taking more time than we expected to sort through it all. But we all agree that we want to do it right the first time. We meet again Thursday to narrow down the recommendations."

See the difference? The first quote simply answers the question and leaves a perception of contentious bickering. The response, however, addresses underlying factors and portrays the committee as a group of knowledgeable but varied people struggling to solve a difficult problem. The response also builds a perception of things getting done.

An effective response gives the listener the right fact and the right feeling. It tells the truth, but goes further. It gives depth, justification, and understanding. Here's another example of a response:

> **Customer:** "I told you that your employee treated me rudely. Are you just going to let him get away with that?"
>
> **Manager:** "I believe that you have been offended, and I promise you this will not happen again. I'm going to look into this as soon as we're done talking here. That is not the way our associates have been trained to deal with customers."

The manager accepts the customer's view (perception) but without condemning a possibly innocent employee. She does not answer whether she will discipline the employee as the customer expects. The manager's response promises action and assures the customer that the company maintains high standards of treatment.

Imparting the right feeling like this is easy once you get the hang of it. What's important is that you keep sight of your goals and how you want the other person to react based on the perception. (Refer to sections 14.2, 20.1, 30.2, and 33.2 for examples.)

1.4 SETTING GOALS— MAINTAIN, SWAY, AND NEUTRALIZE

If you don't know what your goals should be in your responses, you are guaranteed not to achieve them. You will fumble around and look confused, because you are. You cannot master a tough question if you don't take the step of setting a goal for your response. Response goals don't have to be complicated or terribly difficult, but you must have one if you want to win instead of lose.

The easiest way to begin setting goals for your responses is to take a lesson from the public relations, advertising, and political strategists, who believe there are three powerful and attainable goals for swaying and holding opinion.

❏ Maintain the support you already have.

❏ Sway the undecided.

❏ Neutralize the unreachable.

Here's a brief summary of these notions, and how they apply to the workplace:

1. *Maintain the support you already have.* Your responses should include points your friends can use to maintain and build upon their support for you and your views. Your supporters are your political base, and like it or not, office politics is much the same as governmental politics, only smaller. You need a base of friends and supporters to succeed.

2. *Sway the undecided.* Issue strategists believe that perhaps 80 percent of the public is ambivalent on an issue, not caring one way or another and not likely to pay much attention to discussion. That leaves 10 percent who are pivotal. They are concerned, but not fanatical or interested enough to pay attention to the discussion.

Your workplace is probably no different. Your audience may well include a few key people who haven't yet formed an opinion, at least not a strong one, but who are interested enough to have an open mind and pay attention to your ideas. It is doubly important if these people belong to the "dominant coalition"—individuals who are the opinion leaders and power centers of your organization. (Refer to section 7.2 for related comments.) Add to your response key facts and words that appeal to the reason and emotions of the undecided.

3. *Neutralize the unreachable.* On any given issue there tend to be people with extreme viewpoints. Their hold on their opinion is strong, and they aren't likely to be swayed. Society often refers to them as fanatics, zealots, and extremists.

This is also true of the workplace. People with relatively the same knowledge, background, and experiences can be all over the spectrum on a policy, program, or idea. Don't try to persuade the unreachable. It's better that your response neutralizes them so they don't undermine the support you're getting from the first two groups. Here's an example:

> "Some very knowledgeable and well-intentioned people on one end of this issue are saying we are doing too much. Some very knowledgeable and well-intentioned people on the other end are suggesting we are doing too little. I'm proposing we choose a middle ground that will enable us to do what's *just right.*"

So according to this theory, changing opinion doesn't mean your response must transform the viewpoint of the entire group. It doesn't mean your comments must even directly change the viewpoint of a majority. Changing a group's viewpoint starts out by creating responses that convince a comparatively small number of aware but passive people—as few as 10 percent—to reflect on the question and form an opinion they haven't had.

How do you reach this pivotal 10 percent?

❐ Avoid confrontation.

❐ Focus on the positive.

❐ Direct your responses at those who have an identifiable self-interest in the subject.

❐ Tie your message to the context of the audience: What's in it for them?

❐ Pay particular attention to those who belong to your organization's "dominant coalition." They are the ones who grasp the seriousness of the issue and can get others to follow. See section 7.2 for more on dominant coalition.

❐ Keep control of your emotions so you are not reacting to hostile questioners (and thereby being controlled by them).

❐ Push the right emotional buttons that will generate cooperation and understanding.

❐ Avoid words and phrases that inflame emotions even more.

To maximize the power of your responses, include the three major persuasive factors found in most great comments, ranging from a sentence to a full speech. These three factors are:

Logos: Logic, facts, numbers, analyses, studies

Pathos: Emotions, feelings, illustrative examples, personal experiences

Ethos: Ethics, standards, rules, laws, mores, and other behavior codes

If you just throw facts at people, their minds tire quickly of listening to you. They may think your comments are "just a bunch of numbers that don't mean anything." But if you have only emotions or examples, your comments lack the depth that numbers can provide. Even with the logic of numbers and the feeling from examples, however, your responses need something to tell the listener what is normal or what's too extreme. That is why you need a reference to a code such as ethics, rules, laws, or other standard set by whatever community you are dealing with.

See Chapter 4 for more on inflammatory words. Also see sections 11.2, 11.3, 18.1, 23.2, 23.6, 26.5, 28.2, 29.2, 30.1, 32.3, and 33.1 for related comments.

1.5 TAKING CONTROL BY BRIDGING TO YOUR GOALS

Bridging is a tactic demonstrated throughout this book. It is the most important technique for mastering difficult questions. You've seen it used a thousand times by politicians, actors, reporters, and other skilled communicators. They consciously use bridging to steer discussions in the direction they want.

With bridging, you use a bridge of words to draw attention away from the question and direct it toward the points *you* want to emphasize (again, a response instead of a simple answer). Done right, the method transfers people's attention from your alleged mistake or problem to your correction or solution. After all, rarely do people remember the question after it's been asked; it's the response they remember. Bridging is the best means for doing that.

When you are being questioned, you almost always have at least some control over the situation, and perhaps more than you realize. Just as people feel the right to ask you just about anything they want, you, in turn, have the right to answer in any way *you* want.

After you have briefly addressed the tough question, you can use some of these effective bridging remarks in almost any circumstance. Sometimes you may judge it best to skip the first part and go directly to the bridge. Listed here are simple bridges.

- ❏ "I understand what you are asking; lots of people are concerned about that, but they need to know . . ."
- ❏ "An important point about that is . . ."
- ❏ "Your question is built on a common misconception. Let me explain the real problem . . ."
- ❏ "The heart of the matter really is . . ."
- ❏ "Actually, that relates to a larger concern . . ."
- ❏ "If you look at the larger picture . . ."
- ❏ "It's much more important to realize . . ."
- ❏ "That's one of many concerns about this issue; however, we're focusing on solutions, not just problems. One of the solutions is . . ."

If you just react to the questioner, he or she controls you. But bridging puts you back in control. With practice, you can bridge without appearing to evade the question. And don't evade for the sake of evasion. Done too often, it's annoying and eventually fails. Usually it's best to answer the query with a few words, then quickly bridge to your points.

Successful politicians (i.e., those who win reelection) learn early to employ bridging. Those who don't usually don't survive the political arena. Office politics are no different.

Points to remember:

- ❏ Bridging won't work every time—no method does.
- ❏ Bridging won't win over everyone—nothing does.
- ❏ Bridging will work *most* of the time for *most* people in *most* situations—nothing works better.

Proven bridging methods that boost your power over hostile questions are detailed throughout Chapter 2: "Bridging Formulas that Really Work." They are also demonstrated often in Chapters 5 through 33.

1.6 ACKNOWLEDGING MISTAKES TO GET PAST THEM

Common sense dictates that it's best to admit to a mistake, particularly when it's glaringly apparent to others. Don't pretend it didn't happen. Not admitting to an obvious error anchors everyone's attention to past mistakes. It prevents you from directing their attention to the future, where you have more influence. Unfortunately, millions of bad responses, regarding issues of all types, come about by a decision-making process lacking a critical element: common sense about the obvious.

Refusing to admit to an obvious mistake also encourages people to wonder what else you're hiding. In our society and workplaces, friends, bosses, and colleagues don't grant forgiveness until we confess and atone. Get rid of the drag by briefly acknowledging obvious errors; then bridge to corrective actions. Switch the focus to solutions as quickly as you can. See Chapters 28, 29, and 30 for sample responses and additional tips. See sections 14.3, 14.7, 23.1, 30.1, and 33.4 for specific examples.

1.7 SHOWING UNDERSTANDING TO GAIN MORE CREDIBILITY

One way to ensure that no one accepts your response is to ignore or insult other viewpoints. A common characteristic of an ignorant manager is his or her compulsive insistence on "we-versus-them" answers to complex questions.

This type of manager reduces everything to simple dualities—right or wrong, good or bad, friend or foe, guilty or innocent. The other person is guilty, shady, arrogant, selfish, stupid, misguided, and so forth. If you bring up something to discuss that the thick-headed manager doesn't want to hear, he or she bluntly says, "That's irrelevant. It doesn't have anything to do with anything." We have all worked for people like that. A manager who responds that way loses credibility fast, even with friends and supporters.

You, on the other hand, gain advantage with the people you seek to persuade by acknowledging other viewpoints as you respond. You gain credibility by demonstrating your respect of the other person's opinion. Our society deems it a virtue to have an open mind and show respect for other ideas. The virtue doesn't require you to agree with them, but to recognize them respectfully.

Recognizing other views will alleviate tension that blocks other people from listening to your responses. For example, how do co-workers, employees, and customers respond when their feelings and comments are ignored? With more intensity; they argue more, listen less, and yell louder. An acknowledgment won't eliminate their emotions completely, but it will reduce their determination to focus on them, again providing your response a better chance of getting through. See sections 2.1, 7.3, 15.2, 25.1, 26.4, and 33.4 for specific suggestions, and generally review Chapters 5, 25, 27, and 33 for model responses and detailed techniques that include the advantage of acknowledgments.

1.8 DEPERSONALIZING RESPONSES TO REDUCE CONFRONTATION

Just about everyone has learned to make letters and speeches more personal ("touchy feely") by using pronouns such as you, we, I, and us. Their use is intended to make recipients feel closer to the author or speaker. In apparent frustration over this, Mark Twain long ago wrote: "Only kings, editors and people with tapeworm have the right to use the inclusive word 'we.'"

In responding to hostile questions, however, you may not want to introduce an emotional connection. Use a general third-person statement to create a buffer space between you and the antagonist.

Hostile question: "Why don't you ever listen to me!"

Personalized response: "I listen to everything *you* tell me."

Depersonalized response: "I try very hard to hear what *any employee* has to say."

See how the personalized response intensifies the emotional stress between you and your antagonist. In contrast, the depersonalized response subtly creates a buffer space between the two of you by generalizing attention to any and all employees, not just the one in front of you at the moment. Another example:

Hostile question: "Is this chemical leak responsible for our illnesses?"

Personalized response: "I don't doubt *you* have these illnesses. *I* do doubt your illnesses are caused by the chemical leak."

Depersonalized response: "I don't doubt *some people* have illnesses. But testing by both government and independent laboratories has not detected a link between the two."

The depersonalized response is less confronting because it does not directly threaten the questioner as the first response does, "*I* do doubt *your* illness. . . ." If the questioner wishes to challenge your *de*personalized comment, he must begin talking about distant third parties. Even that would help you further because it keeps the focus away from the questioner.

In the second example's personalized response, the respondent unnecessarily takes on responsibility for the government's position that there is no proven link between the illnesses and chemicals. By doing so, she invites criticism directed at her also, which otherwise could be limited to the findings reached by other people.

Which is better, personalized or depersonalized? Neither. What works for a given situation is best, and what aggravates it is not. If creating a closer feeling will help establish rapport and not likely threaten the questioner, then a personalized response probably will help you master the tough questions.

However, if your response will refute the questioner so strongly that he or she will be intimidated, you may be better off using the third-person depersonalized approach. In regard to deciding whether you should use personal pronouns in responses, consider the rule of thumb for journalism (and, some say, surgery, too), which says, "When in doubt, take it out." See sections 5.2, 6.1, 13.1, 19.1, and 32.1 for additional examples of personalized and depersonalized responses.

1.9 THE TACTICAL ADVANTAGE OF TELLING THE TRUTH

When you formulate a response, don't say it if it isn't so. That isn't a lesson in morality; it's excellent tactical advice on handling tough questions. If you decide on the spot to starting lying, you immediately weaken your capability to win the contest.

While you already know the truth, you don't know much about other information that you'll have to instantly invent to support your false statement as follow-up questions are thrown at you. At that point, you have to remember the first false statement, invent new information to support the first one, remember the new false information, and also think of what methods you will use to respond. Not even an Olympic gymnast could keep his or her balance very often with that much to handle.

The methods and responses in this book assume you will tell the truth. If the idea of telling the truth frightens you, your problems go far beyond your need for skill in handling tough questions. Again, you need substance and skill; having only one of the two won't work. The realization that you don't have good answers because you don't have good policies or programs should be a red flag. Consider making changes or improvements so you can justify your actions when the tough questions hit. Refer to sections 11.2, 33.1, and 33.4 for additional examples and comments.

1.10 BUILDING SKILLS BY PREPARATION, PRACTICE, PATIENCE

If you read a diet book but never act on its advice, would you lose a pound just because you read the book? Of course not, and the same principal holds true with mastering tough, trick, and hostile questions. Just reading this book but taking no action will not make you a skilled master of verbal gamesmanship. You must put your good intentions into action by building skills through preparation, practice, and patience.

Use the work sheets at the end of each chapter to reinforce what you have learned. Taking a few minutes to do that after reading a new chapter will ingrain this knowledge in your mind for years to come.

If you want to develop even more sophisticated tough-question capabilities, then get your own tough questions Tool Kit. To assemble your kit, get a stack of index cards, a rubber band, and a pencil (not pen). This is your tool kit. Don't be deceived by its simplicity—great things don't have to be expensive or complex. (Hey, that's a great response to a tough question.)

On one card, write down a thorny question that you'd have trouble answering. Using only pencil, on the back of the card jot down a few points you might include in your responses. This is only draft, and you're using pencil, so you can and should change them later. Don't try to get it perfect at this point or you'll lose the entire effect.

The beauty of this method is that the small space of the 3×5-inch card forces you to be brief, so keep it brief. Repeat this process with several more troublesome questions—one question per card. Place the rubber band around the cards and carry them and a pencil with you for the next few days. When you have a few moments, pull out a card, ask yourself the question and practice giving your answer *aloud* but without reading it.

Do you doubt that you can boil down your message to the limited space of a 3×5-inch card? Is your message so complex and important that you require at least one full sheet of 8×11-inch paper? If you think so, consider the phrase that "all emphasis is no emphasis." If you don't select a few points to be most important, your listeners will make the selection for you, or they'll ignore you. If leaders of government and corporations can learn to reduce the message to its bare essentials, so can you, if you practice. (Refer to sections 14.4, 16.2, 18.7, 33.1, and 33.5 for additional comment.)

1.11 USE WORKSHEET, TOOL KIT TO EXPAND REPERTOIRE

Practicing with the worksheets and your tough-questions tool kit will expand your repertoire of great responses. Make extra copies of the worksheets as you progress through the book, so you'll have extras on hand for convenient practice. Because practice will embed the new responses in your long-term memory, they will be available to you instantly any time you're caught off guard. It's a great confidence builder. Almost certainly you'll be less defensive.

Finally, the most important reason for taking time to prepare is to make the mistakes during your preparation so you don't make them, or as many of them, when the real time comes. A sports team practices so it makes its mistakes *before* the game, not during it. (Refer to section 15.2 for related comment.)

1.12 AVOIDING DISCOURAGEMENT

Be nice to yourself in your efforts to master tough questions. Be patient. You are developing new thinking habits while embedding new response phrases into your memory. It will take awhile to create responses that you will like and will be comfortable with.

Moreover, it takes time to break old habits that you used to use in making impromptu responses and then replace them with new habits from this book. Although you are building new habits, you should not try to become like someone else whom you may admire for his or her skills in handling tough questions.

Always be *you*. If you try to act like someone else while you are also trying to think of crucial responses while under hostile fire, you probably will mess up your replies or your act, one of the two. You will either come across clumsy or you'll sound phony and insincere. So just be yourself while you concentrate on the method and substance of your responses.

Be patient. Don't be discouraged by the first few times you feel awkward about employing your new skills. They will come quickly enough; just keep preparing and practicing.

2

Bridging Formulas that Really Work

You can take control of hostile questions and turn them around to actually help instead of harm you. The all-time best method for that is "bridging." With this technique, you use a short phrase or sentence to respond to the threatening question while you deftly move attention to the points you want to get across.

When you are under fire, it may seem too difficult to implement bridging, but you can do so easily by putting a few formulas to work. Bridging formulas are simple frameworks or speech patterns to which you add your important information. Skilled use of these formulas will help you avoid the trap many people under fire fall into: rambling aimlessly while stumbling around trying to figure out simultaneously what to say and how to say it, and often burying main points and boring listeners.

Don't confuse the formula for the content; a formula shows you only how to mix and deliver information. But you have to have substantive content for it to be effective. This chapter provides many impressive bridging formulas for you to test. Find a few that fit your style. Practice them, and after a while they'll come naturally to you.

2.1 REMOVING BARRIERS WITH 3-STEP EXPLANATIONS

If they aren't listening, they can't hear you. The best response in the world won't help if the people you want to reach are too upset to listen.

This three-step bridging formula ranks among the best ever for removing emotional barriers that can block your message. In three short response sentences you can regain your critics' attention while steadily and convincingly moving toward your explanation.

1. "I understand what you are asking and why it concerns you so much."

2. "Other people who had your experiences probably would feel the same way."

3. "However, I would like to explain a little about this problem . . ."

Each step in this response formula can achieve very specific results when a manager is confronted with hostile inquiries. The first step (I understand) tells the questioner that you have heard him. She realizes that she doesn't have to yell expletives to gain your attention. You've said, in effect, I have heard you and I'm listening. Countless surveys show that customers and employees often feel that "no one is listening;" therefore this step is important for regaining her attention.

The second step (others would feel the same) tells the angry questioner that it's okay for her to think that way. She's normal, because other people (our frame of reference in life) would think the same if faced with similar circumstances. The second step can lessen the emotional barricade even more, because you've told her she isn't insane for saying such things.

It's risky to make the second step more personal by saying, "If that happened to me, I would feel the same way." Although that may make both of you feel like great buddies, it may also cause the listener to jump to the conclusion that since you would feel the same way, you must be agreeing with her point of view. By saying "others" would feel the same way, you reduce the chance of that misunderstanding.

The first two steps regain the angry questioner's attention. Now you are ready for the third step—leading to your explanation. Keep control of the floor by immediately going into your explanation; don't pause for a moment.

Picture yourself with a new employee whose work is not meeting your expectations. You have just told him that he must improve or he won't pass probation. He really needs the job and feels he isn't being treated fairly.

> **Tough question:** "I work very hard and don't goof around. How can you make that judgment when you see only part of the work I do?"

> **Three-step response:** "I *understand* that you work hard, and I haven't seen you standing around wasting time. *Other new employees* in your situation probably would *feel the same* way you do. Your job is just as important to you as anyone's job is to them. However, working hard by itself isn't enough; *each employee needs to produce results that meet company standards.* You have not done that yet. So let's focus on what you need to do so the quality of your work improves and you keep the job we both want you to have."

This three-step formula works superbly as a prelude to other bridging formulas. It is also a great stall when you need more time for your panic-stricken brain to assemble an intelligent response. See the end of this chapter for a list of great short stalls.

2.2 CREATING RAPPORT WITH FEEL-FELT-FOUND FORMULA

Like the three-step explanation formula, the feel-felt-found formula makes your response personal while creating a rapport between you and the hostile critic. However, the feel-felt-found formula brings you closer emotionally to the questioner.

With this method, you tell the questioner that you have some idea of how he feels, and that you have felt similar concerns yourself. If done honestly, you may impart to the critic that the two of you share common feelings, which may help both of you understand each other better.

Once the rapport has been established, you should move to the third stage. There you note what you have found to be true in your past experiences, which were inferred in the I-have-felt part of the response. Don't overreach using this formula. For example, if you are a middle-class white male talking to a low-income African-American female struggling to get out of poverty, you cannot feel what she feels. But that doesn't mean you can't understand some of her problems (rent, food, car repairs, etc.).

Make sure your attempt with feel-felt-found is based on genuine common experiences. Think of what it would be like to tell a young employee that her position is being eliminated as part of company-wide job reductions. She is very fearful of what will happen to her.

> **Tough question:** "Why did you guys bother to hire me if you knew that this might happen? Why couldn't you have at least told me a couple of months ago so I could have started looking for a job?"

> **Response:** "I'm sorry this is happening. I feel I know what you are going through because it happened to me years ago. I felt the same way myself when I lost my job. I won't kid you and say it's easy, but I found that when it was all over I could see that it wasn't as bad as I thought it would be. It's hard for awhile, but there are lots of ways to cope and move on to other jobs as thousands of people do every day. . . ."

When used with sincerity, the feel-felt-found formula is one of the best responses for creating a productive dialogue based on the common understanding revealed in your response. As it is true that success breeds more success, initial understandings can lead to more understanding and then agreement. (Refer to sections 19.4 and 33.1 for additional examples and comments.)

2.3 STARTING SAFELY WITH PAST-PRESENT-FUTURE FORMULA

One of the easiest and safest bridges is past, present, future. When asked a tough question for which you don't have a ready answer, use this formula to safely draw people's attention away from the past problem and move it toward the future solution.

Past: Tell what happened.

Present: Explain what's happening now.

Future: Outline what may happen next.

One advantage of this formula is that when you are ambushed by a really hostile inquiry, you can buy extra seconds to gather your thoughts by actually explaining how you are going to respond at that moment.

"I understand your question. I'm going to summarize what happened, what's happening now, and what I expect may happen next. . . ."

When used to the fullest, the past-present-future moves everyone's attention powerfully to the future. As an example, when a utility shut off electricity to an elderly woman in the middle of winter, contributing to her death, things looked very bad for the utility. Here's how one of its managers used the past-present-future formula most effectively.

Hostile question: "How could you make a mistake like that?"

Response: "The accidental disconnection was a tragic mistake, and we take responsibility for it. We have expressed our sincere regret and condolences to the family and offered any assistance. We will be reviewing all of our procedures *to see what changes need to be made so nothing like this can happen again.*"

In a few words, the manager did a remarkable job of bridging from the terrible incident in the past to the "positives" in the future. She sincerely apologized for the mistake, moved on to present corrective actions, and then to future solutions. You certainly want to consult with your lawyer before admitting a mistake like this, but remember to balance the court of public opinion with the court of law—both deliver verdicts.

The big benefit of this approach is that it rarely backfires but almost always allows you to fill awkward silences until you've thought of a good rejoinder. Make sure you don't waste too much time on explaining, apologizing, or defending. You'll lose the precious seconds you need to maintain support and sway the undecided. Don't ignore the past; but don't dwell there very long because you want to move the focus to the "solutions" you have to offer for the future. See sections 7.3, 14.7, 20.3, 21.1, 23.1, and 23.6 for specialized examples.

2.4 FAST RESPONSE WITH PROBLEM-TO-SOLUTION FORMULA

The method that moves the fastest from the hostile question to your positive-response goals is the problem-to-solution formula. With just a few words, you acknowledge a problem exists and then immediately switch to the solution without spending time on explaining the problem. You might even say, "I agree we've got a problem, but I'd like to go directly to a proposed solution."

Sometimes this method can turn a mistake into an opportunity for you to demonstrate something positive, like corporate responsibility. For example, when asked by passengers, employees, and the media to comment on the illegal dumping of waste into the ocean from a cruise liner, a company executive responded to environmentalists.

> **Hostile question:** "Don't you think you deserve to be fined for polluting?"

> **Response:** "The fine, if there is a fine, is of less importance to us than the actual incident being brought to our attention, because it allows us to take the appropriate action to ensure this doesn't happen again."

Can you see how this method has the extra benefit of not repeating the negative suggestions of the hostile question? Repeating the hostile words would only deepen a negative image, possibly establish it in the listeners' long-term memories. With this approach, you get deserved credit for being forthright and then extra credit for offering a solution (or at least mitigation). Refer to section 24.1 for another example.

2.5 CREATING SUPER RESPONSES WITH 4-STEP PCST

If you like the Problem-Solution approach and know you have at least two minutes to respond, try the more elaborate four-step formula: problem, cause, solution, timing (PCST). Using the four steps, you can build a more solid and persuasive reason for your listeners to accept and possibly agree with your response.

At a normal rate, you can speak 200 words in 2 minutes. A manager can say a lot in that time, if he is prepared and not wasting words.

> **Trick question:** "Why has your department missed its deadlines for the past three months?"

> **Response:** "We missed three of five deadlines despite some pretty hard work. The *primary causes* were vendors delivering supplies late and

two employees who were out on unexpected medical leave. One of the *solutions we're putting in place* is to call vendors to remind them of their obligation two days before we expect delivery. We are also pulling in an employee from another department; he used to handle this work and is very good at it. We've also gotten another employee to agree to postpone her vacation a month. We'll have the rest of the plan in place *by Friday."*

After directing everyone's attention to the solutions, you can exit by describing the three choices in timing to implement the solutions.

❐ Cite solutions that have been implemented.

❐ Point out solutions that are being developed.

❐ Forecast when future solutions will be ready.

Because this formula starts with "knowns"—a problem and then a cause, it allows you breathing room to pull together your thoughts while also building the foundation to support your solution and timing. The first two steps are safe, because you cite what generally is already known. It's the wording of the solution that needs a minute to take shape in the back of your mind. See sections 7.1, 14.3, and 23.8 for additional examples and comments.

2.6 DEFENDING AGAINST IGNORANCE WITH SIA FORMULA

Questions are even more difficult when the questioners don't know the background or understand the issues. The simplify-illuminate-advance (SIA) formula works effectively with critics who don't share your knowledge or appreciate the complexity of your work. Use this formula to help make their comprehension possible.

Simplify: You simplify the discussion in one or two sentences. Sometimes an analogy will achieve that.

Illuminate: You illuminate (reeducate) the antagonist explaining—in your terms—a few simple facts and principles that can be readily understood by most people.

Advance: The third and most important step is to advance your points, which help reveal the complexity of your assignments. The more you advance your points here, the more you undo the false premise that endangers you as long as it exists in the listeners' minds.

After you are sure that at least some of the listeners have understood your explanation, move to your recommendations. The first two steps obviously set up the listeners for the third.

> **Tough question:** "Doesn't the higher carbon dioxide level prove we have global warming that will damage crops?"

> **Response:** "The average CO_2 level is irrelevant without knowing the high and low of each day. It's like telling a cop who caught you speeding at 90 that your average speed since starting at zero was 45 miles per hour. What do the numbers mean? Well, the bottom line is that . . ."

SIA works best when you can prepare ahead of time. If caught off guard, you may want to employ one of the easier formulas. Refer to sections 25.2 and 33.3 for additional examples and comments.

2.7 GENERALIZATIONS OR SPECIFICS: ALL-PURPOSE ANTIDOTES

Two effective all-purpose antidotes to hostile questions are natural opposites: generalities and specifics. These are as easy to use as they are to remember. If your nemesis asks you a nasty specific question, you might be able to dodge it by employing generalities. In reverse, if you are attacked with a generalized inquiry, you may be able to overcome it by citing specifics.

> **General question:** "With all of the complicated statistical stuff involved in the Quality Improvement fad, and all of the QI failures in other places, how can you expect it to work here?"

> **Specific response:** "Some of the Quality Improvement methods can be pretty complex, but it doesn't always have to be that way to work well. If, for example, we look at how teams can be more effective than standing committees, we could gain a lot in that area alone. The advantage of teams is that they . . ."

Instead of responding to all the alleged problems of QI techniques, the preceding response goes from the general issue to a specific example in one sentence. Without pausing for anyone to interrupt, the response moves directly to illustrating the advantages of teams over committees. The specific response does not get stuck in the quagmire of the general condemnation but instead uses the hostile query as an opportunity to sell the best parts of the QI methods. Picture yourself as a listener at the table and think how much you would rather hear a short explanation of teams instead of a quarrelsome debate over alleged QI failures and numerous complex QI methods.

> **Specific question:** "Why do you want us to continue the team fad when we all saw that process bombed last year?"
>
> **General response:** "I certainly wish the QI teams would have worked better last year, but I also recognize that the team approach is like other QI methods that can produce great results once we master them. It has been proven in many organizations that efficiency and customer satisfaction can increase significantly when QI methods are fully developed."

In the general response, you move from the specific problem to broad generalities that contain many positive examples for you to bridge to. (Refer to sections 14.5, 14.6, and 32.1 for additional examples and comments.)

2.8 CONTROLLING DAMAGE WITH WRONG, RIGHT, AND WHAT IT ALL MEANS

When all hell breaks loose and tough questions bombard you from every direction, you may elect to employ this formula, which is akin to battle-field triage: Let go of what's gone and save what you can. This is called what we did wrong, what we did right, and what it all means.

You do this by letting go of issues that are damaged beyond hope. In other words, you don't defend what won't be accepted by the people who support you or the undecideds whom you wish to sway your way. Next, you point out what you have done right. This lays the foundation for re-building your image and status. You bring this all together by explaining "what it all means" to create a new perspective.

Here's a space agency executive using this formula.

Hostile question: "Doesn't this last failure mean the program is faltering?"

Response: "We do very difficult things, and sometimes we have failures. In 52 missions over the last five years, there were only three or four major failures. I don't think our charter is to guarantee 52 successes out of 52 tries, because it would say we're loading the deck and weren't pushing the boundaries."

Note that the response does not refute or explain away all of the criticism, which would be nearly impossible for anyone to do. But the space agency executive does create a feeling of prudence and then acceptance by using this formula to focus on the larger picture.

Inexperienced managers flounder when they futilely spend their limited response time trying to salvage what's damaged beyond repair. Not only do they fail to resurrect what's dead and gone, they waste short-lived opportunities to highlight what was done right. And they never get to the essential goal of giving their own perspectives about the problems. Those compelling reasons make it clear why this formula, or one like it, should be used when all hell breaks loose and you are left with saving what you can.

Sometimes you cannot escape tough questions without some bumps and bruises. Too often inexperienced managers fantasize that they could get away unscathed if they only knew a few clever lines of rhetoric. That is not true in real life. But you can do effective damage control with responses that cite what you did wrong, what you did right, and what it all means. (Refer to sections 14.3 and 30.1 for additional examples.)

2.9 TALKING ABOUT THE QUESTION IS LAST-RESORT BRIDGE

What about the awful moment when you don't know how or where to start a response? You don't have a good understanding of the problem and almost nothing about what caused it. You don't want to look foolish by misstating it. On the other hand, perhaps you know that merely listing the causes would be explosive. Maybe the solutions on the table are more like land mines than anything else. How do you handle this situation?

Simple. Talk about the question until you think of a bridge to a safe place. Talking *about* a question instead of answering a question is an art that successful high-level executives and politicians (is there a difference?) master early in their careers.

Talking about the question instead of the answer does not come without a price. It buys you time, but it will quickly irritate your questioners if that's all you do. Use this as a last resort.

How do you "talk" about a question without talking about the issue? Talk about the who, what, when, where, or how of the question itself. The following examples show how easy it is.

> "Your question is very *important to me;* I've been greatly concerned about it for a *long time.* As anyone can see, we must be very careful *how* we address this question. The implications are serious. You are asking about one of the most *important responsibilities* I have, and if we are going to talk about it now, we need *to consider . . ."*

> "The question you just asked touches on problems that worry a *lot of people I know. They* are asking some of the same questions. In order to answer them, we need to know more about *where* the problem exists and *how long* it really has been going on. We need the *best advice* we can get from *people* close to the problem itself. . . ."

> "That's one of those tough questions that's easy to ask but *extremely complicated to answer.* The *question is tied* to the experience and knowledge of hundreds, maybe *thousands of people* in dozens of *locations.* I've learned a lot from them, and I'm still getting more information."

> "With hindsight, I'm sure all of us wish we would have raised and answered that question *long ago.* It's obviously *time* we respond, because *it is too important* to delay much longer. At this *time,* I can provide a little insight but will have to *defer* other parts until we get more complete information. What I can say is that . . ."

Don't use the talk-about-the-question formula only as a dodge, because that approach won't work very well with most hostile questioners. This formula works best as a longer lasting stall while you organize your thoughts on how to bridge to the points you think up during the delay. Imagine you are in a board meeting and an outside executive catches you off guard by asking point blank why so many errors have appeared in your department's marketing brochure.

> **Hostile question:** "Have you even looked at the stuff you are mailing out? Does anyone bother to proof this embarrassing material?"

> **Response:** "You've asked a tough question that has to be answered. A lot of people have been asking themselves *how* those mistakes could

have gotten past our editing and proofing process. I'm sure our customers are wondering the same thing. And I have been concerned with *finding out what* needs changing or fixing so those errors are stopped. [Up to now, you haven't said anything substantive and therefore haven't made a substantive mistake. And now you find a bridge to get out of your predicament.] Although I wasn't prepared to talk about the brochure errors in detail today, I can say that, yes, we do look closely at marketing materials, yet obviously not well enough. However, we have begun looking more closely and more thoroughly at every item. We won't stop this effort until we fix the process *and the brochures come out error free.* I will keep you informed of our progress."

Of course, you can't keep the stall going for more than a minute or two, but that's plenty of time to collect your thoughts and build a bridge to safety. Try it a few times with co-workers. The effectiveness of this seemingly unglamorous formula is surprising the first few times you use it. (Refer to section 7.3 for a related comment.)

2.10 WHEN ALL ELSE FAILS, STALL SOME WAY, SOMEHOW

When absolutely nothing comes to mind, when no formula fits the question, your mind goes blank, and you are too upset to talk about the question, just stall for time somehow. It may seem like an hour, but stalling for 10 or 20 seconds can give your brain enough time to come up with something intelligent to say. If you try to speak substantively before you have come up with something worthwhile, you are guaranteed to fall flat on your face or your butt—take your pick, the result is the same.

Here are some of the time-tested stalls that work very well—indeed everyday—for people who are masters of handling tough questions. They provide examples of how to stall in different ways for the same question. (Refer to section 13.1 for related comment.)

❐ Restate the question as though you are clarifying it.

❐ Ask the questioner to clarify the question. (Then you can think awhile.)

❐ Rephrase the question to your favor.

❐ Use an opening phrase such as the following:

"I am frequently asked that question wherever I go." (Old cliché that still works.)

"I did not hear you clearly. Would you ask that again?

"I'll be covering that point shortly. . . ."

❐ Tell an anecdote about the issue.

"Before I answer that, I'd like to tell you a brief story about . . ."

Won't the questioner and other listeners see the transparent stalls? Perhaps, but so what? This is your last resort, and you don't have much to lose. The worst case is that someone would accuse you of stalling. Again—so what? You could say that, yes, you were stalling a moment so that you could collect your thoughts and say something a bit more intelligent.

Remember that your goals are to maintain the support you have and to persuade the undecided to believe you. Neither group will turn against you just because you use an obvious stall to compose yourself. Don't worry about the hostile, unreachable group. No matter what you say to them, they are determined not to like it. So don't bother trying to accommodate them in your response.

Although the stalls by themselves don't provide you with a framework on which you can hang your information as do the bridging formulas, the stalls nevertheless keep you in control of the conversation. As long as you control the flow of words, you limit the hostile questioner from beating you up more. The generic stalls also have the additional benefit of buying you time during which you can come up with something substantive. (Refer to section 7.3 for a related comment.)

2.11 IF NOTHING ELSE, TAKE CONTROL WHEN UNDER FIRE

When under fire from hostile questions, always remember to take control some way. This applies for every situation and formula given in this chapter. Even if you can't recall any of the formulas from this chapter, remember to tell yourself to take control in whatever way you can. If you don't, you will get mowed down eventually.

After you get control (even if only by asking for everyone's attention and patience for a moment), remember to think of a goal or direction where you want to take the discussion. Trust yourself to think of something. While it may seem like an eternity, most people will think of something worthwhile in about 20 seconds, which is typically how long most bridging formulas take, or how long most stalls will gain for you.

Be confident that you can and will get through the tough question. It can't last forever. And as long as you keep looking for bridges, you'll keep finding your way out of the hot spots.

3

Exploiting Weaknesses
in Tough Questions

No matter how intimidating they seem to be, all tough questions have weaknesses you can exploit. But before you can do that, you must first recognize the type of question you are dealing with. This chapter identifies and analyzes major types of hostile questions and demonstrates how to thwart them by taking advantage of their weaknesses.

Knowing this information will give you immense power over your hostile questioners. It's like being a fighter pilot with radar fighting an enemy who doesn't have it. You are able to see the shape of what's coming and thus will know how to maneuver out of harm's way while he can't see what's happening.

With the knowledge from this chapter, you'll find yourself saying mentally "Oh, yes, I recognize that type, and now I know just how I'll handle it. . . ."

3.1 THE BENEFITS OF DUCKING HYPOTHETICAL QUESTIONS

When you hear "what if," get ready to duck; a hypothetical question full of supposition and assumption is on the way. By answering a hypothetical question, you give the hostile questioner the chance to follow up with more "what ifs" until you finally stumble.

The weaknesses of hypotheticals are their unproved assumptions about the future. Because neither you nor the questioner is in control of the future, the best answer is to say you don't want to assume anything and you can't predict the future. Point out the "iffy" premise of the question, noting there are numerous uncertainties. Suppose you were at a department meeting to discuss your plan to overcome your section's production lag, and your nemesis asks this taunting question:

> **Hypothetical question:** *"What if* we have a lot of employee turnover next year or the union contract is changed? How can we be sure your section will meet its deadlines and not slip again?"

> **Answer:** "That's a hypothetical question based on a lot of unknowns. If any of those factors change, or if any other major surprises happen, we will have to regroup and adjust our plans accordingly. *But for today I'd rather stick to what I know for sure.* Let me explain my plan based on what we really do know. . . ."

The result of this response is that you'll get back on track quickly while also having adroitly resolved a tough question thrown at you in front of your peers. The first part of the comment presents a logical basis for *not* giving a substantive answer. The second part of the response swiftly moves everyone's attention back to where you want it to be, your proposals to catch up on the work schedule.

Another major benefit of this response is that you don't pause for the questioner to speak; you quickly bridge to where you want to go. In most cases, rules of etiquette will inhibit her from interrupting as you bridge back to your topic. However, if she ignores those and attempts to pull you back to the hypothetical question, others at your meeting may voice their displeasure at her wasting time discussing uncertainties that aren't relevant today.

But if the group or the meeting leader doesn't cut off her second effort, you can still avoid answering the hypothetical by turning it around. You do that by asking her what specifically she sees happening and why. Then you (and possibly others) may ask her to explain her predictions more, which probably will cause other colleagues present to voice their disagreements with some of her views. That puts the conflict between her and other staff present, but keeps you out of it.

However, if you choose (you always have a choice) that for some important tactical reason you want to answer the hypothetical, make sure you create a back door. Condition your answer like this:

> **Conditional answer:** "I really don't like to deal in hypotheticals because any big change in circumstances could alter my answer entirely. In response to your *hypothetical question, I'll give a hypothetical answer* that shouldn't be generalized to any other set of circumstances."

The conditional response gives you a back door through which you can easily escape hostile follow-up questions. If the challenger attempts to pick apart your hypothetical response, remind her that what you just said was hypothetical and the real answer depends on future circumstances that no one there knows. For additional examples and responses involving hypothetical questions, refer to sections 8.5, 22.3, and 24.5.

3.2 SIDESTEPPING THE TRAP OF SPECULATIVE QUESTIONS

The risky speculative question is a close cousin to the hypothetical question. Your antagonist asks you to speculate about a future outcome (while he's getting ready to argue with your answer). Speculative questions often include such traps as "Isn't it likely that . . ." or "What's your best guess. . .?"

Even if you are qualified to speculate, is this time the time and place to do so? If the questioner is being hostile toward you, then give him a response rather than an answer. Of course, there are many situations where speculative answers are fine, where you are free to openly discuss possibilities. But if you are in a situation where your antagonist may use your speculation against you, it's best to not give him a club with which to hit you in the first place.

Suppose you were talking with other managers and a few subordinates, one of whom had been a thorn in your side for years. He casually asks you about possible job cuts.

> **Speculative question:** "Whose job do you think will be eliminated? How many are going to be cut?"

Response: "We're talking about people's jobs and paychecks. *I don't want to speculate about something so important.* I want to be careful to keep my comments limited to what I know. I don't want to guess about something and cause unfounded rumors or worse."

In addition to the obvious rumor potential your answer would have, it would also likely become distorted as it was passed along the grapevine and back to the CEO's office. There is no planning or operational need for you to speculate whose job, if any, might be cut. The biggest benefit of this approach is what you don't get—a lot of grief later caused by your speculation about serious concerns, which fed rumors and emotional reactions.

The antagonist may not be pleased and suggest that you are holding back on what you know. If so, tell him that he is free to believe or not believe whatever he wishes; you still are not going to participate in potentially harmful and pointless speculation. The respect for you by others present probably will rise a notch as you demonstrate your character (not a rumor monger) and intelligence (smart enough not to walk into a trap). See sections 24.5 and 29.1 for more on responding to hazardous speculative questions.

3.3 GRABBING CONTROL OF QUESTIONS BASED ON MISQUOTES

The question based on a misquote of you ranks at the top of the "false premise" inquiries by employees, customers, bosses, and colleagues. The antagonist misquotes one of your earlier statements; she begins with "Well, didn't you just tell us that . . . ?" You realize she's got everything backwards and you can't let the misquote stand as truth. But how to do that without creating more tension?

If you say she wasn't listening, you start a second argument over whether she can prove she was paying attention. If you tell her she didn't quote you correctly, she may quarrel over how accurately she quoted you. Worse, you might sound as if you are calling her a liar.

If you tell her she didn't understand your comment, you imply she's pretty stupid, among other things. There is an honest and easy way out by using the question's intrinsic weakness. The question is vulnerable to the power *you* have to define what *you* meant to say.

Question: "How can you sit there and tell me that none of what I turned in was acceptable? Didn't you just tell me you haven't even reviewed it?

Response: "If that is what you heard, *I didn't say things very clearly.* I'm sorry it came across that way; it's not what I meant to say. Let me tell you what I intended to get across. . . ."

By taking the blame for the "misunderstanding," you regain control of the discussion. With that control, you restate your position. The questioner has little choice but to let you clarify what you meant to say. Even if you know for certain that you had spoken very clearly and the questioner really has gotten it all backwards, it does you no good to point that out to her. You would only create another issue to argue about. If you ever settled the second argument, you would still need to go back to try to settle the first.

By deftly sidestepping useless quarrels, you achieve a second chance to drive home your points. The questioner won't know what happened but will realize that she wasn't correct and hasn't got much to argue about either. Finally, your colleagues will be awed by your ability and ask you later "How'd you do that?" Refer to section 25.5 for an additional example and comment.

3.4 DISARMING LEADING QUESTIONS AIMED AT YOU

The name of this false-premise question implies its threat—it is loaded with something dangerous. Unless you disarm this question, it may blow up in your face.

The antagonist fills the query with negative terminology and suppositions that uninformed observers might believe unless you unload the question. The weakness in the loaded leading question is that you can dismantle it quickly by showing that its premise isn't correct. Having done that, you are free to take the conversation in any direction you want.

Be sure *not* to use the hostile questioner's negative terms in your response because that only reinforces the impact he's trying to have.

Hostile question: "With all the grievances filed against your division, why haven't you done something to improve the bad morale?"

Response: *"I want to correct the premise of your question.* The number of grievances in my division is about the same as others in the long run. I continue to meet individually with most of my staff, and most tell me things are going fairly well. We've had more incoming transfer requests than ever before. I'm looking forward to hiring some pretty good talent for the two new vacancies."

See how the response does not repeat the allegation, even when refuting the false premise. If you repeat a false premise, you drive it deeper into the minds of the listeners. The primary result from this approach is that you can dislodge the negative perception of "bad morale" with the picture of a manager on top of things and in communication with her staff. For more on turning around false-premise questions, see sections 9.2, 10.4, 14.1, 21.2, and 23.2.

3.5 BEATING "COATHOLDER" QUESTIONS WITHOUT FIGHTING

A "coatholder" holds your coat while goading you into a brawl with another person by claiming that person said something bad about you. Coatholders can be employees, colleagues, and even bosses who ask your reaction to harsh comments supposedly made about you by third parties.

Coatholder questions serve little purpose except to cause arguments and hard feelings. The weakness in the coatholder question is your convenient ignorance—you haven't heard the comment, so you don't really know what was said.

> **Coatholder's question:** "Al, did you hear that Mr. Benton said your cost estimates weren't worth the paper they're printed on?"

> **Response:** "Tom, I haven't personally heard that from Mr. Benton and I'd rather not respond to something like that until we've had a chance to talk. . . ."

If the coatholder got the gossip thirdhand and you want to be firm in your response, consider saying this:

> **Response:** "Tom, I don't know what Mr. Benton said, and really, neither do you. Let's not get ourselves in an uproar over rumors."

It takes strong self-discipline to make this method work, because your anger is triggered quickly upon hearing supposed slanders from absent parties. However, you will be glad you held your tongue. (Refer to section 29.2 for an additional example and comment.)

3.6 MAKING LIMITED-CHOICE QUESTIONS WORK FOR YOU

Some hostile questioners will try to corral you into a trap by building limits into the false premise. The either-or question insists there is only one way or another, and nothing in between (my way or your way).

The yes-or-no question demands the same choice. (The customer is right or wrong.) The weakness is obvious: Work problems are not that simple. The same goes for a question that is based on a premise that is too extreme to be credible. Step outside these questions by pointing out the false limitation.

> **Question:** "Either I work faster and make more mistakes or I go slower and have better quality. Which do you want me to do?"

> **Response:** "It may seem that it has to be speed or quality, *but those aren't the only choices.* We can go slow and do good work or bad, and it's possible to move faster and still maintain quality. If we keep doing the same things, yes, we'll get the same result. So let's look at doing the work differently and also try to save time while improving quality. We won't know until we review all the options."

Refer to sections 8.5 and 20.2 for additional examples and comments.

3.7 ANSWERING HELPLESS VICTIMS WITHOUT FEELING GUILTY

It's usually an employee or a frustrated customer who poses the helpless-victim question: "How can I live (feed my family, pay the rent, or do my job) if you let this happen?" The helpless victim wants you to feel guilty and use your power to help her in a way you shouldn't. Many helpless victims get through life by instinctively pushing off their responsibilities onto other people, often through pleading questions.

No doubt some of the helpless victims really have serious problems. Nevertheless it's a slippery slope once you step toward answering *what* they should decide or *how* they should solve their personal crises. Stick to your managerial roles and advise them where to get help with the other issues.

Is that being cold and uncaring? Not really. A helpless victim really doesn't want you to make her decisions or tell her what to do. Nevertheless, if you did answer the victimhood questions, and her subsequent actions led to more grief, whom do you think she will blame?

The weakness in the helpless-victim question is the hidden premise that tries to push the victim's responsibility onto you. Your response should show her where the responsibility is, and always will be—on the questioner.

> **Question:** "What am I supposed to do? Should I pay the rent first or make the car payment? Maybe you think my son should quit college and get a job?"

> **Response:** "I don't underestimate your situation; I know it's darn tough, but *only you can make decisions about running your life.* I can refer you to counselors who may help you make those decisions. My duty is to meet the responsibilities of this position. *Only you can answer the other questions.*"

Certainly you can offer to help someone and support her with whatever means you have, but that does not mean you should take on her responsibilities to make her own decisions and be responsible for her own life. Don't "enable" the helpless victim by answering her pleading questions with suggested decisions. Give options and choices but leave her responsible for deciding. (Refer to sections 15.1, 16.4, 16.6, 18.7, and 21.4 for additional examples and further comments.)

3.8 EXERTING POWER OVER MULTIPLE-PART QUESTIONS

New managers with little experience facing hostile questions tend to age rapidly when clobbered by multiple-part questions. Because the novice manager still believes she has to answer all the questions, the multiple-part query can cause real panic.

But learn to love multiple-part hostile questions, for they are kinder and gentler (and weaker) than all the rest. Why? Because you can pick the part to which *you* want to respond and ignore the rest.

Most questioners and listeners will not be able to recall what parts you don't answer, particularly if you bridge to something else. The more turbulent the discussion, the better this works.

Imagine you were at a raucous staff meeting, and a rival sniped at you.

> **Question:** "Why was your report so late, and how come I didn't get a draft to review? Are you really sure you've gotten enough input from other departments?"

> **Response:** "I sent an e-mail message to all eight departments, asking for their comments as soon as possible. I received two by Monday, and one really helped improve the report. Tom Getlewski said he wanted a new section of specific procedures. I agreed to meet with him. Would anyone here like to attend? *What do you think we should tell him we plan to discuss?"*

This response ignores the sniper's question of lateness and why he supposedly wasn't sent a draft copy. The response instead concentrates on your goal (showing that you asked for input) and then bridges to your meeting with Tom Getlewski. You thus picked the one part of the question you wanted to comment on, not the others that might damage you and open up new lines of trick questions.

If the sniper tries to get you back into the open field by returning to parts of the question you haven't answered, tell him you want to clear up this first point, then you'll get back to the others. Odds are you'll never get back to the sniper's hostile attack before time runs out at the meeting.

If the hostile questioner stubbornly won't relent in his antagonistic questioning, you can reverse the pressure by using a tactic often used by the Pentagon's military spokespersons. Sometimes when a lengthy multiple-part question is asked, one of the Pentagon staff takes down each part of the question. The spokesperson responds to each segment, at length. In a room full of reporters all wanting to talk—or at least get on with things—this turns the room against the questioner. It's something you should consider doing only as a last resort. If you really wish to get others in your meeting to turn against the hostile questioners' waste of time, make a point of taking down each part of the question, so you show how seriously you're taking the questions.

> **Beginning for lengthy response:** "You've asked a bunch of questions, so let me write them down so I don't forget. . . . Okay, you want to know why the report is late, why you haven't seen it, and if I got sufficient feedback from everyone. Does that cover it? Well, I hadn't planned to revisit every facet of this action in this forum, but if that's what everyone wants, I'll be happy to. I'll take them one at a time. . . ."

If it's not the boss asking, this would be a good time to look at the boss for guidance or approval, or to look around the room, giving people a chance to butt in and save you by saying this stuff should be handled in another forum. This also reinforces your role as the reasonable person. It also reinforces the perception that your antagonist is being unreasonable and keeping everybody from work, lunch, home, and hearth. If nobody saves you, and you see no other way out, proceed and keep smiling. Refer to section 25.7 for an additional example and comment.

3.9 NULLIFYING INSULTS OF ATTACK QUESTIONS

The insulting attack question isn't really a question: It is a direct attack put in question form. These usually come from angry customers or people who want to make you look bad by insulting you:

> "Don't you ever do anything right there?"

> "How the hell can you keep a job with such incompetence?"

> "Do you know what everyone thinks of your lousy service?"

Because the nonquestion is an attack, don't respond as though it were a question. Unless it is imperative to your job or organization to blunt the assault, simply ascertain the issue at hand and address just that.

Take a slow deep breath, ignore the insult, and discuss the facts and solutions.

> **Attack question:** "Aren't you supposed to 'serve' the public? Do you call this 'service'? Didn't anyone ever teach you how to do your job right?"

> **Response:** "Mr. Jones, your shipment was late because the delivery truck's transmission broke. I am very sorry this happened. By the time we got another truck over there, we were already late. I can't change that but I do want to make it up to you by . . ."

Too often new staff members and managers alike are compelled to feel they are supposed to answer the literal question. They futilely attempt to explain that they do serve the public quite well most of the time, or that they were trained thoroughly, and so on. But that only makes things worse, as it gives the angry customer more to argue about. Instead of lasting only 5 minutes, the unpleasant incident will go on for 30 minutes. And probably nothing will be settled then either. Indeed, the customer probably will be even angrier. Remember that attack questions are rhetorical, so just bear with the situation and respond to the main issue while the angry customer vents his emotion. Refer to sections 21.1 and 23.1 for additional examples and comments.

4

Don't Throw Fuel on the Fire:
Keeping Incendiary Words
Out of Your Responses

4.1 *You aren't paying attention. You aren't listening.*

4.2 *You should have . . .*

4.3 *That's irrelevant. That doesn't have anything to do with this. That question doesn't make any sense. Why in the world would you ask that?*

4.4 *You must . . . You have to . . . You have no choice . . .*

4.5 *That's not what I said at all. You really have that mixed up. I don't know how you could get that from what I said. You didn't quote me correctly.*

4.6 *That's not my responsibility. It's not my job.*

The words you choose for responding to tough questions can mean the difference between putting out a fire or fanning the flames higher. Angry questioners become incensed when they hear certain words or phrases they feel insult or demean them or otherwise make them look bad. They rarely think about the actual offending words; they just react at the emotional level.

Well, it should be easy then. Right? If you know a word or phrase might fan the flames of anger even higher, just don't say it! But it isn't that simple. Though this chapter lists many words and phrases you should avoid, just reading it won't do you much good by itself. Your vocabulary is deeply rooted with your speaking habits, developed over many years—words often pop out without much thinking.

When you are being hit by tough, trick, and hostile questions, your habits automatically take over as your emotions rise. Even if you could remember the words and phrases to avoid, it would be hard for you to avoid them. That's because you haven't developed and practiced other choices to build new habits. Take ten minutes to reread this chapter monthly for six months. Put it on your calendar as a reminder to replace the aggravating words and phrases with neutral ones. (Refer to section 13.1 for other comments on word and language choices.)

Here are words and phrases to avoid. Each one is followed by alternatives, but you will be better off if you modify them or invent new ones to suit your style. It is imperative to your effectiveness that your responses blend in with your natural speaking manner.

4.1. YOU AREN'T PAYING ATTENTION. YOU AREN'T LISTENING.

If you include these comments in your responses, you won't add one bit of information to the discussion, but it sure insults the listener. Who first used those scolding phrases? Your parents? An angry teacher? The phrase can make you sound like a bossy adult talking to a child.

Better alternatives:

"I may not have been clear when I spoke earlier, but I had hoped to say that . . ."

"I did explain that somewhat a bit earlier, but apparently I didn't get it across very well. Let me try again."

"Maybe you weren't able to hear me but I said earlier . . ."

4.2 YOU SHOULD HAVE . . .

These three words cause more unnecessary grief than almost any others. They tell the other person he failed to do something important, and now it's too late. They also make people feel inferior to the person who feels superior enough to claim others "should have." Additionally, they set the stage for additional argument, because the questioner may wish to explain in angry detail what he "shouldn't have. . . ."

Better alternatives:

"One option you could have considered . . ."

"One thing you could have done if you had the chance was to . . ."

4.3 THAT'S IRRELEVANT. THAT DOESN'T HAVE ANYTHING TO DO WITH THIS. THAT QUESTION DOESN'T MAKE ANY SENSE. WHY IN THE WORLD WOULD YOU ASK THAT?

These phrases hit the questioner with similar effects; they are like a slap in the face. They imply you think the questioner is too stupid to ask a worthwhile inquiry. Moreover, these comments callously dismiss the feelings and concerns that led the questioner to ask the original question in the first place. Using these phrases can only make the confrontation worse, probably unsalvageable. Such insults make emotions skyrocket and nearly guarantee no communication or understanding will take place for a long time.

Better alternatives:

"I am not sure how that is connected, but I will try to answer your question."

"It may just be me but I don't see how that question relates to the main issue here, but let me explain based on what I think you are asking. . . ."

4.4 YOU MUST . . . YOU HAVE TO . . . YOU HAVE NO CHOICE . . .

Most people, especially Americans, resent being told what to do. And they burn with red-hot anger when you tell them what to do in a pushy, authoritarian way. These grating phrases come across like a poke in the chest just before a bar fight breaks out. They almost beg a person to push back by saying something like "I don't *have to* do anything, and *you* can't make me."

Don't use these phrases in your responses if you don't want your listeners to shut you out. If indeed they "have to" do something, you needn't use command imperatives such as these. Give your listeners credit for enough intelligence to recognize what they have to do and what they don't. (Refer to section 19.2 for additional comment.)

Better alternatives:

"To comply with the law, you would want to . . ."

"If you want this service, you need to follow these procedures . . ."

"Yes, you technically have a choice, but it's limited to meeting all of the requirements or paying a penalty. . . ."

4.5 THAT'S NOT WHAT I SAID AT ALL. YOU REALLY HAVE THAT MIXED UP. I DON'T KNOW HOW YOU COULD GET THAT FROM WHAT I SAID. YOU DIDN'T QUOTE ME CORRECTLY.

All of these retorts imply the questioner can't paraphrase worth a hoot, is an incompetent listener, or is lying about what he heard you say. These stinging barbs provoke another issue to argue about, thereby blocking any hope for good communication until feelings subside days or months later. The following alternative cleanly points out that the questioner isn't quoting you correctly but does it without insult.
Better alternative:

"If that is what you heard me say, well, I didn't explain myself as well as I would like. Let me tell you what I had intended to get across. . . ."

This is a powerful approach. In a few words, you disarm the hostile question by saying its premise is incorrect, but you take the responsibility for that result. Then you skillfully take full control of the discussion by restating what you want the listener and everyone else to know is your exact view. It happens so fast that he won't realize what you did. Try it once, and you'll never forget this method as one of the best of them all. See section 3.3 for more on this approach to help you avoid the preceding inflammatory phrases.

4.6 THAT'S NOT MY RESPONSIBILITY. IT'S NOT MY JOB.

Although these infuriating phrases are identified most often with government bureaucrats, they apply to the private sector as well. How many times have you asked for an answer only to hear back, "That's not my responsibility" or some variation of the phrase, which essentially is heard as "I am not going to help you."

You can let the questioner know that it may, indeed, not be your responsibility while you direct her to the appropriate office or work site where she can get her question answered.

Better alternative:

> "Because this isn't my area of expertise, I would like to help you find the right people in another department. They have the information and responsibility to answer questions like yours. I could help you locate them if you would like."

PART 2

5

Defending Company Policies Even When You Disagree with Them

5.1 How can you defend such a terrible policy?

5.2 Why don't you just admit this is totally wrong?

5.3 Why didn't you just tell them no?

5.4 How can you expect us to go along with this?

5.5 Are you just going to lie about what you really think?

If you're a middle manager (they call it *middle* management because that's who always seems to be caught in the middle) you've probably been called upon to defend policies with which you don't agree. That usually means defending them against harsh comments from staff and co-workers who think they know your real feelings. You may be caught between your integrity and your preference to keep your job (not to mention the ancillary thing called a paycheck).

Upper management sometimes creates policies with which we disagree (and usually don't fully understand). Nevertheless, we are paid to carry out those policies, even when the policies are unpopular.

A big part of how employees react has to do with the trustworthiness of the management team. Management needs to be credible and to speak with one voice. If you're part of that team, they expect you to act a certain way, as do those who work for you. If you deride the policy, you're not only damaging the management team's credibility, you're hurting your own, or at least saying a lot about how loyal you are to the team.

On the other hand, if you blindly enforce a policy with which you are known to disagree, your credibility is weakened. It might also stain both the management team and their image if your employees feel management stomped you into dust and made you do something you knew to be wrong. This cuts both ways. So what do we say when a tough question such as the following comes from a trusted colleague who knows you well?

5.1 HOW CAN YOU DEFEND SUCH A TERRIBLE POLICY?

The advertising manager reports to you, and you both work at a financially struggling advertising firm that has loosened its policy on clients it will accept. The advertising manager is furious at the new policy that led to the firm taking on an antiabortion campaign. The advertising manager knows you are pro choice, and she says you should have stood up to the vice president and told her you won't do the work because "it's wrong."

The antiabortion ads are supposed to portray abortion as both wrong and sinful. Some of the women working on the campaign support it while others agree with the advertising manager. It might seem that you have only two choices for a response: tell the advertising manager you agree with her and trust she'll understand your dilemma, or keep your views private while you carry out the task. However, there's a third choice for your response:

> *"I'm not defending or criticizing anything.* I am, however, trying to explain what was decided and how it's expected to work. I've got seven weeks to meet both of those goals. *It's my assignment, so I'm going to get it done the best way I can.* I could use a little leeway here and some help, too. This is something that happens to every manager; your turn may be next."

This response is intentionally transparent to the advertising manager, who can reasonably reconfirm that you still hold your old views, but it also says that you are going to do the assigned work. Giving such transparent responses doesn't reveal anything new to people who already know what you have said in the past. You aren't going to fool them anyway.

"Don't Tell Anyone, But . . ."

Even though this response is transparent, it nevertheless uses words that are likely to get you into trouble with upper management. If you don't want your CEO to know that you think the policy stinks, don't tell your

---

**Tip: Don't be a buddy
when responding to tough questions.**

Loyalty will make up for a lot of shortcomings, whereas **almost nothing will make up for a lack of loyalty.** So instead of agreeing with the critics so you can be a buddy with the staff, politely tolerate their disdainful looks and comments. It's part of your job description.

---

staff or anyone else. How many times have we all uttered the words: "Don't tell anyone, but . . ." or "I'm not supposed to say anything, but . . ." only to have the boss call us in to explain why we said something we knew we shouldn't have said?

Juicy gossip travels fast, to all levels. More than that, your actual resistance becomes ammunition for those who want to scuttle the program. It can also play into other existing, but not related, office politics. In either case, you're handing people bombs and hoping you don't get hit with any shrapnel.

If you reinforce the criticism of the unpopular policy, your words are absolutely guaranteed (or your money back on the price of this book) to find their way back to the CEO's ears. Even better, those words will gain strength and colorful distortion by the time the CEO hears them. You may never know the CEO heard them, but the big boss isn't likely to forget. Her doubts over whether or not you are dependable when times are tough will last for years.

5.2 WHY DON'T YOU JUST ADMIT THIS IS TOTALLY WRONG?

The advertising manager is sure you really believe the policy is totally wrong in every way. She and others standing around now demand you confess how "wrong" it is. With your admission, they can feel "right" about themselves while reaffirming that the CEO is really a bad guy after all. All of them know you well enough that their guess is probably right.

What harm would it do to just say so? Plenty. In every gossip exchange in the company, your response would be used as justification for recalcitrance. Your words would undermine the ability of the firm to provide timely and quality service to this client. And that would harm your career, maybe even end it at the firm. Consider this response as a better alternative:

> *"I don't get to decide what is right or wrong* in every situation. And I don't know everything the chairwoman knows. I'm not saying I'd make the same decision, but I don't know that I wouldn't. The CEO considered every angle on this problem, and *she used her best judgment.* And now it's my job, and yours too, to get this going the way she wants it."

You could give the same response if you wanted to use a depersonalized response to lower the level of emotions. Refer to section 1.8 for others.

> "No manager gets to decide what is right or wrong in every situation. A manager doesn't always know everything that the CEO considers when she is reviewing every angle of an issue. Sometimes it comes down to knowing it's a manager's job and the staff's, too, to get something done the way a CEO judges it should be."

"Wrong" by Whose Standards?

Does the staff really know the policy is "wrong?" By whose standards? Notwithstanding those people graced with divine guidance, our everyday run-of-the-mill wrong is generally decided by community consensus (or at least acceptance). We enact laws, establish cultural norms, set office policies, and so on. Rarely are these clear, even though everyone talks about "right" and "wrong" as though they are easy to distinguish from each other.

The Policy Just "Is"

Assuming the policy isn't a clear crime like murder, usually the "wrong" in the context of this question means the company's action goes against what your colleagues believe in. Therein lies the first opportunity to respond. You can point out that their opinion of what is wrong may not be shared by everyone else. Further, you can choose *not* to debate the issue of what's right or wrong about the policy—the policy just "is." You don't have to agree or disagree on what is wrong or right—the firm has a new policy, and you are going to follow it.

5.3 WHY DIDN'T YOU JUST TELL THEM NO?

The advertising manager reminds you this is *still* a free country. She says that anyone with character would refuse to implement such a policy. She wants to know where your backbone is and whether you ever stand up for yourself. To her it's just that simple: All you have to do is open your mouth and say no.

In logic reminiscent of youthful idealism, she concludes that because you are right and they are wrong, they wouldn't dare to say anything back, that is, "You're fired." By now you can't help but be concerned about losing respect from her and the staff. You can also respect yourself for taking a reasonable, albeit unpleasant order and carrying it out. Someday you may be part of upper management and giving such instructions. Our entire civilization depends on reasonable order, so there's nothing to be ashamed of when you don't just tell upper management no as your colleague urges. Try these responses.

> "Amy, it might be fun to think we can just say 'no,' but life doesn't work that way. I made my alternative proposal, and they turned it down. *I'm not going to defy authority and get fired for nothing.* That would be heroic but nothing would change—someone else would still have to carry out the policy. *I don't have to like it to do it.*"

> "If everyone here *obeyed only the directions they liked*, we'd have chaos in an hour. I gave my opinion, they made a decision, and it's going to be done by me and done very well. If you're as wise as I think you are, you will do the same."

5.4 HOW CAN YOU EXPECT US TO GO ALONG WITH THIS?

The advertising manager has been joined by a few more rankled colleagues—the Moral Majority of the office—who also protest the policy. They feign mutiny, implying that maybe they simply won't go along with it. Maybe they'll all leave en masse. And because you should also know how wrong it is, how could you expect they would do otherwise?

As the advertising manager and her buddies stand on their high moral ground, you realize this is one of those days that actually will last longer than 24 hours, maybe a lifetime.

Leave It, Try to Change It, or Accept It

We have only three reasonable choices when faced with just about any situation. We can leave the scene and avoid the problem. We can change the circumstances (or attempt to). Or we can accept the situation and get used to it.

In the following response you use that logic to lead the group's thinking to its only reasonable choice, unpleasant as it may be. It's very similar to St. Francis of Assisi's famous prayer that begins "Lord grant me the wisdom to accept those things I cannot change. . . ."

> "I understand what you're feeling, but I am not going to join you in those feelings. I didn't ask for this situation, *but I can't just wish it away either.* When we accepted our jobs, we knew there'd be things we might not like. There are three choices in these situations. We can quit our jobs, try to change the situation, or we can accept it. I don't intend to quit, and we know the policy decision is final. *So that leaves accepting it, at least for now.*"

In the preceding response you purposefully duck the antagonistic question and thereby duck the verbal punch that might start another round of quarreling. Instead, you gain attention by showing your awareness of their concerns, but then you bridge the discussion to the reality of reasonable acceptance.

5.5 ARE YOU JUST GOING TO LIE ABOUT WHAT YOU REALLY THINK?

As you begin to explain and promote the unpopular policy, you're accused of lying about what you really think. The advertising manager and your colleagues allege that you don't really believe what you are saying. They know what you have said previously, and it doesn't match up with what's being said now.

The easy way to resolve the issue of whether you are going to lie about what you really think is not to talk about your views. Instead, report what the CEO and the vice presidents think, say, and do regarding the policy. And it's not a bad idea to preface your remarks sometimes with the notion that "wiser heads than mine. . . ."

"There's nothing to lie about. The truth is very simple—the CEO set a policy and she gave her reasons for it. I'm telling the truth that *it's my job to explain the policy and see that it gets implemented on time*. We have all witnessed situations in which an initially unpopular decision actually turned out to make good sense after implementation. *Let's do what we're paid to do* and carry out the new policy in a positive and capable manner."

Tough Questions Worksheet

Create responses to the difficult questions you could face on this chapter's topics, using the formulas below. Use **logic, emotion,** and **ethics** whenever possible. Experiment by answering the same question with different formulas to learn which best fits your natural style. Use pencil so you can erase and refine your answers.

Past, Present, Future:

What happened was:

What's happening now is:

The way we'll prevent it from happening again is by:

Problem to Solution:

*The **problems** we have are:*

*I'd like to go directly to a proposed **solution:***

Problem - Cause - Solution - Timing (PCST):

*The **problems** we have are:*

*They were **caused** by:*

*The **solutions** we may implement are:*

*Our **timing** is:*

Wrong, Right, and What It Means:

*This is an extremely complex area and our track record has **overall** been very **good**:*

*We do very difficult things and sometimes we have failures. What **happened** is that:*

*What this **means** for us now is:*

Three-Step Explanation:

I understand what you are asking and why it concerns you so much:

Other people who had your experiences probably would feel the same way:

However, I would like to explain a little about this problem:

Other formulas and responses I want to use for tough questions related to this chapter:

6

Establishing Your Authority with Former Co-Workers

6.1 *Well, Boss, what would you like us peons to do today?*

6.2 *You used to do this work and you had the same complaints. So why are you deaf to our complaints now?*

6.3 *Whose side are you on now, ours or theirs? It didn't take you long to sell out, did it?*

6.4 *Has all your authority gone to your head?*

6.5 *Have you forgotten what it's like to do real work here?*

When you're promoted to manage former peers, how you handle the first signs of resentment or anger can mean the difference between succeeding at your new job or failing miserably.

It's a very complicated task, managing people who used to be co-workers, even friends. The challenge is twofold: You have to continue to empathize with your former peers while also establishing your new authority.

Some former co-workers may be genuinely happy for you and thrilled that one of their own is now in a position to make some improvements. Others, however, will have a hard time overcoming their envy of you without showing some signs of trouble. You're no longer one of them, you're one of *them!*

There may even be some (who you once thought were friends!) who act as competitors. Others may become opportunists and take advantage of the friendship with unreasonable requests or favors. When opportunists succeed in taking advantage of you, their successes become your failures.

When the tough questions start to fly, it's critical that you manage such behavior skillfully. Get the message across tactfully before the employee has a chance to do any real damage.

6.1 WELL, BOSS, WHAT WOULD YOU LIKE US PEONS TO DO TODAY?

A co-worker who has worked with you for years is the first to test you. He was vying for the position alongside you and has been half-teasing and half-taunting you with these "peon" questions. You don't want to come across heavy-handed your first week as the boss but you feel you can't let him pose these disrespectful hostile questions either. Consider these openings; one is depersonalized, and the other is more direct:

> **Depersonalized:** "When someone gets promoted there usually are a couple of candidates who are disappointed they didn't get the job. That is understandable, *but what matters after the decision is made is how well they work together afterwards.* The new manager needs the staff's support to do a good job just as the staff needs hers so they can do good work."

> **Personalized:** "Greg, I understand that you were interested in this job, and you're probably disappointed that I got it. What matters now is how well we work together. *I'm asking for your support,* because without that, I can't do the job as well. In return, I'll do my best to be a good manager. *Can I count on you?*"

The depersonalized response can be less threatening because it puts a little distance between you and the former co-worker. Sometimes you need a buffer like that to lessen the impact of your words when you don't want to sound heavy-handed. Refer to section 1.8 for more comments on depersonalized response.

Now suppose the question in 6.1 was asked by a colleague who didn't compete for the supervisor's position. But you're uncertain whether he's uncomfortable with the new circumstance or if he's purposefully trying to be difficult. You decide to give him the benefit of the doubt while your response lets him know you're uncomfortable too.

> "I have to admit, though I'm excited, I'm a little uncomfortable at the same time. *Circumstances have changed, and I hope for the better for both of us.* What's important is that I know firsthand that you care about being a good employee, and I want you to know that I care about being a fair

---

Tip: Stop it before it starts.

Just as important as knowing how to field critical questions is knowing how to **avoid the situation in the first place.** Day one is key. From the moment you walk through the door, your former peers, perhaps friends, will be looking to see if you act differently. You're now a "them," not an "us."

It's a good idea to hold a group meeting first thing to let them know how you're feeling about things and to get both their support and feedback. Start off by telling them you recognize that it could be an **awkward situation for all of you.** Ask them how they would feel in your situation. Get their feedback on what are the qualities they'd most like from a supervisor. Finally, let them know that even though things have changed, you're committed to being a fair boss, and a respected one.

---

supervisor. *We're both going to need some time to get used to this new relationship.* Can I count on your support in the meantime?"

This up-front approach may both surprise and move him to see you more as an ally, not an enemy. If not, and the sarcasm continues, maintain your composure and toss the ball into his court with one of these responses.

"If you were my supervisor, how would you expect me *to treat you?*"

"Seriously, what kind of supervisor are you hoping I'll be?"

Depending on how he reacts, you might want to finish with a response that clearly communicates the legitimacy of your authority:

"If the tables were turned and you were my manager, *I doubt you would tolerate my treating you with such obvious disrespect.* And I won't tolerate it from you either. Everyone has to answer to somebody, and that somebody is me. *I'd like for us to respect the position each of us is in* and work at getting along in this new relationship. We worked well as co-workers. There's no reason that should change now."

6.2 YOU USED TO DO THIS WORK AND YOU HAD THE SAME COMPLAINTS. SO WHY ARE YOU DEAF TO OUR COMPLAINTS NOW?

The transition from employee to supervisor is a difficult one and carries a big possibility of failure, particularly if it is a promotion within the same department. Generally speaking, your people will be curious as to how you will handle your new relationship. They will look to you for "clues" as to your management style and probably will be as anxious as you to get off on the right foot.

Coming on too strong at the outset will upset morale, but at the same time your manner should leave no doubt that you are now in charge. But always remember the old adage "If you're nice to people on your way up, they'll be nice to you on your way down."

So now you are faced with a vexing question from an employee who had worked alongside you for 12 years before you were promoted to manager. You were once openly critical of some things for which you are now responsible. He wants to know why you aren't listening to the staff complaints on the same concerns you had voiced.

As you prepare to respond, you don't want your responses to brush over problems lightly that were especially irritating to you as a line-level employee. You know that otherwise you will lose his respect and that of your other new subordinates. You don't want them to consider you shallow and insincere.

Your response should tell them you are going to follow through on making improvements—that you sincerely have their best interests foremost in your mind. If the proposed change is within your authority to act on, your reply could be like this:

> "As you know, this is an area that bothers me too, and believe me when I say that *I will give this priority* just as soon as I can get my feet on the ground in my new job. I need to figure out what effect this change could have on the other departments and possibly get their input. In any case, I'll get back to you on the results—probably within 30 days."
> (Then make sure you do!)

If you are in a position to at least push for changes, this is your chance to let your new employees see the benefit of having someone with direct experience in a management position.

> "You know as well as I do one of the reasons I complained is because I didn't think anybody was listening. Well, I am listening and I'm going to try and improve conditions. *But one thing I am learning is that it's not that easy.* It's more complicated than you or I thought it was. There are certain ways to go about making changes, and *I need time to work within the system or we won't get anywhere.*"

Tip: Be friendly—not friends.

When you face these inevitable questions from former co-workers you now supervise, be friendly but not a friend. Your new authority and duties will distance you from them, so accept it as a fact of life. Don't try to be a buddy and make quick promises in your responses. You're still learning the ropes. New managers have a **tendency to want to prove themselves** too early and try to change the system. Respond openly and live up to your new role.

For those suggestions that would affect people and systems throughout the company and therefore require approval by upper management, have your response recommend that your employee make a formal submission, possibly through your company's employee suggestion program if it is a functional one.

> "I don't want you to think that I'm putting you off on this—quite the contrary. Your suggestion involves other departments, system changes, company-wide policies that *require upper management approval.* I think that you should receive recognition at the highest level for your ideas, and maybe it will put some money in your pocket. I'll be glad to help you put your ideas in writing, maybe on the suggestion form."

If you haven't got the authority or leverage to make things any different at the moment, because the situation is unsolvable or a sacred cow, you can at least say you are listening.

> "What's different is that I agree with you, and will at least listen to your complaints, which is more than we had before. When the opportunity comes by, we'll push for a change, but now isn't the time."

But if you have come to realize in your role that circumstances dictate that no change will or should take place, you might respond directly:

> "You're right. I did complain quite a bit and tried to do something about the policy. *Now that I've had the opportunity to see how and why it was put into place,* I realize it's the only workable solution for now. You may not like it, but let me explain what I've learned . . . ."

6.3 WHOSE SIDE ARE YOU ON NOW, OURS OR THEIRS? IT DIDN'T TAKE YOU LONG TO SELL OUT, DID IT?

Too often "management" and "labor" separate themselves into different camps, like royalty fighting with revolutionary peasants. As soon as you start making decisions some former co-workers don't like, you'll undoubtedly hear these accusatory questions.

One friend has just asked if you weren't "taking their side" and if you have "sold out already." It's time to separate the facts from her opinions. The facts are that you have a new job and must make decisions, including some that former co-workers may choose not to like. She chooses to interpret your actions as "selling out already."

Have your response let her know that just because she creates a meaning (opinion) around a fact (your decision), it doesn't make her interpretation real—it's just her opinion, her perception. She is choosing to see it a certain way, and you can show her that she has a choice in how she chooses to interpret your decisions. As the new manager, you can join the growing ranks of team leaders by avoiding picking sides:

> "Hey, that's not really fair. The fact is I got a promotion, and you know I've got a job to do. I guess *you can choose to interpret* that as 'selling out' or taking sides. But you know someone's going to make these decisions, and I'm trying to be as responsible and fair as possible. *I wish you'd choose that interpretation instead.*"

6.4 HAS ALL YOUR AUTHORITY GONE TO YOUR HEAD?

Has it? Are you one of those new managers who overexert authority to the point of being overbearing? If so, the best response is to apologize to her for sounding too bossy and start over, smoothly. But that isn't the case for most of us, so we can honestly say something else. Something's bugging her to cause her to ask such a hostile question, so try to find out what the complaint is behind the question. Maybe you have overlooked a mistake.

> "Wait a minute, you seem to be *really bothered by this decision.* What is it? Do you think I made a mistake? *Is there something I should know?*"

"Have I decided something too quickly without giving you the chance to come forward with your ideas? *If so, I apologize. What are your thoughts on this?*"

6.5 HAVE YOU FORGOTTEN WHAT IT'S LIKE TO DO REAL WORK HERE?

This question reveals the age-old attitude that front-line workers producing the goods and services do the "real" work while managers do superfluous things—you know, important things like watching subordinates work and creating useless paperwork to make their lives miserable and less efficient.

Whether true or not, she perceives that in the rarefied air of management you have lost touch with the reality of the workplace. Certainly, it indicates her frustration, which may extend to others. If the employee is sincere, it may be an opportunity to head-off a morale problem. You might try something like this:

> "I don't think so, but why don't you *tell me what causes you to ask that.* Sometimes a manager gets too involved with the detail work of his job and loses sight of problems that may be affecting production. Is this what's happening, in your opinion?"

On the surface, her question is an insult (to be ignored), and underneath may lie a complaint about a problem unknown to you in the workplace. Listen keenly for what perceived or real problem exists; then respond.

> "It might not seem like it, *but I work pretty hard too.* So what's really bothering you? *You wouldn't be asking a question like that if something weren't going on.* What are you trying to tell me?"

> "I remember very well what the work here is like. No doubt about it, you work hard. *Granted, my new work is different, but it's no less difficult and no less important.* I used to just have to worry about keeping my own end of the job up. Now I'm responsible for other people's jobs, on top of production levels, marketing, and personnel problems. *I know you work hard, just as I do.*"

Tough Questions Worksheet

Create responses to the difficult questions you could face on this chapter's topics, using the formulas below. Use **logic, emotion,** and **ethics** whenever possible. Experiment by answering the same question with different formulas to learn which best fits your natural style. Use pencil so you can erase and refine your answers.

Past, Present, Future:

What happened was:

What's happening now is:

The way we'll prevent it from happening again is by:

Problem to Solution:

*The **problems** we have are:*

*I'd like to go directly to a proposed **solution:***

Problem - Cause - Solution - Timing (PCST):

*The **problems** we have are:*

*They were **caused** by:*

*The **solutions** we may implement are:*

*Our **timing** is:*

Wrong, Right, and What It Means:

*This is an extremely complex area and our track record has **overall** been very **good:***

*We do very difficult things and sometimes we have failures. What **happened** is that:*

*What this **means** for us now is:*

Three-Step Explanation:

I understand what you are asking and why it concerns you so much:

Other people who had your experiences probably would feel the same way:

However, I would like to explain a little about this problem:

Other formulas and responses I want to use for tough questions related to this chapter:

7

Deflecting Sniper Attacks to
Protect Your Back

7.1   You're finished with the project, aren't you?

*7.2   Whom does the client blame for losing his business? (The sniper
        knows the client blames you.)*

7.3   What's causing so many staff problems in your division?

You don't have to be in the work force very long to know that unreasonable deadlines, demanding bosses, and stressed-out co-workers are a natural part of the terrain. If you've been at the game longer, you're probably aware of a far deadlier hazard lurking in just about every organization—vindictive colleagues.

With downsizing corporations cutting away at salaries and positions, there are too many managers competing for too few jobs. One management association reports that the number of managers has been cut in half in many organizations during the past decade.

As competition and stress increase, so does destructive office behavior at all levels, from the secretarial pool to the corporate boardroom. Seeking to ruin your credibility, these "snipers" can embarrass you in meetings or undermine you to supervisors and peers. It may be an insecure boss, a jealous peer, or an ambitious employee.

The worst mistake you can make is to think it will never happen to you. Here are some ideas on how to protect yourself when the sniper strikes.

7.1 YOU'RE FINISHED WITH THE PROJECT, AREN'T YOU?

You're in a Monday-morning meeting with the management staff. Things are going smoothly until one of your colleagues turns to you and casually inquires how one of your projects is going.

It seems like an innocent enough question on the surface—just a concerned colleague inquiring about your workplace welfare—and all faces turn to you for a reply. The trouble is, *you know* it's not an innocent question. You know it's an underhanded attempt to put you on the spot. You just discussed the project in private with your colleague so she knows darn well you've hit snags. She has begun a game to embarrass you in front of others.

The games played in the corporate arena are similar to those in the sports arenas. In sports players beat the tar out of another person to win. All sorts of behavior is tolerated to help make that possible, as long as you don't get caught: nasty clips, punches below the belt, a stick in the face, and a knee to the groin.

On the corporate playing field, nasty behavior can also prevail; but it's more subtle because it's a mental game and not a physical one. So what are your options when a colleague hits you with a vicious clip? Well, it's tempting, certainly. But you'll have more success with *Problem, Cause, Solution & Timing* (PCST).

Using the PCST formula will help you keep your professional composure. It focuses your remarks on solutions, not problems and thus takes the momentum out of the underhanded move.

1. State the problem very briefly to focus everyone's attention on it instead of on you. Don't repeat the sniper's loaded terminology, for example, she refers to "your failure" instead of "the delay." Every time you use the sniper's loaded terminology, you drive the negative image deeper into the minds of the listeners.

2. Point out the cause. Cause is not blame or fault. Cause is "what happened." Fault and blame show who was wrong, but those terms don't tell the facts—what happened. Stick with the objective facts of what happened.

3. Outline your solution. Draw a positive picture of things getting done, now or soon. Emphasize what you are actually doing or what you plan to do. This shifts the focus away from what's gone wrong to what's being done and forces others to respond to you, not the other way around.

4. Give the timing, that is, the new project completion date you're sure you can meet (and then make sure you meet it).

Here's an example of the formula in action:

"The problem was we were held up temporarily. *It happened because* some staff weren't available and several vendors missed their delivery dates. *We're solving* this by taking a team approach to bring it back on line. We've temporarily reassigned staff, and we're making our vendors meet our schedules. We've set a *new completion date* for the end of the month, and we're sure we're going to make it."

Yes, of course, someone at the meeting might hear this as just diversion. But not most people. Even bosses become uncomfortable when others around them feel foolish. Unless the boss uses that moment to press you on the tardiness, you're probably off the hook for now.

Knowing When to Counterattack

Should you ever counterattack when asked a sabotage question? Should you ever snarl biting retorts such as the following?:

"John, I'm unclear why you are asking me that now. I explained things in detail a little while ago. I even sent you a memo on it."

"What value do you find in asking me a question for which you already know the answer?"

"If you had been involved with this project from the beginning, Joyce, as the rest of us have been, you would know that . . ."

Don't counterattack just because it feels good and you have the immediate urge to vent your anger. Counterattack only as a last resort and only when you need to neutralize the sniper's credibility. For example, if the listeners seem to be accepting the sniper's allegations and it is tactically vital that you prevent more damage right at that moment, you should consider counterattacking.

Your counterattack responses can be aimed at the same targets the sniper goes after: credibility, knowledge, motives, and so forth. See section 1.2 for a detailed list. You can allege that the sniper doesn't have complete or current information and therefore doesn't know what she is talking about. Or you could point out that Mary has made incorrect statements in the past, which indicates her current statements are suspect. Additionally, you could imply that she is making these unfair comments because of past conflicts with your work unit.

As you can see, counterattack responses may get quite unpleasant. However, if the sniper looks credible and you look fully at fault, your counterattack may succeed in reducing her standing (and credibility) in the eyes of the listeners you don't want to side with her. Because the risks are high, don't counterattack unless there is absolutely no other choice and the issues are very important to your life, family, or career.

Knowing When to Cloud the Issue

If you're not off the hook yet, then consider an old and cunning strategy that works so well for courtroom lawyers and politicians: confuse or blur the issue. (Refer to sections 2.9 and 2.10 for related comments.) Here is an example of blurring:

> "You refer to it as one project. Actually, the project has been more like several projects under one name. Some schedules were only tentative in the beginning—others were revised as we gained direct experience. And there were changes in some of the milestones as we went along. We've met most of the target dates that were set once we found how difficult it was going to be. . . ."

Tip: Lashing back is too costly.

You can't afford the luxury of lashing back to a sniper's undermining hostile question. Don't allow yourself the luxury of even mentally cursing the other person. Angry thoughts hurt you in two ways. First, they show on your face, consequently causing everyone else to react emotionally to you. That raises the tension in the room and puts the conflict in the emotional realm, instead of in the professional. It also focuses on the conflict, when a skillful answer might deflect that.

Second, you waste the priceless milliseconds your mind needs to quickly develop damage-control responses. You've got to create a new picture to replace the one your colleague just painted. **Use the PCST (Problem, Cause, Solution, Timing) formula** to paint that picture while you regain your composure. (Refer to section 2.5 for more on PCST.)

7.2 WHOM DOES THE CLIENT BLAME FOR LOSING HIS BUSINESS? (THE SNIPER KNOWS THE CLIENT BLAMES YOU.)

Losing a client is worse than missing a deadline. The lost revenue threatens everyone, including your boss. When this sabotage question is presented, grab hold of center stage and move everyone's attention away from fixing the "blame" to fixing the "problem."

Consider these two response options: the "punishment-forgiveness" method; and the "normalizing-comparing" method.

The first option relies on the cultural belief that you must be punished before others will forgive you and let you be restored in their eyes. When you employ this strategy, you confess that you really screwed up and are at fault. Do this only *if* you are to blame for losing the client and you can risk saying that publicly.

For example:

> "I think I should *accept responsibility* for that. I made some mistakes and certainly didn't satisfy the customer's expectations. I know what I'll do differently *the next time* I have a customer like this. Have any of you ever faced a customer who demanded . . . ?"

Don't Excuse Yourself

Don't offer excuses in this approach; excuses suggest you are forgiving yourself. Only others can grant forgiveness. Remember that most people tend to forgive, because they can picture themselves in your position—or they've been there before. Once they signal forgiveness, that begins your restoration while you promise not to mess up again.

Caution: The risk of this method is that others may not forgive you, but could use your unconditional admission as additional evidence that you should be penalized. If you are on fairly good terms with the boss and most co-workers, this method can end the issue right then and there. However, if you're already on shaky ground from previous events, consider the next approach.

Using a Compare/Normalize Approach

Put the matter in perspective by using the comparing-normalizing method. Compare your experience to other people's similar experiences. By com-

---

Tip: Get to your *reasonable* goal.

Think boldly and symbolically when talking about your actions. Talk about changing things for the better, being willing to find new ways, helping others out, and so forth. This says something positive about you even while you are talking about a failure or problem. Then bridge to your action plan. **The goal is not to show you're right, but that you're *reasonable*.**

---

paring your problems, you show that they are not unusual and are, in fact, within the norm. This should open up "normal" avenues of fixing things.

A typical comparing-normalizing response might look something like this.

> "I had some problems with his account, but *not more* than sometimes happens with any of our staff. I did everything possible to satisfy him—a heck of a lot *more than we do* for most customers. I went as far as I could to patch things up, but nothing would appease him."

What's the standard for doing enough for the unreasonable client? Does it cost so much in time and money to satisfy him that it's not worth the effort? Then it becomes a conclusion that "he" is unreasonable and really can't be satisfied. Hence, the loss isn't much of a loss, if at all.

What's reasonable depends on the makeup and belief system of the organization's "dominant coalition." The dominant coalition sets up the values, standards, and acceptable behavior for members of the organization. (Refer to section 1.4 for related comments.)

If you know who belongs to that coalition (a.k.a. the ruling clique) and what they consider reasonable, you can use that knowledge to put the loss of the client in perspective. It will help you to portray yourself as having prudently done all that your boss and neutral colleagues would do in a similar circumstance.

7.3 WHAT'S CAUSING SO MANY STAFF PROBLEMS IN YOUR DIVISION?

As with most work divisions, your unit has its share of staff problems. When another manager becomes a sniper by purposefully bringing up the subject in an open meeting and implies you are to blame, she is making double trouble. Her first implication is that there are, in fact, a great many staff problems, which may not be true. The second implication is that you, as the captain of your division, must be to blame.

Don't let the sniper put you on public trial over whether your division is about to mutiny. Instead, make the point that your problems are no different from anyone else's. Notice how the responses not only refute the premise, they turn the hostile question into an opportunity to brag that you're handling things just fine.

> "Oh, I don't believe the staff issues in my division are particularly different from other divisions. People were rewarded and people were disciplined, and the rumor mill grinds a little faster when the latter happens. *We've got our share of challenges* like everyone else; however, most employees say they're pretty happy in their work. We've got a few who aren't really happy campers at the moment, but I think we can resolve most of their concerns, too. We're *making good strides* toward becoming a very team-oriented division."

> "We view the changes that have been taking place as real opportunities. We've got some very talented and ambitious people in the division, and we're *creating ways we can all work together* more effectively. One of the things we're doing is . . . after that we're going to . . ."

Are there prima donnas in your division? If there are (and everybody has got them at some point in their careers) admit that you are challenged to bring them together working as a team. You're confident this will be accomplished and will produce one of the strongest divisions in the organization. You might also want to point out that if people didn't care, they wouldn't argue. You might just have a very passionate group that, once they agree on something, will be a force to reckon with.

How to Respond to Implications of Strife

If, however, you believe your boss and colleagues generally think there is an unusual level of dissension in your division, you could make things worse by ignoring or sidestepping the implication.

In that case, consider the following:

> "We've definitely had *our share of tough situations* in a relatively short period of time. It's demanding much of my attention now, and though

I know *it will be settled*, I expect it will take some time and possibly personnel changes. Some of you have been through similar times, and I'd appreciate any suggestions you might have."

This response acknowledges what the others already believe—the division is having a tough time—without convicting yourself of incompetence. Dissension indicates the possibility, or at least the "perception" (and perception is reality, in one way or another) of weak leadership. You had better impress upon the group that you are ready to take tough action—if called for.

The response shows that you recognize the problems, have begun to evaluate them, and that you're committed to improvement—employ the past-present-future formula. (Refer to sections 1.7 and 2.3 for related comments.)

You have now shifted the focus to your audience by asking for their expertise. There is a good chance they will accept your request and share their seasoned experience. The discussion could then shift to their old war stories and advice—thus the focus is not on whether you let things get out of hand in your division.

Tough Questions Worksheet

Create responses to the difficult questions you could face on this chapter's topics, using the formulas below. Use **logic, emotion,** and **ethics** whenever possible. Experiment by answering the same question with different formulas to learn which best fits your natural style. Use pencil so you can erase and refine your answers.

Past, Present, Future:

What happened was:

What's happening now is:

The way we'll prevent it from happening again is by:

Problem to Solution:

*The **problems** we have are:*

*I'd like to go directly to a proposed **solution:***

Problem - Cause - Solution - Timing (PCST):

*The **problems** we have are:*

*They were **caused** by:*

*The **solutions** we may implement are:*

*Our **timing** is:*

Wrong, Right, and What It Means:

*This is an extremely complex area and our track record has **overall** been very good:*

*We do very difficult things and sometimes we have failures. What **happened** is that:*

*What this **means** for us now is:*

Three-Step Explanation:

I understand what you are asking and why it concerns you so much:

Other people who had your experiences probably would feel the same way:

However, I would like to explain a little about this problem:

Other formulas and responses I want to use for tough questions related to this chapter:

8

Collaring Staff Who Go Over Your Head

8.1   *Are you saying I can't talk to the top boss? Just you?*

8.2   *You're hardly ever around! How could I check with you when you're so busy?*

8.3   *How was I supposed to know you wanted this information directly?*

8.4   *Aren't we supposed to have open communication here so we can talk with anyone?*

8.5   *Do you want me to check every little thing with you first, even if it causes delays?*

8.6   *Are you saying I should not respond to the vice president's request but just give you the information?*

When someone goes over your head, there's only one word to describe the intense emotion such a move provokes—betrayal.

It's embarrassing to learn that one of your employees has sidestepped your authority and gone directly to a superior. It's deliberate; it's risky; it's a very strong statement of disrespect.

Those are the thoughts that are bound to run through your mind. But you have to cool off and evaluate the real cause of the employee's action. If your company has an open-door policy, employees may well have been indoctrinated with a philosophy that the door is always open to the top bosses' offices for discussion of their ideas or complaints. This is an excellent way to keep lines of communication open, but it can cause confusion as to the proper chain of command.

In one company the president let it be known among all employees that she welcomed their visits at her table during morning coffee break to discuss their questions and ideas. When you have an open system like that, you have to allow for the fact that there will be some confusion and misunderstanding. Don't overreact! You, too, must work within the system.

The end run reflects on your abilities as a manager. Right or wrong, it can imply that you are unapproachable, too aloof or busy to deal with problems, or you are being unfair in some way. Usually these complaints are directed down the chain of command to you for handling and follow-up reporting. It's time for some self-analysis. Are you occupying your time with "busy work" instead of leading/supervising your staff? If so, this incident is your signal that something might be wrong with your management style.

There are always a few souls who don't think of an end run as an improper means of settling a dispute. However, when an employee bypasses you, the boss, it's usually for one of two reasons. He wants to give you a very strong message (warning) that he can make life difficult for you, if he chooses. Or second, he believes the two of you are at an impasse and there is nothing more to lose by taking his suggestions or gripes elsewhere.

8.1 ARE YOU SAYING I CAN'T TALK TO THE TOP BOSS? JUST YOU?

Even when you are assured of your authority as well as support by upper management, this hostile question poses potential harm to your reputation as a manager. If your response gives rise to rumors that you are suppressing your staff, the gossip can make you look insecure and unsteady in your leadership. Upper management probably won't believe the first rumor. The second rumor will make them wonder, and the third will start to make them believe it. That is a principal reason why you want your response to define you as a strong manager with an open mind along with an orderly process, not as a petty manager who uses fear instead of respect to lead.

In this scenario, an employee has worked for you for two years, and the two of you clash from time to time. He has pulled another end run without giving you a chance to address his latest concerns. When you ask to speak with him about going over your head, he poses the explosive question cited above.

On the surface, his question sounds like an implied threat. But before you lay down the law of the land, find out what his motivations are. If you don't have a good idea of what he's thinking, then you have very little chance of determining a workable course of discussion and action. How you handle his argumentative questions will test your authority, skill, and resolve. Consider it first an opportunity for you to reassert the boss-employee relationship, strengthen your authority, and give him a clear message of what you will and will not tolerate concerning the chain of command.

It's conceivable he's naive and doesn't know any better. It's also possible he misunderstands what "open communication" and "open-door" policies are all about.

Here are good opening questions to elicit feedback:

"I am interested in *why you felt it necessary* to go directly to my manager with this matter?"

"What did you *hope to accomplish* by going directly to my boss?"

If you discover he's simply naive about how organizations function, consider this response:

"I'm saying that this organization, like almost every organization, has *a structure, has a chain of command, so to speak.* If an employee wanted a vacation day, that employee wouldn't go to the president, he would report to his supervisor. Everyone, including my superior, expects you and all the rest of us to *follow this procedure.* She was glad you talked to her, but she's asked me to make you aware of this. If you ever feel I'm being unfair, you should tell me. If we can't come to an agreement and you want to appeal this further, *let me know* and I'll arrange a meeting for you with my boss."

If his remarks lead you to believe it's clearly an end run and you are *certain* you have the support of your superior, consider these:

"I am very disappointed that you would go directly to my superior with your complaint. Though she didn't say it bluntly, she was disappointed in you, too. I am your supervisor. That means you need to deal with me, on everything, *unless I tell you otherwise.* If you do this again, I will have to take disciplinary action. Now, I'd like to start over by beginning with what the original problem was. Let's get that in the open and let's settle it clearly and fairly."

"You need to understand that you answer to me, not my boss. In the future, if you feel it necessary to go to my superior because you are unhappy with a decision I've made, you may do so *after informing me first. We are expected to settle as much as possible at this level.* I think that if you give this another try, you'll find it will work for both of us."

"When you went behind my back, *you put both of us in a difficult position.* My boss was rather amazed and troubled that you felt it necessary to speak with her directly, without approaching me first. In the future, this will not be tolerated by either one of us. Is this clear to you?"

If you don't have the support of your superior because of her egalitarian open-door policy, you'll need to try another tactic because she might pull the rug out from under you.

Working with an Open-Door Policy

In theory and sometimes even in practice, open-door policies work and help keep everyone—supervisors too—on their toes. Open-door policies encourage employees and managers to carry out the universal duty to communicate.

Where there actually is an open-door policy, make sure you communicate in your responses how it really *should* work, so as to avoid clogging up the time of upper management.

"Yes, we have an open-door policy in this company. And I agree, it's great. *But the purpose* of having it is so that your ideas aren't blocked from people who could benefit from them. It's not there as a means for you to ignore the employee/manager relationship."

"Are you aware that this will make things more difficult for you because *you didn't exhaust all the remedies and options at this level?* Not only was it unfair to me to bypass me entirely, but you forced me to inform my superior of my dissatisfaction with parts of your job performance. That was something I had hoped we could resolve between us."

"How can you expect me to deal openly with you when *you aren't dealing fairly with me?*"

Experience has shown that many well-intentioned new CEOs can't keep up with the results of their open-door policies. They get bogged down with numerous lower-level disputes and pretty soon tell division managers to "take care of it." So, have patience, as the open-door method—good as it can be—often does not last more than a few months.

Recognizing When You Might Be at Fault

If this isn't the first time an employee has bypassed your authority, ask yourself whether your management style is perhaps the reason. Do you explain the rationale behind decisions? Do you give employees an opportunity to voice their full concerns before making decisions? Do you really listen to what they are saying instead of listening for what you can argue against? If you make a mistake, do you own up to it and set things right?

If, after you have listened to the employee, you sense you might be the primary cause for the end run, consider backing off somewhat while you rethink what you want to accomplish with your responses to his original question. Consider using remarks such as these:

> "I always thought we talked freely. Why didn't you come to me with this?"

> "Good heavens, no! That's not what I'm saying at all. I'm sure you can understand the difference between casual conversation as opposed to airing complaints that haven't been discussed with me. It casts a bad light on me—it makes it look like I'm too tough on my people. *Do you and I have a problem that I'm not aware of?*"

> "You know I'm concerned about why you bypassed my authority and went to my boss on this matter, *but I'm more concerned that perhaps I have done or said something that led you to believe it was your only course of action. Have I?*"

Tip: Base responses on solid information, not assumptions.

Don't assume you know why the employee would go over your head. If you believe your assumption and it is incorrect, your erroneous guess will lead you to responses that could possibly make the situation even worse. An employee's apparent end run could be intentional, it could be innocent, it could be something you inadvertently caused. **You can't respond well unless you know which one is the *cause.*** If you're stuck in the crack of the open-door policy, make sure your employees understand what that really means. It doesn't mean they can saunter into the president's office any time they feel like it to discuss whatever's on their mind that day.

8.2 YOU'RE HARDLY EVER AROUND!
HOW COULD I CHECK WITH YOU WHEN YOU'RE SO BUSY?

Yes, the employee is right. You are darn busy. You tell people that all the time. Everyone knows you're endlessly pulled from meeting to meeting. So does the employee have you cornered? Does he have a point? Is it your fault that he pulled an end run?

Don't make yourself guilty, but don't argue against the truth either. His statement uses a true premise to reach a false conclusion. Don't argue whether you were so busy he couldn't reach you. Don't say, "I wasn't that busy." That just opens up a second issue to debate.

Accept the truth that you've been very busy, just like many managers. But don't let him make busy mean unreachable. You'd have to be out of the solar system nowadays not to be accessible by phones, faxes, telegrams, notes, e-mail, messengers, the Internet, and so on.

Make it clear that it's his responsibility to find a way to get a message to you when he's got something important that needs your immediate reaction.

> "I know I've had a hectic schedule lately, and sometimes it's been tough to catch me in my office. But you could've *at least tried to see me first.* You could've called; you could've left me a note. That would have given me a chance to respond to you. I'm asking you to come to me first next time. I've always got time to read a note or take an urgent phone call. *Are we agreed on that?*"

8.3 HOW WAS I SUPPOSED TO KNOW YOU WANTED
THIS INFORMATION DIRECTLY?

A question like this is maddening, especially when the employee acts surprised at your attitude and is clearly pretending all innocence. More often than not it's a desperate and foolish move meant to pass some of the blame for his actions your way. Don't accept it.

Here again, begin with a question to get him talking, and, undoubtedly, watch him back himself into a corner.

> "Why would you *assume* I would not want information directly?"

Allow him to explain himself without interruption—unless he goes on for ten minutes and gets repetitive. Then you might say:

Tip: Make them say it back to gain clarity.

Asking an employee to repeat back the instructions embodied in your response has quadruple value.

1. By having him repeat the response's instructions in his own words, **he confirms** for you that he understood them.

2. His feedback gives you a chance to respond again to **correct any misunderstandings** immediately.

3. His restatement gives you **evidence** that the instructions contained in your response were given and that he understood them.

4. The first three steps limit the options he might want to offer the next time, because it will be harder to say he didn't get the message or misunderstood it.

"To prevent any future misunderstanding, I will let you know *when and if it is appropriate for you to bypass me* and take information directly to my boss. If I don't specifically say something should go directly to my boss, you should *assume I want to see it first. I'm held responsible* for what gets done here, so I have a good reason for this policy."

If he still questions your need or right to stop end runs, using a firm statement like this may get the point across:

"Because I am your supervisor, *I am accountable for what you do here.* That means that any information you think should be discussed with my superior is information you should discuss with me first. That is my direct instruction to you. *Tell me what you think this means,* so I'll know we understand each other."

8.4 AREN'T WE SUPPOSED TO HAVE OPEN COMMUNICATION HERE SO WE CAN TALK WITH ANYONE?

Here again, the employee is trying to excuse unacceptable behavior. He's pretending to be the innocent subordinate unfairly reprimanded for playing by the "open-communication" rules. Most people have worked in traditional hierarchies where information and authority flowed up and down the chain of command. Many people don't even distinguish the difference between authority and information. Consequently, when a progressive CEO adopts the open-communication policy, the new sense of freedom in communications induces a few subordinates to mistake that for freedom from *authority.*

Use your response comments to educate your employee on what an open-communications policy really is. Explain to him that the freedom to *say* what he wants does not mean freedom to *do* what he wants. Help him understand that the organization still must maintain a chain of command as the integral structure of the organization. Make it clear that obedience is not an option, now that he understands better. Also, have your responses point out that any permissive option like open communications will fail if it's taken to the extreme. Prudent judgment is imperative, which is part of what you contribute as the manager.

The following reply makes the rule clear, with a shrewd threat of what will happen if all the rules aren't followed.

> "I will be as clear and direct as I can be here. I want you to understand what open communications means—*and what it doesn't mean.* Open communication here means that you don't have to go through channels to get your ideas or suggestions heard by *people who could benefit from them.* For example, you've got access to engineering, quality control, and purchasing. But open communication does not mean you can circumvent lines of authority. It doesn't mean you can bypass your supervisor's authority that goes with his responsibilities. Open communication is fine, but *if you abuse it, you'll lose it."*

8.5 DO YOU WANT ME TO CHECK EVERY LITTLE THING WITH YOU FIRST, EVEN IF IT CAUSES DELAYS?

This is a predictable fallback question the end runner. He attempts to make your demand seem unreasonable by taking it to the extreme. It is an age-old technique to make something look absurd by making it absolute in some fashion. Questions such as this usually include extreme words like never, always, nothing, or everything.

If you follow his tack away from the real issue, he sets you up, you're hooked on the bait. It will be difficult to get back to reality. The theoretical

> ### Tip: Avoid the traps of *absolutes.*
>
> In the last tough question and any other, don't argue whether the extreme situation *will* happen; that would be just as futile. Let the questioner know that **you don't deal in absolutes**, particularly hypothetical ones. Move the discussion back to the realm of realistic possibilities and address the issues in that context, not in the context of extremes.

extreme situations are not reality, and therefore it would be a waste of time arguing about a theoretical extreme that isn't going to happen. (Refer to section 3.6 for related comments.)

Tell him you will discuss what really happens, and then stick to that.

> "I can't give you an answer for *an absolute question like that.* What I can and will tell you is that if it's important enough for my boss to know about it, then it's important enough for you to tell me about it first. If you're not sure, ask me first."

> "I trust your judgment a lot more than most. You have the authority to do many things. Most don't require my approval or involvement. As a rule of thumb in the future—if it's something that *involves my boss, then I want to review it first.*"

8.6 ARE YOU SAYING I SHOULD NOT RESPOND TO THE VICE PRESIDENT'S REQUEST BUT JUST GIVE YOU THE INFORMATION?

This hostile question is an obvious trap. The employee would just love you to say he isn't allowed to respond to the company vice president; the next time the VP calls for information, he could say he can't respond because bad ol' you said so.

Your reply should let him know what his responsibilities are to you, without stepping on the vice president's toes.

> "No, I'm not saying that you or anyone else shouldn't respond to the vice president's request directly. But I am saying *you must alert me to the request.* If I'm not here, at least try to reach me somehow. If you can't reach me first, then respond immediately to the vice president and then let me know as fast as you can afterward."

Tough Questions Worksheet

Create responses to the difficult questions you could face on this chapter's topics, using the formulas below. Use **logic, emotion,** and **ethics** whenever possible. Experiment by answering the same question with different formulas to learn which best fits your natural style. Use pencil so you can erase and refine your answers.

Past, Present, Future:

What happened was:

What's happening now is:

The way we'll prevent it from happening again is by:

Problem to Solution:

*The **problems** we have are:*

*I'd like to go directly to a proposed **solution:***

Problem - Cause - Solution - Timing (PCST):

*The **problems** we have are:*

*They were **caused** by:*

*The **solutions** we may implement are:*

*Our **timing** is:*

Wrong, Right, and What It Means:

*This is an extremely complex area and our track record has **overall** been very* *good:*

*We do very difficult things and sometimes we have failures. What **happened** is* *that:*

*What this **means** for us now is:*

Three-Step Explanation:

I understand what you are asking and why it concerns you so much:

Other people who had your experiences probably would feel the same way:

However, I would like to explain a little about this problem:

Other formulas and responses I want to use for tough questions related to this chapter:

9

Defending Your Decision to Promote Younger Workers

9.1   *I've waited a long time for this chance. Don't you think it was my turn?*

9.2   *Why should I bother working hard anymore? What does it get me?*

9.3   *How can you pass me by when I know ten times as much as she does?*

9.4   *How can you possibly call this a "fair" decision?*

9.5   *Isn't this age discrimination?*

Few things are as divisive as promotions. Double that when you select younger employees to leapfrog over senior staff. It's a safe, albeit unwanted bet that you will be subjected to emotionally wrenching questions when you appoint a youthful wunderkind to the new administrator position.

You must consider myriad factors when deciding whom to entrust with the heavy responsibility of running the shop. Who knows enough? Who is dependable? Who is responsible? Who can see details and the big picture? Who can lead instead of push and punish? Who shares your vision? And then when it's clear the applicants with 20 years experience fall short, how do you answer their questions without crushing their egos and inviting a lawsuit?

Not only will the passed-over veteran employees say it's unfair, some will contend it's illegal. Caught between the court of law and the court of public opinion at your work place, it's imperative you handle these land mines without triggering a lot of collateral damage. After you've talked with your lawyer and your human resources director, consider molding their advice with these responses.

9.1 I'VE WAITED A LONG TIME FOR THIS CHANCE. DON'T YOU THINK IT WAS MY TURN?

After years of devotion and consistently hard work, a senior staffer feels it is finally time for him to get the big reward. He knows the company's bottom line looks good partly because of his expert skills and quick responses during major screw-ups. The senior staffer has saved your butt more than once. Both of you feel you "owe" him; despite that, you picked the 32-year-old sales manager. The senior employee is asking why it wasn't his "turn."

How you respond to him will affect how well or how poorly he does his job for months or years to come. No response you can give will instantly stop the hurt he feels, but your response can shorten the duration of his emotional pain, or it can prolong it. The senior employee may be looking for a rational explanation to settle his own mind, or he might want to hear a response that he can use to prove you made a mistake, or he may be embarrassed. He might be feeling all those things and other emotions also. He probably doesn't know for certain what he is feeling, and you can only guess.

Nevertheless, you must respond. It seems best to gently lead the disappointed applicant to the general reasons why the successful applicant got the job.

"I know you've been here a long time, and you've done some great work. I can say the same about other candidates as well. I'm being honest when I say I know how you feel, because this has happened to me too. *But none of us has a 'turn' for a position like this.* Getting appointed to administrator *isn't a reward the company gives for exceptional performance.* The candidate we selected has the best qualifications to do the administrator's job."

"The person we selected isn't being rewarded for his past successes as much as he's being put into a job that he's very qualified to do. When you were hired for your job, it didn't have anything to do with whether it was your 'turn.' *You were hired because you were the best candidate for the position, and that's what we did in filling the administrator's position.*"

"The administrator position isn't a special reward given to recognize good service. *You've done excellent work and we've compensated you for that in other ways. But this process isn't about someone's turn at bat or a means of giving recognition.* The administrator position is crucial to our overall operation, and we selected the person whose abilities best fit the duties."

Only time and acceptance will help him get over his disappointment, but a well-chosen response could help both of you feel better. A wise counselor once said, "No matter how bad you feel, that feeling can't last forever." Alas, he said the same was true for good feelings.

9.2 WHY SHOULD I BOTHER WORKING HARD ANYMORE? WHAT DOES IT GET ME?

This is a rhetorical question, yet it nevertheless requires a wise response from you. On its face, the question may seem stupid to a callous manager; the reasons for continuing to work are too obvious not to be seen: paycheck and benefits. But the vexing question is more of an attack on the system that didn't reward the senior employee as he feels it should have. The tough question needs a two-tier response that handles the literal and emotional concerns.

In his disappointment, the older employee sounds off by suggesting he might not work so hard anymore. After all, what did he get for it? No pro-

---

Tip: Don't rush 'em when they're on the ledge.

If someone is standing on a ledge and thinking about jumping, that isn't the time to rush him. **You might trigger the action you don't want.** It's the same with hollow threats by disappointed employees who insinuate they might not work hard or obey orders. **It would be a mistake to pick that emotion-filled moment to remind him of the obvious, that he has to be productive, or else.** Such a reminder could precipitate the petulant behavior neither of you really wants. As you would with a potential jumper, keep him talking about something positive until you lead him to a safe place where reason will replace emotion.

motion, no increased pay, no increased status, no deserved recognition like a higher title, and so on. While the mutiny he's hinting at may not be real, the disappointment certainly is. You need to deal with that as gently as you can.

> "I don't know any fancy words that would really satisfy you. Each of us has a different reason for working hard. I do it because I like to get things done—I do it for me—not because someone tells me to. Yes, I've got a job and I get a paycheck, and that's important, too. But I work hard because I want to, and I believe *you have the same work ethic.*"

9.3 HOW CAN YOU PASS ME BY WHEN I KNOW TEN TIMES AS MUCH AS SHE DOES?

You can't deny it. Most of the senior staff know a lot about the ins and outs of the company. The veterans often have great rapport with important customers as well. Most production processes were created by the older staff, so they know the operational methods well. They know the history of product development.

How could you have promoted the younger staff member when the older one knows so much more? Don't debate how much the older employee knows or doesn't know, or any other specific attribute of any of the candidates. It's too subjective and only invites more argument about what's done and over with. Then there's the little thing about being sued if you start down the road of comparing how each applicant measures up against others. You can't win, but you sure can lose big time. Listen to your lawyer and human resources director on this one.

To be on the safe side, your response to the older employee should focus on the general and not on the specific. Explain that the best candidate was selected because she possessed the most and best of what was needed for the job, and not because she was the most knowledgeable.

> "*I'm not going to make a comparison between the two of you.* But you've earned the right to some straight answers. Just because you weren't selected doesn't mean we can't see you are very valuable to this company. You know a good deal about what goes on here. Our choice has absolutely no reflection on how much you know or don't know. The person we hired, however, *fits all the qualifications, and she simply had the best combination of knowledge, education, and skills for this particular position.* It's that simple."

9.4 HOW CAN YOU POSSIBLY CALL THIS A "FAIR" DECISION?

Most employees, managers, and bosses would agree in principle that everything should be "fair." But when senior employees are passed over to hire one of the young and restless (and hopefully genuinely qualified), they call "foul" because it's not fair that one of them didn't get the job after years of loyalty and hard work. Of course, the young and restless would not think it fair that a "worn-out old-timer" got the promotion "just because of age." Damned if you do and damned if you don't.

When the disappointed senior staffer appeals to the ethical standard of "fairness," she has moved away from objective measures of qualifications to the highly subjective judgment of fairness. Once again, don't refer to the substance of the hiring decision, but reply to the context, which in this case is the process.

> "Believe it or not, this was a very open-and-aboveboard process. We'd all like to think decisions are fair, but often making a decision means to pick from two or more choices—and that will always look unfair to the ones who aren't selected. *This was a fair process that produced a good decision.*"

Tip: Showing fair process gets you to safer ground.

Most promotion decisions can't really be "fair." One person gets promoted and the other doesn't. Before you disagree, think about the difference between the **process** and the **result**—they are not the same. **The process can be fair**—the rules are followed fairly for all alike, each party has its fair chance to present its case, and so on. Does a fair process create a fair decision? Only in *your* mind. But the passed-over senior employee probably won't agree with your logic. **Far better you demonstrate that the "process" was fair**; you have some chance of being believed on that point.

9.5 ISN'T THIS AGE DISCRIMINATION?

Like most "mature" adults (nice euphemism for old), senior employees equate age with knowledge and experience. Yet, we know that a person can have 25 years of many experiences or 25 years of one experience. Of course, we learn the most from experiences, but if a person has 25 years of one experience, her expertise may be too narrow.

But now the senior staffer and her co-workers argue that common sense says nobody "that young" could possibly be capable of the administrator's duties. Her question takes you to the edge of a lawsuit. It's safer to respond in a general context instead of the specific circumstances of the recent promotion.

> "Just because a person is younger than the other applicants doesn't automatically mean she's too young to be capable. The reverse is true too—just because a person is older, doesn't mean she is too old for a job. *It has little to do with age. What counts is who has the best combination of knowledge, skill, and capabilities.* That's how we hire and promote—age is not a factor in our decisions."

The tough questions posed in this chapter are prime examples of the type for which generalized instead of specific responses can be the best replies. The generalized response can contain the essence of what you want to get across without giving the questioners a specific to target in their next queries.

The generalized response is particularly advantageous whenever you face possible legal consequences. The fear of legal consequences often makes many managers say nothing, which can be as bad or worse than the possible lawsuit. "No comment" can cause as much damage to morale and productivity as a lawsuit and can be longer lasting. Using the generalized approach allows you to say something worthwhile and limit your exposure at the same time. (Refer to section 2.7 for related comments.)

Tough Questions Worksheet

Create responses to the difficult questions you could face on this chapter's topics, using the formulas below. Use **logic, emotion,** and **ethics** whenever possible. Experiment by answering the same question with different formulas to learn which best fits your natural style. Use pencil so you can erase and refine your answers.

Past, Present, Future:

What happened was:

What's happening now is:

The way we'll prevent it from happening again is by:

Problem to Solution:

*The **problems** we have are:*

*I'd like to go directly to a proposed **solution:***

Problem - Cause - Solution - Timing (PCST):

*The **problems** we have are:*

*They were **caused** by:*

*The **solutions** we may implement are:*

*Our **timing** is:*

Wrong, Right, and What It Means:

*This is an extremely complex area and our track record has **overall** been very **good:***

*We do very difficult things and sometimes we have failures. **What happened** is that:*

*What this **means** for us now is:*

Three-Step Explanation:

I understand what you are asking and why it concerns you so much:

Other people who had your experiences probably would feel the same way:

However, I would like to explain a little about this problem:

Other formulas and responses I want to use for tough questions related to this chapter:

10

Handling Diversity Questions Effectively

10.1   Why are you forcing me to take "sensitivity" training when I'm not a bigot?

10.2   You said, "We are all prejudiced." Are you saying I'm a racist?

10.3   Hasn't there been enough special treatment of certain people already?

10.4   When are <u>we</u> going to get special treatment?

10.5   You're not black or a woman. How can you pretend to understand what it's like to be me?

To describe the amazing and unparalleled diversity of our country, somebody once said we're a "melting pot." Yet others call it a mosaic, swirling with the vibrancy of diverse groups that retain some degree of their identities. Those are pleasant images, but to many people's way of thinking, the analogies suffer. While there might have been some melting or swirling going on in America, reality shows that many of the "ingredients" haven't mixed well. Some have tended to remain on the bottom while others rise to the top.

Few of us admit to being bigots or having prejudice. But how else do you account for the great gaps in jobs across the board? More dramatically, how else do you account for the incredible discrepancy in salaries between white men, women, blacks, and other minorities for the *same jobs*?

As of the writing of this book, legally imposed efforts to lessen the gaps, "affirmative action," are on the Congressional chopping block and despite calls for an overhaul, chances are it will be a long time before the issue is resolved, either practically or philosophically. The issue is just too divisive.

Critics argue that efforts to recruit women and minorities lead to lowered standards and encourage reverse discrimination. They claim it's about time all of America judged people on merit, not quotas.

Supporters of diversity agree that in an ideal world, color and gender-blind merit should be the rule (and should have been all along). However, given America's history of discrimination and the reality of a mostly white male leadership in most industries, that goal is still a long way off. They insist that America continues to need a period of forced gender and race preference.

Both sides acknowledge the difficulty in determining when equality is reached. Critics fear that once an equal threshold of preferential treatment is commonplace, those who benefit will refuse to acknowledge an end.

In the meantime, managers have their hands full as they attempt to make workplace equality a worthy goal, not an obsession.

Many organizations are quick to stress that their programs are based on *diversity* and shun the "affirmative action" words because the terms are so loaded with negative connotations. Some companies have bought into diversity thinking mostly for pragmatic reasons. It hits them right in their self-interest (pocketbooks). They know they are selling to an increasingly diverse customer base.

So for both economically and politically correct reasons, many organizations are making sure women and minorities are invited to apply for opportunities that were previously closed to them. This doesn't necessarily have to mean giving any group preference, but it does mean making certain the same opportunities are offered to both.

Because of the angry rhetoric present in issues such as race, sexism, and homosexuality, managers are facing a lot of resistance, sometimes even rage, in trying to get everyone's cultures "accepted" in the workplace. As the responses and insights in this section point out, the best approach to tough questions on this subject is to show that your organization pursues diversity reasonably and unapologetically.

10.1 WHY ARE YOU FORCING ME TO TAKE "SENSITIVITY" TRAINING WHEN I'M NOT A BIGOT?

Many companies are requiring their employees to take some form of diversity training. It's about what it sounds like: an attempt to make people more aware and sensitive to the needs, struggles, and humanity of others.

But a middle-aged white male who has done outstanding work for the company since he came on board five years ago bristles at the requirement to attend diversity training scheduled for next month. He keeps his views to himself, doesn't use racist or sexist language, and is generous to local charities benefiting all segments of the community.

His hostile question indicates that management's directive requiring everyone to attend the training has become a double-edged sword. On the one hand, you are attempting to make all employees aware of the consequences of past discriminatory practices in workplaces, and to rectify them. On the other, employees hear a different message, that you think they are insensitive.

Worse yet, since the training is obviously directed at helping them be more sympathetic toward women and minorities, they wonder if you are also accusing them of discriminating against these groups?

How your employees react depends to a large degree on how you phrase your response. The key is to let them know that you are talking about everybody: white males, older workers, people with disabilities, women, and people of color.

> "Our company *cares enough* about the people who work here to take steps to ensure that *nobody is denied a job or is underpaid* for a job because of his or her race, sex, age, or sexual preference That includes white males. This training is designed to help us all become more aware of the problems and issues involved in understanding and treating *one another fairly* in the workplace.

> "We all know that there are people out there who for whatever reason refuse to treat certain people with fairness and respect. They don't want to work for a woman, or they don't want to take orders from somebody younger than they or they don't want to do business with people of another race. *I'm not saying that's true of you or me. But we can all benefit from an open and honest discussion* of how we can all get along better. We can also talk about what this company can do to try and prevent people who have these prejudices from making *decisions that are based on ignorance and stereotyping.*"

> "We shouldn't kid ourselves that any of us knows what it's like for other groups of people. Racial, ethnic, religious, and gender differences *are realities that all of us need to learn more about.* Certainly we all intend to be fair and considerate of one another's differences, but just wishing it were so won't make it come true. We are holding this session to help us work toward *converting those good intentions into reality.*"

"Our goal with our diversity program is not to show preference; it's to create a workplace *that reflects America—that means diversity.* Creating diversity means breaking down barriers that have existed for a long time. The *biggest barriers* have always been a lack of awareness, understanding, and appreciation of the feelings and rights of others. *Education* has always been a good first step toward achieving that goal."

"We consider it important and *smart business* to teach our employees about differences ranging from age and race to sexual orientation. Why? Frankly, this is not a social experiment. *We're here to make a product and to make money, and we need all of you working together.*"

"We consider it good business for everyone to spend a little time learning more about the diverse nature of one another and of our customers. All of us bring our *cultures into the workplace.* And when we react to one another, we often respond based on our cultural conditioning. Sometimes we assume our reactions are 'normal and right.' *But there's really no way you can understand how people are reacting to you until you learn about their cultural conditioning.* And that's the purpose of diversity training."

The foregoing responses should remind skeptics of an accepted truth: No one can completely escape society's thousands of positive and negative influences, particularly children. Point out that all of us carry some degree of prejudice caused by mass-media stereotyping and individual experiences. That goes for "minorities" of all types as well as the stereotypical middle-aged, Protestant, white, heterosexual male with a crew cut.

Tip: Stress your respect for individual differences.

Muster up the courage to be clear and honest (still the best policy) about your organization's position on this sensitive topic. In your response, **avoid the temptation to sugarcoat the truth** by saying what is obviously untrue for most of us, such as "Oh, of course, none of us here is prejudiced and we wouldn't dream of stereotyping people." We all carry prejudices instilled in us when young by socialization, but we don't have to let it direct our thinking and behavior all our lives.

10.2 YOU SAID, "WE ARE ALL PREJUDICED." ARE YOU SAYING I'M A RACIST?

Many white males are particularly resistant to diversity programs because they believe they stand to lose the most. They must also contend with the implied or spoken blame for society's problems. White males quite logically feel threatened and uncertain of their own future in this diversity thing.

So when your employee expresses his fear by trying to turn your words around and imply you are calling him a bigot, don't rise to the bait. (Refer to section 3.3 for related comment.) Don't let him take your words to an extreme that can provoke a serious confrontation between the two of you. Keep the discussion focused on the real issues and the clear objectives of the training.

> "I will be bluntly honest with you. I'm saying that *life builds some degree of prejudice* into each and every one of us. A racist is a person who *lets that prejudice* control his thinking or direct her behavior. No, I don't see you talking or acting like a racist."

> "No, I don't believe you are a racist. Nothing in your behavior has given me any reason to think that. However, I am saying that *none of us escaped* being influenced by good things like morality and by bad things like prejudice. No one grows up in a vacuum. We are all part of a society that has major problems because of ethnic and gender differ-

---

Tip: We're all perfect—honest.

Few people recognize the enormous difference between socially induced prejudices and the racist behavior caused by **letting those feelings control behavior.** One is a "feeling" and the other is an "action"—thinking versus doing.

If you can, lead the challengers to the realization that you, I, they, and everyone else has **uninvited** prejudices, yet that by itself does not make any of us bad or wrong in any way. It's okay, really it is. Then use your response to help them see that life gets bad and wrong when we let those prejudices steer our behavior; that's where racism starts. People may honestly believe they are fair, but until they understand and accept other people's values and cultures they will continue to act with some prejudice.

ences. *We all need to step back and look at ourselves objectively.* We're asking everyone to take this training session with the hopes that we can all learn to see each other as we really are, not as stereotypes."

Make certain that no one is calling the challengers "bigots," even if they act like bigots. Acknowledge them as good people, too. Your job isn't to call anyone names, whether the shoe fits or not. It's hoped that it's still true that most of us have a core set of decent values, including racists.

10.3 HASN'T THERE BEEN ENOUGH SPECIAL TREATMENT OF CERTAIN PEOPLE ALREADY?

The notion of righting past wrongs and shortening the present gap is a noble one, but solving an inequity (discrimination) with an inequity (reverse discrimination) is causing rage across America. With this hostile question, your employee is like many people across the nation who react against diversity policies.

He joins many white males complaining they are being discriminated against. He is not thinking about how white males have dominated numerous societies and civilizations for thousands of years. Only in the phenomenally short time span of women's rights, affirmative action, and civil rights (30 years), have your employee and some other white males become aware of how it feels when someone else gets "special treatment."

At present, although many people are covered by civil-rights laws, white males included, organizations can legally give preference to women or people of color to make up for past discrimination practices. That has created an impression in his mind that when you hired the African-American woman for the new position you did so because of her gender and color, not her abilities.

To reply, you can explain how some of the more successful diversity programs have a system for identifying candidates with potential and then create ways of helping them compete for positions. Let them know this is accomplished through support groups, mentoring programs, career-planning initiatives, and targeted training (such as sexual harassment, language skills, and college-level instruction).

"Frankly, we don't consider *trying to make our workplace reflect* the community and America special treatment. *We consider it smart business.* Let me be clear, however, that we are not giving preferential treatment as some companies have done. We are merely taking steps to encourage certain people to apply for positions they were discouraged from seeking in the past. *These are all things most of us have had access to all our lives."*

"I think you're confusing our diversity program with affirmative action. Our policy is *not to give special preference to anybody,* including white males. We do, however, realize that our work force, for whatever reason, simply *doesn't reflect the community we live in, nor the people we do business with.* For this reason, we have created a system for identifying candidates with potential and then help them compete for positions. We do this through support groups, mentoring programs, career-planning initiatives, and targeted training. But we don't hire or promote them unless they are the most qualified for the job. Period."

If your organization is practicing affirmative action, and does give preference to minorities or women in hiring practices, these responses may be more appropriate:

"Let's look at it as *simple math.* Our customer base (consumers) is made up of 82 percent women (major purchasers), 28 percent men, and 22 percent people of color. Our work force is made up of 85 percent white men, 15 percent women, and 8 percent people of color. The numbers just don't ad up. We believe, and many other companies are proving, that making an organization reflect the community is a great way of *boosting sales and boosting morale.* We like that a lot, and I hope you will too."

"Our program will end when people really can see not that the numbers are perfect, *but that the system has become fair and open.* It will end when we can, with confidence, stop counting and turn our attention to other important things."

"Our affirmative-action program is intended to correct the effects of past practices. It's going to take a lot more understanding and commitment to rectify what happened *during decades and centuries of discrimination* in all of our communities and in every workplace. *You are welcome to take part in our focus groups or planning programs if you'd like to help us reach our goal of creating an environment that works for everybody."*

"Affirmative action means many things. It means making sure *everyone is invited to participate and that no one is blocked* from sharing equal opportunities. It also sometimes means hiring certain people *today* who were kept out of jobs they should have gotten *yesterday.* The goal is to have a free society where the work force truly reflects the entire populace. We aren't there yet, but we will be someday."

10.4 WHEN ARE *WE* GOING TO GET SPECIAL TREATMENT?

People who ask this kind of question apparently don't feel the first three thousand years of civilization were enough of a head start. Your disgruntled employee sees your push to narrow the discrimination gap as unfair treatment. It's tough to argue with an employee who uses that kind of logic.

So don't argue, just focus on the positive goals of providing a level playing field for all.

> "While some people may choose to see some aspects of diversity (or affirmative action) as unfair or special preferences, I wonder how many of us really would want the kind of *"special" treatment that women and minorities received* before affirmative action was begun."

> "I think the facts speak for themselves. The fact is that 95 percent of this company is made up of white males. And white males make up only 35 percent of this community. Somewhere along the line, somebody's being shortchanged, left out, or ignored. And I don't think it's white males."

> "Our purpose is not just to make up for past discrimination. It's to increase the strength of people who have been held back, so they have the *same opportunities you have enjoyed in educational facilities and positions of power.* It also means helping to make sure people are represented in the work force in numbers similar to their representation in society. White males have been the recipient of special treatment in society for several thousand years. I don't think *a few years* of attempting to treat others equally is unfair *special treatment.*"

> "Let's look at the facts, shall we? The facts show that white males continue to be promoted at *three times the rate* of other groups in our company, despite our very aggressive diversity goals. I'd say that shows women and minorities are *not getting* a disproportionate amount of advancement since most promotions are going to white males."

10.5 YOU'RE NOT BLACK OR A WOMAN. HOW CAN YOU PRETEND TO UNDERSTAND WHAT IT'S LIKE TO BE ME?

To demonstrate your concern, you attempted to relate to what the female African-American employee is going through. Instead of accepting the dialogue, she rejects your empathy with an accusing question that locks you out of the African-American world. You are a white male of European descent, so how can you possibly know what she feels or thinks? She rejects your empathy because it sounds impossible and thus insincere to her. Do you apologize or should you ignore the slight? There's a better way.

When minority employees question how you can possibly understand what they're going through or make decisions that affect their unique situations, don't recite your experiences. If you are white and they are black or female or otherwise different, you will not convince them you know what life is like for them. For everyone's sake, don't try to be cool or awkwardly use slang terms that don't fit your background.

Don't kid yourself into thinking you really do understand—chances are you will only make a fool of yourself. Instead, your response should point to things that you both value: paycheck, insurance, opportunity, security, respect, dignity, fairness, and two-way honesty. You can be of any color, gender, or shape and still need and appreciate the importance of those things.

> "Regardless of how I may sound, I don't pretend to know what it's like to be a woman or an African American. It's impossible for me to have those experiences. *But I don't have to be female or black to know why it's important to have a job and health insurance.* I can be who I am and realize how wrong it is to deny a job to someone because of gender or ethnic background. If it's tough for a white male like me, it must be worse for people who are still subjected to discrimination. *We can't trade genes and ancestry, but we can understand what's important to each other.*"

Tough Questions Worksheet

Create responses to the difficult questions you could face on this chapter's topics, using the formulas below. Use **logic, emotion,** and **ethics** whenever possible. Experiment by answering the same question with different formulas to learn which best fits your natural style. Use pencil so you can erase and refine your answers.

Past, Present, Future:

What happened was:

What's happening now is:

The way we'll prevent it from happening again is by:

Problem to Solution:

*The **problems** we have are:*

*I'd like to go directly to a proposed **solution:***

Problem - Cause - Solution - Timing (PCST):

*The **problems** we have are:*

*They were **caused** by:*

*The **solutions** we may implement are:*

*Our **timing** is:*

Wrong, Right, and What It Means:

*This is an extremely complex area and our track record has **overall** been very good:*

*We do very difficult things and sometimes we have failures. What **happened** is that:*

*What this **means** for us now is:*

Three-Step Explanation:

I understand what you are asking and why it concerns you so much:

Other people who had your experiences probably would feel the same way:

However, I would like to explain a little about this problem:

Other formulas and responses I want to use for tough questions related to this chapter:

11

Good Reasons Why You Didn't Do More

11.1   *Couldn't you have done more?*

11.2   *Why aren't you making more progress?*

11.3   *Why didn't you act sooner?*

When you are asked why you haven't done more, or sooner, be alert. Nothing you do is ever enough to some people, even to yourself at times. There's always a gulf between what people expect and what reality permits a manager to do.

Whatever enough may be for each of us, it is constrained in every manager's workplace by the limits of time, energy, money, and other resources. These realities frequently stymie all managers. When you fall short of your goals, few people are close enough to know why. Top executives and uninvolved colleagues typically never fully understand which barriers blocked your best efforts.

But your critics—armed with their hostile questions—do they understand or care? Probably not; nevertheless you must respond in some fashion. Otherwise, everyone will be left with the impression that you are to blame for why goals weren't met. How do you explain without sounding as if you're making wimpy excuses?

11.1 COULDN'T YOU HAVE DONE MORE?

You work so hard you literally can't see straight. Despite one setback after another, you succeed at getting something done and are working to prevent further foul-ups. Certainly you would like to have the project kept at full size, the report longer, or the products shipped out in larger volumes.

Your critic, however, thinks he can put you on the spot and demands to know why more wasn't done.

Create a New Frame of Reference

Since "enough" is usually a matter of perspective, your response should hinge upon that reality. Reshape the mental picture by creating a new frame of reference.

❒ Have you just begun?

❒ Did you do as much or more than anyone else could or would?

❒ Have you done all that time and resources would allow?

❒ Did you at least resolve the most important problems and needs?

❒ Have you gone as far as a reasonable person should on this problem?

"Throughout this project our goal has been to do what was both *possible and acceptable* to the many competing interests involved. We strongly believe we have *accomplished what time, resources, manpower, and circumstances have allowed.*"

"No one could have anticipated the huge and unexpected problems that developed. They were *impossible to predict,* and they were new to us. *We responded as well as anyone could have under the circumstances.*"

"We've had to balance our willingness to *pursue change* against the willingness of others to *accept change.*"

"Have we done enough? Perhaps. Perhaps not. On an issue, however, where any action is considered an intrusion by someone, what we have accomplished in such a short time is certainly a *bold improvement over what previously existed.*"

"From being closely involved with this issue, we have found that what is 'enough' is totally *a matter of perspective.* From some we have been accused of doing too much. From others, not enough. *Perhaps that means we are doing just enough.*"

You usually can say in hindsight that you wished you had done more, but you did as much as was possible, feasible, and ethical under the circumstances.

Tip: Don't cite rules, laws.

Avoid emphasizing that rules or laws wouldn't allow you to do more. Even if true, most people will not accept such an explanation. Most people **judge you** according to your **capabilities,** not by your **responsibilities.** Intuitively, people ask themselves "could you have done more?" Show them why you were not capable of doing more.

11.2 WHY AREN'T YOU MAKING MORE PROGRESS?

Co-workers and executives are concerned because you haven't progressed as far as they expected. And the one manager who never misses a chance to embarrass you implies with her question that you're dragging your feet.

You know you are being careful and deliberative in each step of your work and are trying to balance speed (the American way of rush, rush, rush) with the need to take time to do things right. You are well aware of the old phrase, "There's always time to do it over, but never time to do it right."

Your three goals in the face of this type of question are to maintain the support you have, sway the undecided to accept your reasonable answer, and maybe neutralize the unreachable critics. Don't spend time or words trying to reach the unreachable—they don't want to understand, so they won't regardless of what you say or do. But if your response sets the mark for reasonableness, you can prevent the critics from swaying the undecided and undermining your supporters. (Refer to section 1.4 for related comments.)

By itself, a two-sentence response to this tough question won't entirely satisfy your supporters or your critics, but it can set up a new perspective on which to build your persuasive answer. These model responses create excellent bridges to which you can add your substantive facts and explanations:

"We are making progress. *We didn't, however, get into the problem overnight, and I don't think it can be solved overnight.* Our plan is a long-range plan that will create lasting improvements."

"Whenever you make a decision of this magnitude and begin taking action, you have to get it right, and you must take the time to *get it right the first time. There may be no second chances.*"

"These are extremely complex problems. We would all like to see things progress faster, *but not if it means we take the wrong paths and make major mistakes.* That would *cost* everyone a heck of a lot *more in the long run* than it would to take the time to do things right in the first place."

"We're not shirking our responsibilities, but at the same time, whatever we do *will set a precedent* for others, so we want to *get it right the first time.*"

"What we are trying to do is change the culture of our organization. *Cultures don't change overnight, however.* We know we're making solid progress and will continue to make even more."

"I think that *the slow pace reflects the difficulties, as well as the progress, in the process.* It's like a lemon. When you squeeze in the beginning, the juice comes out quickly; it's harder on the second or third try."

"This is an ongoing process, and therefore you *can't have a scorecard at every stop.*"

Don't try converting these stage-setting responses into glib phrases without solid follow up; everyone will see through it. They create a space of reasonableness; it's up to you to provide the informational material to widen and preserve that space. Just make certain your remarks are honest. (Refer to section 1.9 for related comment.)

These responses emphasize why complex issues can't be resolved overnight. Most reasonable people understand this. And remember, your audience is the "reasonable people;" they will decide when to listen to you or your nemesis.

11.3 WHY DIDN'T YOU ACT SOONER?

This question gets thrown at every manager sooner or later. Sometimes you need to determine that it's time to hit your critic with a verbal punch to back him up a bit, so that he understands he could pay a price if he continues his not-so-hidden attack. (Refer to section 1.4 for related comment.) You might use this one-two rendition:

One: "We are seeking to *arrive* at conclusions, *not jump* to them."

Two: "If we acted in a knee-jerk fashion, we might make mistakes and we might have compromised someone's integrity in the process. We're dealing with people's reputations here. *That's not a commodity we're willing to sacrifice for speed.*"

Whether or not you used this one-two punch, these next two responses create perspectives on which you can place your substantive explanations.

"What we have done thus far is an *extremely important first step.* It had to be done carefully and thoroughly, *without rushing, because it laid the foundation for everything that follows.* We are now prepared to move to the next step, to produce the results we've all worked hard for."

"I think we can accomplish what people are asking for. With hindsight, we recognize how we might have done things sooner, and *we are learning from that. Next time we will be able to a better job,* and that's exactly what we are going to do."

There is always somebody who wants something sooner than when you can or should provide it. The preceding responses illustrate the age-old struggle between waste from haste and quality with time. However, don't think you can use these effective responses to cover up habitual procrastination.

If it's obvious you procrastinated, a good response like the aforementioned will come across like a lame excuse. If sooner wasn't possible or advisable, say so directly and back it up with facts. But say it in a way that shows you really believe what you want others to believe. That requires sincerity and concise information.

Tough Questions Worksheet

Create responses to the difficult questions you could face on this chapter's topics, using the formulas below. Use **logic, emotion,** and **ethics** whenever possible. Experiment by answering the same question with different formulas to learn which best fits your natural style. Use pencil so you can erase and refine your answers.

Past, Present, Future:

What happened was:

What's happening now is:

The way we'll prevent it from happening again is by:

Problem to Solution:

*The **problems** we have are:*

*I'd like to go directly to a proposed **solution:***

Problem - Cause - Solution - Timing (PCST):

*The **problems** we have are:*

*They were **caused** by:*

*The **solutions** we may implement are:*

*Our **timing** is:*

Wrong, Right, and What It Means:

*This is an extremely complex area and our track record has **overall** been very **good:***

*We do very difficult things and sometimes we have failures. What **happened** is that:*

*What this **means** for us now is:*

Three-Step Explanation:

I understand what you are asking and why it concerns you so much:

Other people who had your experiences probably would feel the same way:

However, I would like to explain a little about this problem:

Other formulas and responses I want to use for tough questions related to this chapter:

12

Staying Safe While Responding to an Overly Demanding Boss

12.1   Don't you think you should be more efficient?

12.2   Your work isn't that tough, so why can't you handle more?

12.3   Are you working at full capacity and putting in enough time?

Before going into any detail on this subject, ask yourself if the boss really deserves the title of "overly demanding." Did he handle your job at one time and now has a thorough understanding of its demands? If he is a high achiever, does he expect equal performance from you?

Looking at this from a positive stance, you could make the circumstances into an opportunity to develop yourself to full potential. It may be an excellent opportunity for self-analysis. You could evaluate your organizational capabilities, prioritize your work better, become more effective in delegating work to others, and generally improve all of the other capabilities that lead to becoming a successful manager/supervisor.

On the other hand, if you have been totally honest with yourself and consulted with trusted colleagues but you still have your doubts, how do you know for sure? Aristotle said that we are what we repeatedly do. Therefore, if your boss repeatedly demands more of you than you sincerely know is fair or feasible, he *is* an overly demanding boss from *your* point of view. Most likely, he probably doesn't recognize that his frequent, unreasonable demands overwhelm and disrupt your work processes time after time.

This rare but troublesome type of boss fails to recognize your superhuman efforts to please him. He apparently considers long days and frequent weekend work as normal, if he thinks about it at all.

In order to deal with him successfully, you need to know how he'll probably react. Does he generally maintain an open mind? Is he willing to look honestly at himself? Is he closed-minded and defensive? Does he take affront when hearing about his own contributions to your work problems? Consider these factors when forming your strategy and responses. For example, if he's closed-minded and defensive, you should not give blunt responses, as they would only convince him that you should be disciplined in some fashion. But if he's an open-minded workaholic, then more direct replies may work, providing you wrap them in diplomatic language.

12.1 DON'T YOU THINK YOU SHOULD BE MORE EFFICIENT?

Your boss's accusatory question deals with the perception that you're spinning your wheels—rush-rush but little output and frequent rework. His perception suggests to him that you're spending too much time and effort to get work done.

You have your regular annual work plan with all its projects, schedules, and milestones. That was fine when it was put together, albeit somewhat overly ambitious at the time. There wasn't much time for slippage. As the year got under way, problems developed as your overly demanding boss began asking for "just this short little rush I need tomorrow" and that "special letter I've just got to have this afternoon."

An overly demanding boss who asks such damning questions is also the one who impulsively makes whatever is in front of him your highest priority, at least for that moment. He proves the truth that all emphasis is no emphasis. You have his long-term top priorities, the short-term top priorities, and then this "one-time" top priority for today.

This guy makes just about everything a priority. His priority switching and memory lapses jerk you around with so many starts and stops that your productivity actually declines.

You try to accommodate the boss to make him happy. But that was yesterday, because now he wants to know why you can't keep control of your work schedule so your time is more productive. In responding, first get control of his question and redirect it toward undoing the damaging premise of the inquiry. Which of these might fit your style?

"Like anyone else, I certainly want to be more efficient. I'm always looking for ways to do that in scheduling, prioritizing work, personal organization, and so on. But I seem to be constantly interrupted with endless high-priority demands on my time. I'd like to *list some of the 'must-do' interruptions* I get constantly. It would help me if you'd suggest *which I should accept and which I should decline or refer elsewhere. . . ."*

"I've been looking for ways to *shorten some of the steps* in my work. I'd like to make it a priority to actually come up with several ideas for you to consider. *Can we meet to discuss the options and then select the ones you want?* I would appreciate any suggestions you may have."

"*I work very hard* but don't disagree that *there are some things I wish I could do faster.* I have thought a lot about making some changes but haven't had the time to think them through. *Got any observations* for me on how I can get things done more efficiently?

Are you inefficient? Of course you are—and so is every other human being. None of us has yet become the perfect worker. Everyone can be more efficient; so don't argue that issue.

The preceding responses intentionally do not include a denial or an admission to the accusation of inefficiency. Don't offer a false, self-condemning admission of inefficiency to curry favor—a false confession will be used against you during your annual evaluation.

Unless proving him wrong is pivotal to keeping your job, skip the potentially damaging argument over what and who is efficient. The boss already believes you are inefficient. At the least, he is stuck with his accusatory comment. He probably won't retract it.

Taking Control Without a Fight

The aforementioned responses subtly take control without a fight. They acknowledge that you also want efficiency and then bridge away from his negative premise. These responses lead him where you want to go. You ask him for suggestions, thereby making him convert his complaints into recommendations. Furthermore, the responses force the boss to reveal his hand, tipping you off as to what his perception is based on.

When he begins responding to your questions, you have gained control. Refer back to section 1.5 where we explain how a person is controlled by the person to whom he reacts. Don't get cocky; it'll show instantly. Use your power over the discussion carefully and skillfully.

Tip: Use bridging questions to grab control.

Generally it's dangerous to answer a hostile question **with** a question. Your antagonist can use the opportunity to chop off your head and hand it back to you as his answer. But when a hostile question is built upon a false and damning premise you don't want to debate, you can use a **directional question to control and move the scene.**

You must learn to listen very attentively to gain this kind of control. By asking the critic for helpful suggestions about something to be done in the future, you **use his own thoughts** to help you **bridge away** from the negative image in the original question. His recommendations for the future help you **create a new space** full of positive images such as solutions and problem solving, even hope. Those images probably will replace the negative perception in time, assuming you keep him informed.

Learning to Control Others by Listening

Listen as though his observations and comments are true. Shut off your judgments and allow yourself to believe what he says, for the moment at least. That will put a convincing expression on your face, plus you just might learn something. You can always throw it out of your mind later if you don't agree.

While he's explaining his recommendations, get ready to complete your bridge. Listen for a "recommendation" that you want to implement. Start discussing that, and soon both of you will forget the original attack question.

12.2 YOUR WORK ISN'T THAT TOUGH, SO WHY CAN'T YOU HANDLE MORE?

Your overly demanding boss can ask this tricky question in a dozen different ways. In any form, its implications are serious. The premise of the question makes you queasy, because you fear your out-of-touch boss hasn't got a clue what your work is really like.

The false premise of his question sets you up for a job-ruining (and health-ruining) workload. You need to reeducate this guy in a hurry, but how? If you tell him how tough your assignments really are, he probably won't listen. His mind is made up, and he isn't the type to admit a mistake. Therefore, instead of answering "why can't you handle more," switch the focus to a discussion that gives you an opening to give him information he doesn't have.

> "Some of my assignments are easier than others, but some are pretty complex at times. Maybe I'm spending more time on projects than they are worth to the company. Let me list a few here *that are taking the most time.* If we could talk about them, it would be helpful for me to know *which ones are your highest priorities* and which ones don't require as much time. . . ."

> "Like many people here, I work longer hours than may not be apparent. Some of my assignments involve customer service or personnel matters *outside my control.* If I *explained some of the circumstances,* maybe you could help recommend ways to reduce these problems."

When the boss throws this tough question at you, don't let it boomerang back at him by arguing about what's tough and what isn't, or whether you can handle more. The more time you spend arguing with him about the impossibly subjective measure of "toughness," the less time you have to reeducate him. Indeed, if you quarrel over his false premise, you deepen his thoughts and may never have the chance to reeducate him.

During the discussion of your many assignments, elaborate on their complexity and difficulty. Steer the follow-up discussion to find out what he wants done first and by when, item by item if necessary. By the time you and the boss arrive at a new understanding of which assignments are most important and most difficult, both of you will probably have forgotten the opening question.

12.3 ARE YOU WORKING AT FULL CAPACITY AND PUTTING IN ENOUGH TIME?

Unless you've kept exceptionally detailed work and time logs, you won't have the documentation to show your overly demanding boss that you put in enough time on the job and work to full capacity. If you were the boss, what could an employee possibly tell you that would change your perception that he is slacking off and cutting corners?

Without data, all either person has is anecdotal recollections. Therefore, use your response to set up an answer in the future. You don't have to agree with his allegation about the past to agree to answer the accusatory question with future data.

An overly demanding boss who asks these questions almost certainly thinks he knows the answers, and is getting ready to jump all over you. You have only a few seconds to respond in a fashion that takes control.

> "I'm putting in a lot of hours and getting a lot done. And I burn the midnight oil when necessary. Obviously, there must be some doubt about that, or this question wouldn't come up. This could be answered fairly easily if I *logged my time—as lawyers and other professionals do.* Would that provide a useful answer to the questions?"

If the overly demanding boss can still be reached with rational discussion, and you sense this is the time to chance that, you could try a longer response to elicit his expertise. Everyone knows something we could benefit from, so your bridge could actually produce worthwhile advice. Are you working to full capacity?

> "I can honestly say that I think that I am, but you may have other ideas. I'm not a clock watcher, and often work additional hours during the week and on weekends. Maybe I should keep a *daily log* of my activities and the time devoted to each function. We could *analyze where I'm spending my time.* Your experience and coaching could be helpful to me in pointing out where my priorities may need changing. *Would you be willing to do that?*"

Tough Questions Worksheet

Create responses to the difficult questions you could face on this chapter's topics, using the formulas below. Use **logic, emotion,** and **ethics** whenever possible. Experiment by answering the same question with different formulas to learn which best fits your natural style. Use pencil so you can erase and refine your answers.

Past, Present, Future:

What happened was:

What's happening now is:

The way we'll prevent it from happening again is by:

Problem to Solution:

*The **problems** we have are:*

*I'd like to go directly to a proposed **solution:***

Problem - Cause - Solution - Timing (PCST):

*The **problems** we have are:*

*They were **caused** by:*

*The **solutions** we may implement are:*

*Our **timing** is:*

Wrong, Right, and What It Means:

*This is an extremely complex area and our track record has **overall** been very **good**:*

*We do very difficult things and sometimes we have failures. What **happened** is that:*

*What this **means** for us now is:*

Three-Step Explanation:

I understand what you are asking and why it concerns you so much:

Other people who had your experiences probably would feel the same way:

However, I would like to explain a little about this problem:

Other formulas and responses I want to use for tough questions related to this chapter:

13

Answering Up When Your Boss Forgets His Own Orders

13.1   Why did you do something so stupid? Who told you to do a dumb thing like that?

13.2   Why did you proceed blindly without double-checking with me first?

If you really want to wreck your relationship with your boss, wait for those vulnerable moments when he asks tough questions or makes blatant accusations based on his forgetful memory. This is, at the very least, your chance to commit career suicide by pouncing on the misstatement—you announce he is "Wrong Again!" (all the time bursting with silent glee; climbing over fallen comrades is the way to the top, right?).

It's a natural human desire, and popular workplace fantasy, to expose the incompetence of an unpleasant superior. You get extra points if you do it in front of co-workers, or better yet, *his* boss.

Exaggeration? Not at all. It's done every day. Unfortunately, most people won't find job security or promotional opportunity by pouncing on the memory lapses of their superiors.

When the boss forgets his past directives and throws tough questions at you, don't announce to him and the world how much smarter you are. Redirect the question to "facts" (the instructions or conversations) as you recall them, and don't engage in a heated discussion of whose memory is right or wrong.

13.1 WHY DID YOU DO SOMETHING SO STUPID?
WHO TOLD YOU TO DO A DUMB THING LIKE THAT?

Your incompetent boss has forgotten his past instructions. You did exactly what he told you to do. Now he hits you with this accusatory question. Your emotions react to the word "stupid," but you choose to ignore it. You are tempted to embarrass him by reminding him of the written instructions he has forgotten. Instead, help him save face.

If you can, lead the forgetful boss to recognize and admit his mistake. It takes just a few minutes for even the most secure and honest managers to bend a little and admit they've erred. It takes longer for an angry boss who is throwing grenades in the form of accusatory questions because he's forgotten his own instructions.

So buy some time—even if it's only 60 seconds—by reviewing your understanding of prior discussions. (Refer to section 2.10 for related comments.) Cite a time or place to jog his memory but keep it vague while your foggy boss recalls bits and pieces. This gives you an opportunity to regain your composure while the boss may be regaining his cool.

> "Actually, I did what I thought I was supposed to do. But now I'm not so sure that I understood what you wanted. *I'd like to go over what I thought your instructions were.* Maybe we can learn where this project fell off track and get it back on."

More likely, though, the department head won't admit anything, so your best bet is to bridge to what should be done in the future. If this is a rare event, and your raise or promotion isn't at risk, it's not worth the fight to prove him wrong.

Depersonalize to Deflate the Tension

In certain highly tense situations such as these, disarm and depersonalize your comments by avoiding the first- and second-person pronouns, such as you, me, I, and we. Avoiding personal attribution lowers the emotional level of the discussion. It creates extra space to temporarily distance yourself from the hothead. Taking the "you" out of responses can help provide the buffer that may be needed to avoid greater friction.

Believe it or not, depersonalized phrases with passive voice is also the language of successful diplomats. Most writing and speech classes tell you to use active voice because it's snappy and fast—the way Americans like just about everything. Although passive voice and depersonalized comments seem weak and wimpy, they help prevent triggering worse confrontations during explosive situations. Look at the following contrasts:

> "*I* think *we* have a communications problem here. *I* did *not* intend to do anything wrong. *Your instructions told me* to . . . If *you* could clear up *your* instructions . . . *I* could start . . ."

Now read the depersonalized response below. Do you feel less emotional tension from it?

> "*There may be* a communications problem here, and *not an intentional decision* to do something wrong. The *instructions seemed* to be . . . *Maybe* that's where a misunderstanding occurred. If that could be cleared up, then this project can be done correctly."

The depersonalized, passive-voice response is less direct and actually a bit dull. But dull, indirect, and boring are just fine when snappy and fast might stir emotions and foster more acrimony. However, if used too frequently, the passive-depersonalized method will make you sound cold, distant, and uncaring. Save it for the times when you want to make sure you don't sound superior or threatening. (Refer to section 1.8 for more on depersonalized replies and then to Chapter 4 for additional comments on word choices.)

13.2 WHY DID YOU PROCEED BLINDLY WITHOUT DOUBLE-CHECKING WITH ME FIRST?

In this era of empowerment, you're being told to use your discretion, exercise your initiative, and make decisions by yourself or with your team. Your boss is very busy and said you should run your department as you see fit, checking only when you think it's needed.

But then one day you hear about the consequences of a decision you were empowered to make. Your boss is aghast that you would choose to act without his approval. He has forgotten he empowered you to act. At this point, do you point that out in your response?

You have two choices here. You can quietly accept misplaced blame or politely defend yourself. If you choose to accept the criticism, you might say:

> *"Maybe I exceeded my authority. If I did, I'm sorry about that.* At the time, I didn't think it was a decision you would want to review. Do you have time now to go over what types of decisions you want to review before I make them? That would give me a better idea of what your expectations are so I don't do this again."

On the other hand, if you want to defend yourself diplomatically, this response might be more effective:

> "I know you've *been very busy* lately, so you *might not remember exactly,* but I thought we did talk about this beforehand. It was sometime last month . . . I have a copy of the e-mail in my desk . . . It says something about . . . ."

Peace signals can help, so don't start your response by protesting loudly "What do you mean? Ask you? You told me to make my own decisions!" Instead, signal that it's okay he has forgotten his previous approval. You thereby give the insecure boss a face-saving way to escape his mistake.

CEOs and higher-level managers, even with all their presumed power, can be just as insecure as the rest of us. Offer them a face-saving escape route and let them take it—unnoticed. Do they deserve it? Doesn't matter. The issue is how to defuse the explosive moment, not make someone look wrong and foolish.

Here are more variations you may adapt to your own style.

> "Actually, I thought about checking with you. But this seemed to be the kind of decision I thought you'd expect me to handle. *Sorry if I presumed too much.* Next time I'll consult with you first. If you've got the time now, *can we talk about your expectations on decision making,* so I can get a better understanding?"

> "This honestly seemed like something I thought you'd want me to *take care of without taking up your time.* Perhaps we need to decide when I should make decisions on my own and when I need to pass them through you first."

The *careful* use of self-effacing humor can help you grab control of the situation in a hurry, if you are dealing with a halfway reasonable boss (and we hope they outnumber the others). One veteran executive's proven way to handle the forgetful boss was to slap his palm against his forehead and say something like:

Tip: Diplomacy first—fisticuffs second.

For the first several times your boss tosses hostile questions because of his repeated forgetfulness, duck when he takes a swing at your ego and work performance. A few subtle reminders about his past instructions may help him learn to **make real inquiries instead of using attack questions.** Try diplomacy first. Don't concern yourself with looking weak or submissive. If you need to fight back to protect your job, you can always use the more powerful and **direct active voice along with evidence later.** It's much harder to switch to the diplomatic approach after you've started a fight.

"How stupid can I get? I thought you told me to . . ." (He'd then repeat exactly what the boss had directed.)

When he saw his boss's eyes glaze over for a moment (in recognition) he knew he had him, regardless of what might follow. What else could be said after the executive had already called *himself* stupid? A halfway decent boss will stand corrected, or will agree it was a simple misunderstanding.

Tough Questions Worksheet

Create responses to the difficult questions you could face on this chapter's topics, using the formulas below. Use **logic, emotion,** and **ethics** whenever possible. Experiment by answering the same question with different formulas to learn which best fits your natural style. Use pencil so you can erase and refine your answers.

Past, Present, Future:

What happened was:

What's happening now is:

The way we'll prevent it from happening again is by:

Problem to Solution:

*The **problems** we have are:*

*I'd like to go directly to a proposed **solution:***

Problem - Cause - Solution - Timing (PCST):

*The **problems** we have are:*

*They were **caused** by:*

*The **solutions** we may implement are:*

*Our **timing** is:*

Wrong, Right, and What It Means:

*This is an extremely complex area and our track record has **overall** been very **good:***

*We do very difficult things and sometimes we have failures. What **happened** is that:*

*What this **means** for us now is:*

Three-Step Explanation:

I understand what you are asking and why it concerns you so much:

Other people who had your experiences probably would feel the same way:

However, I would like to explain a little about this problem:

Other formulas and responses I want to use for tough questions related to this chapter:

14

Defending Yourself During an Unfair Job Evaluation

14.1   Why are you giving everything to your staff to do? Don't you think these duties are your responsibility?

14.2   How come I see so many of your staff standing around talking all the time?

14.3   Why isn't your department catching and fixing mistakes before they get out?

14.4   Why do you have an excuse for every mistake your department makes?

14.5   Why don't you do your reports better so I don't have to fix them all the time?

14.6   Wouldn't your section produce better quality and meet deadlines if you trained them as you should have?

14.7   Why don't you delegate more? Why do you try to do everything yourself?

Isn't it ironic that our ability to think clearly abandons us when we need it most? A good example is when we're expected to answer critical questions from an unfair boss during the necessary evil known as the annual job evaluation. It's no wonder, because we think so much is at stake: our paycheck, promotion, career, self-esteem, and so forth.

This chapter will help you work through the emotional overload that arises when an unfair manager poses trick questions or makes assertions that threaten your life, liberty, and the pursuit of your paycheck. It demonstrates how to answer back without sounding as if you're talking back.

However, don't make the mistake of believing that a clever talker can escape these or other tough questions with glib phrases. That's a Hollywood myth. The skill of responding to tough questions refers only to the method of delivery, not the content. You need both skill and content to respond effectively, especially over the long term. This book provides the basis for that skill; your brain and files provide the content.

In any case, an unfair evaluation stirs up unwanted emotions in us all. It's twice as bad when the boss conjures up surprise questions. What can make an unfair job evaluation even more difficult to handle is when you are faced with a manager who has had little managerial training. Often managers rise in an organization because they possess some important technical skill or are friends with higher-ups, not because they show great potential at managing people.

Many managers mistakenly use the evaluation to give essential guidance in the form of harsh criticism, rather than using positive methods to seek improvement or correction. This is called fixing the blame instead of the fixing the problem.

Regardless of how difficult and unfair the evaluation may be, it's crucial you learn how to handle the appraisal and the boss's tough questions positively.

14.1 WHY ARE YOU GIVING EVERYTHING TO YOUR STAFF TO DO? DON'T YOU THINK THESE DUTIES ARE YOUR RESPONSIBILITY?

When your boss poses a question like this, she has asked an absolute false-premise question. Her question uses an absolute term (everything) and therefore the premise is almost certainly false.

You can easily knock down an absolute premise in a debate, but an unfair evaluation is not a contest with an impartial judge. You should hesitate to pull the proverbial rug out from under your boss by proving that you don't pass down everything. Instead, bridge to the high road. (Refer to section 1.3 for related comments.)

See how the following quote attempts to undo the premise subtly by bridging very quickly to your interpretation of what has been going on.

> "I know I am accountable for all activities in the department. I do delegate authority and responsibility for some of my duties to those who

hold promise as future leaders. If and when I leave this job, *there will be someone ready to take over my position.* This is not only good for morale, it provides a *pool of talent* you can draw from when openings occur in other departments. I feel that this has the added advantage of *reducing turnover.* These exceptional people are less likely to seek opportunities with another company."

You might add:

". . . as a side benefit, *should I suddenly become ill,* the department will operate on a business-as-usual basis."

Well, maybe the boss isn't always right during your unfair evaluation, but tactically speaking, that's a good place to start. If her criticism is vague, ask her to tell you specifically what you should and should not have delegated.

If she lists items she told you to delegate herself, point that out—but only if she has shown she can admit to a mistake. However, if your manager is like a few we all have known and won't acknowledge errors, then you won't gain much by arguing the past. Just find out what should be done next and get it in writing.

Do your own follow-up to make sure your future delegations fit her expectations. Don't wait for her. Of course, you shouldn't have to do the follow-up; maybe you believe that's her responsibility. Maybe you're right, but so what? What does being right get you? Not much, except an even more displeased boss who still won't admit her mistakes.

If the evaluation you are enduring is unfair, but you still believe your supervisor can be reasoned with, consider a more direct response. If she's the type who can have an impromptu talk over a cup of coffee with an employee to find out what's going on, you may want to meet the unfairness head on. But then bridge to what the two of you can do to replace the image with a new, more accurate and positive one.

"I feel pretty good about the work I have done and the duties I have delegated. But there seems to be a serious difference of opinion here. Maybe I have given you or one of the staff the wrong impression on some assignments. It's important to me that *we talk about it, so we can clear this up right away.* I hope we can resolve this so it won't be a problem in the coming months."

Tip: Take power by empowering yourself.

Here's a method that sometimes helps prevent history from repeating itself: When an unfair evaluation includes a list of **past problems,** ask yourself what you could have done to detect each developing problem and prevent it from happening. Stretch your brain beyond what you **should** have done. What are the craziest, wildest, nuttiest, nearly impossible things you **could** have done?

The answers may help empower you. The more ways you come up with to satisfy your supervisor, **the more you take away her opportunities to be unfair.** Of course, there are a few managers who will be unfair no matter what you say or do, but you can minimize their effect by using these responses and self-empowering methods.

14.2 HOW COME I SEE SO MANY OF YOUR STAFF STANDING AROUND TALKING ALL THE TIME?

This is a no-win question. It's damage-control time.

Your manager believes her own eyes, which tell her that your staff spends too much time talking. Telling her you haven't seen it, or that you know differently adds to your problems. She'll think either you don't know what your staff is doing or you're covering for them. Either way she'll still believe they gab too much.

The last thing you want to do is to give a response that would encourage your boss to keep watching your department. She may be itching to get personally involved in department operations again, and your invitation may be too much to resist. Also, the inference is that maybe you can't handle it alone. Take the issue away from her with a response that puts you in control of what will happen next:

> "Some of this is necessary for interdepartmental communication, but I, too, have the feeling this might be getting out of hand with a few people. I'll bring it up at next week's *department meeting* and, if necessary, on a *one-to-one basis* with those failing to get the message. Consider it handled."

Was your staff talking too long? Take a tip from the advertising and psychology fields to understand why three minutes can seem like an hour

---

Tip: Teach a little psychology to protect yourself and your staff.

Tell your staff that when the boss walks by you want them to make sure she sees an end to the picture of them gabbing. Don't portray her as the bad guy; she is thinking just like any other human being. **Explain to your staff why such impressions occur** and why it's in everyone's best interest to cut the gabbing short—save the longer sports discussions for break or lunch. If you're reasonable about this, you will come across not as an unfair taskmaster, but as a prudent manager.

---

to a boss walking by. Psychologists have shown that the human mind constantly adds information and meaning to what it sees as the brain tries to figure things out. Advertisers use that in ads—they give part of the picture, knowing that our minds will add more, including what might be happening just outside the photo frame.

Now imagine your supervisor walking past your staff at starting time Monday morning after the big game. Three minutes later, as she returns to her office, your staff is still talking. She will likely assume that your staff was talking before and after. If she sees this once, she'll wonder how often it happens; twice makes her concerned; three times is "proof."

14.3 WHY ISN'T YOUR DEPARTMENT CATCHING AND FIXING MISTAKES BEFORE THEY GET OUT?

If your department is making excessive errors, admit it. The worst thing you can do is to try to gloss over it or act as though the problem is not one of your top priorities. (Refer to sections 1.6 and 2.8 for additional comments on mistakes.)

Your manager may be a bit surprised if you admit to the problem, relieved that you're not going be defensive about it, and, it's hoped, open to your ideas as a result.

> "I know some things got out of here with mistakes. I want you to know that *all errors concern me.* I would like to explain the results of our quality control audits *showing* that, while mistakes have been made, they are being held to a bare minimum."

"We have been making too many *mistakes,* and I'm certainly not proud of that at all. I've made it a priority to find out what's *causing* these mistakes and I've come up with some *solutions for you to consider.* Some of these are things that I can make happen, but others need approval from elsewhere. I've prepared a report that I'd like for us to go over *now* if that's all right. . . ."

Using PCST Formula to Turn a Mistake Around

Maybe your department's mistakes are like lemons that can be made into lemonade (admittedly not all problem lemons can be made into lemonade). In this case, make lemonade with the PCST response formula—problem, cause, solution, timing.

The second preceding response makes lemonade by conceding the problem (the pattern of mistakes that can't be hidden anyway). But you sweeten the mixture when you bridge to positive actions you are already undertaking, or are prepared to undertake. That might be a search for root causes, such as high turnover, poor working conditions, inadequate training, quality control, insufficient equipment, and so forth.

The second response moves directly to your plans for solutions, and your recommendations for actions that exceed your authority. Finally, the response addresses timing by asking to talk about the solutions now. The PCST formula, mixed with your knowledge and drive, can show you are capable of managing problems, which happen to everyone eventually. (Refer to section 2.5 for more on PCST.)

Don't be too hard and fast on the time element in your response. You may have to get the job done with what you have at hand now. The important thing is that you make recommendations to higher management when you need action beyond your control.

If you are really organized, you will have done this in writing long before the appraisal—but a late response is better than none. If you have already submitted your recommendations, chances are this subject will not be brought up in the appraisal. If it is, then it should be a simple matter of giving your boss a status report on your progress, showing that action is underway to reduce these errors to an acceptable limit.

Being a good manager does *not* mean you don't have problems; being a good manager means you identify the problems and get them resolved. So don't be too embarrassed by mistakes that slipped through. That happens to every good manager, so you're in fine company. But to stay with that fine company, make sure your responses demonstrate how you are resolving problems.

Tip: Soon you will get *twice* the staff but *half* the time.

In future performance evaluations, managers should expect more tough questions as our private and public organizations get leaner and meaner, often by cutting management positions. In the past many organizations had a manager-to-employee ratio that was optimum, 1 to 6 or 1 to 10, according to some experts.

Under the banner of "empowerment" and "reinventing," some organizations have established ratios of 1 manager for each 15 employees. Managers with **twice the staff** to manage will obviously have **less time to check** for mistakes (and weren't we terribly busy with the old ratio of managers to employees?).

There will be situations in which the boss is really off base with her accusation of too many errors. You can't afford to let the false premise stand unchallenged, because the implications could be fatal to your career.

If this is the case, several possible replies come to mind.

> "I have heard these same rumors, but so far, I haven't been able to track down the cause. Our quality control *results indicate a normal error* ratio, and we are not seeing an increase in items returned to us for redo or repair."

> "I've heard that rumor too, but so far, in tracking those down, they turn out to be *misunderstandings about the product rather than errors.* I'm in the process of making a formal recommendation that we improve explanatory instructions. . . ."

14.4 WHY DO YOU HAVE AN EXCUSE FOR EVERY MISTAKE YOUR DEPARTMENT MAKES?

"Wait a minute!" you say to yourself. You just explained what happened, but the boss turns it back on you by calling your statement an "excuse." Why should she disparage your account about what happened? This hostile question may reveal that she has adopted a negative attitude toward you, and that could threaten your position, even your employment. If you conclude that is what is happening, it's time to take a stand to protect yourself. You might reply:

> "Frankly, this takes me by complete surprise. To the best of my knowledge, *my files on the reports sent to you show few corrections.* I'm using the

same format week to week, month to month, so chances are that my situation *won't improve until I see what you think* I'm doing wrong. Have you got time to go over this now?"

If you want to own up to your responsibilities, but still get your explanation in, consider weaving the two concepts together in this fashion:

"I know that *results count, but excuses don't*. I didn't realize I sounded as if I was just making excuses. *I'm not ducking my responsibility*—not at all. I am trying to explain what happened. I want things to get done right just as much as you do."

"*I am not excusing myself from my responsibilities*. But it sounds as if I might be *overly protective of my department*. The next time you hear me sounding as if I'm making excuses instead of just explaining things, tell me straight out. I'd like to fix that."

If your factual explanations also contain hollow statements that seem to exempt you from your responsibilities, then your explanation becomes an excuse. Results count, excuses don't. As a manager, you cannot be excused from your responsibilities, so you should explicitly own up to them.

A good explanation should move from factual recounting of events to a clear admission of your responsibility. Then list what you've learned and how you're using that knowledge to correct the problem and improve performance (yours or others).

If you are not sure of the difference between an explanation and an excuse, ask yourself if your explanations are factual descriptions of who, what, when, where, and how (skip the why for now). If that doesn't work, write it out after asking a co-worker to listen to you. You'll be surprised at what you reveal to yourself that way. (Refer to sections 1.10 and 1.11.)

14.5 WHY DON'T YOU DO YOUR REPORTS BETTER SO I DON'T HAVE TO FIX THEM ALL THE TIME?

Your boss has asked a specific question that may indicate that she, like many managers, is not well trained or is too busy to give regular feedback. Either way, you get a surprise: All year long the unfair boss hasn't liked your memos or reports (or whatever) but didn't get around to telling you until the evaluation!

Tip: Dispel false generalizations to protect yourself.

A hostile question that includes a false generalization **is just too serious to simply let pass**. In many other parts of this book, we suggest that sidestepping most fights is tactically smart, but sometimes it's better to stand firm. The false-premise accusation built into the preceding question is much **too serious and far-reaching to let stand to become an accepted truth.**

The kind of manager who recklessly makes sweeping generalizations full of hyperbole probably doesn't keep good records. So you may respond to the question by asking several of your own. In answering your questions, your boss may realize she's on thin ice and may wish to skate away. (Refer to section 2.7 for additional comment.)

An unfair boss most of all won't react well if you point out that she failed in her duty to give you timely feedback. She may fire back with something like: "You know you should have done the work right in the first place. . . ."

Sometimes you just have to hold firm and defend yourself, so false statements don't become official and hurt you in the long run. This is such a moment; she is saying you haven't done a major part of your job.

Without a doubt, it's usually wiser to avoid confrontation when responding to hostile inquiries from your boss. But at times like these, you may have too much to lose to simply give in. Be polite, stand firm, and coolly request that she produce the evidence.

> "If I heard you correctly, you're saying 'all the time.' All of my work had to be redone? In the last year, I've written more than 40 reports and memos. Which ones are you talking about? *I've got copies of the drafts and final versions of each one. I'd like to discuss them.* This is a surprise to me, and I'm pretty concerned about it."

14.6 WOULDN'T YOUR SECTION PRODUCE BETTER QUALITY AND MEET DEADLINES IF YOU TRAINED THEM AS YOU SHOULD HAVE?

As the manager, you are responsible for making sure your staff is properly trained. You know that you are supposed to get work done through other people, and that means you must ensure the workers are trained to do their jobs. But too often circumstances and even upper management force you to put off needed training until next week, which often never comes.

In this scenario, your unfair boss has made things worse by making training the first thing to fall by the wayside when time and money got tight. She nevertheless expects you to get the staff adequately trained—in between rushes, rework from previous rushes, and staff turnover. She forces you have to jump from crisis to crisis, rush to rush, and new staff to new staff. You would like to ask her how she could forget about all this. Instead consider one of these options:

> "*I don't recall it the same way you do.* We planned for a lot of training last year but didn't get it all done; that's true. *Let me list what we did get done and then summarize what we didn't and why.* There isn't just one cause, so we need to examine each one. You may not remember at the moment, but I sent several memos to you about what was happening and why we could not go all the way with the training plan. We could have done it if the time planned for *training wasn't used for other priorities.*"

> "Last year, two of my best people quit and we had a 20 percent employee turnover. The *training budget was cut in half.* When I started in-house training sessions for new employees, the vice president gave us three rush projects. I need your help to get the vice president to understand that *everyone has to resist putting a rush priority* on so many projects. I want to get the staff trained, but we need the time and resources to do it; *training should be like any other important goal.*"

Tip: Keep an accurate file to bolster responses.

Regrettably, it's necessary in the real world to keep an accurate file—written documentation—to give your responses more power during an unfair evaluation. You may also need to bring the time-tested file to the meeting.

A boss who conducts unfair evaluations will be swayed (or defeated) only by records and facts. Without hard evidence it is her assertion versus your unsupported response. Her unsupported assertions will **seem like facts** to her, while **your** unsupported responses will **seem like excuses.** You will lose that battle almost every time, unless you keep accurate records and use them when you decide to fight back.

An unfair evaluation is likely to include a question that implies you failed to train your staff. The unfair boss might lead with, "If you would have managed better. . . ." But in almost every instance, training is not done because of the direct or indirect effects of decisions by top executives.

Some bosses will give your department rush projects without asking what will be pushed aside, or they fail to give you enough money to train your employees. By doing this, your boss turns the so-called high-priority training into low priority by default.

Then the unfair boss changes the default to your fault—if you let her. Your response should include facts about the projects that cut into staff time and the decisions that pulled funds out of the training budget.

14.7 WHY DON'T YOU DELEGATE MORE? WHY DO YOU TRY TO DO EVERYTHING YOURSELF?

Delegate more—more than what? That question will probably pop into your mind. But be careful, because your manager—unfair or not—has just brought up a subject that has been the downfall of many managers. Your ability to properly delegate tasks will enable your capable subordinates to grow in their positions. It will provide job enrichment and prepare them for promotion.

This is a good time to use the past-present-future response formula. (See section 2.3 for related comments.)

> **Past:** "I slipped into the habit of not delegating enough, a habit I've seen in many managers. It's easy to fall into *the routine of doing it myself because I wanted it done right.* But I know that by doing so, I tend to overload myself.
>
> **Present:** I am setting up *some reminders* to help me break the habit.
>
> **Future:** I will *keep you informed* of how it's going."

Notice how the preceding response admits to a problem, but then quickly takes control by moving from past problem to future solution—a solution you create and control: you'll keep the boss informed. (See section 1.6 for more on admitting mistakes.)

If, however, you have a good record of delegating appropriate work to subordinates, and this is a time when you feel you must refute your boss, here is a past-present-future response you might build upon:

"Actually, *I did delegate* quite a few of my responsibilities, but maybe not as many as you think I should. Just in case you might not be aware of some of them, *I'd like to list a few.* (Then cite some.) Are these what you were thinking about? *Are there others* you think should be delegated?"

This response states clearly that you are meeting the duty to delegate but are willing to do more in the future, if the boss so orders. You therefore don't lose while also letting her retreat to a safe place—oddly enough, discussing the future.

If the boss takes the face-saving way out by selecting other items she wants delegated, the confrontation is over. If she doesn't, your response has signaled the ground you intend to defend, so be ready to stand firm. Giving in to her false allegations at this point probably would only lead to more "evidence" in her file against you.

However, if your relationship with the boss is still civil, you may wish to sidestep an argument about the past altogether by bridging directly to a solution for the future. You can use a neutral device like a list of duties (i.e., the usually ignored job description) on which to build a discussion that can be safe for both of you.

"Maybe this would be a good time to go over my job description so *we could update what you want me to do directly* and what I should delegate."

Listen First—Then Educate

During an unfair evaluation it's strategically important to keep your mind open. Listen as though everything she says is true—save your judgment for later. If you listen without mentally refuting every word your manager says, you might hear vital information. You may discover ways you can improve yourself, or even learn how you could delegate more. You can't learn a thing when you're the one doing most of the talking.

On the flip side, if your manager's unfair appraisal reveals she doesn't know how much you already delegate, you can try to educate her. Wait until she's done making her points. Don't interrupt; she's not going anywhere. You'll have your turn. And she may even surprise you by appreciating your obvious attention.

If you have to fight back, you will be better able to do that after she has revealed her strongest positions.

Tough Questions Worksheet

Create responses to the difficult questions you could face on this chapter's topics, using the formulas below. Use **logic, emotion,** and **ethics** whenever possible. Experiment by answering the same question with different formulas to learn which best fits your natural style. Use pencil so you can erase and refine your answers.

Past, Present, Future:

What happened was:

What's happening now is:

The way we'll prevent it from happening again is by:

Problem to Solution:

*The **problems** we have are:*

*I'd like to go directly to a proposed **solution:***

Problem - Cause - Solution - Timing (PCST):

*The **problems** we have are:*

*They were **caused** by:*

*The **solutions** we may implement are:*

*Our **timing** is:*

Wrong, Right, and What It Means:

*This is an extremely complex area and our track record has **overall** been very **good:***

*We do very difficult things and sometimes we have failures. What **happened** is that:*

*What this **means** for us now is:*

Three-Step Explanation:

I understand what you are asking and why it concerns you so much:

Other people who had your experiences probably would feel the same way:

However, I would like to explain a little about this problem:

Other formulas and responses I want to use for tough questions related to this chapter:

15

Disciplining a Disgruntled Employee Who Doesn't Measure Up

15.1   *So what have I done wrong now?*

15.2   *Are you going to fire me? Is that what this is about?*

15.3   *What facts do you have to back this up?*

15.4   *I've never had a problem at other jobs. How can you say this is my fault? Frankly, I think it's just a personality conflict between you and me, don't you?*

15.5   *All you've ever done is criticize me! Why don't you ever appreciate or draw attention to the good things I've done?*

15.6   *Why are you blaming me for other people's mistakes?*

15.7   *Are you saying that I'm really that bad? That I'm one of the goof-offs?*

For many managers, the most unpleasant part of the job is disciplining employees. Few people relish the idea of sitting in critical judgment of a co-worker, especially one who believes she is being unfairly reproved.

Worse yet is the future possibility of incurring the daily wrath of an angry subordinate. Faced with the latter, some managers may opt to put up with mediocre work, rather than confront a ticking bomb. This is especially true of civil service and large private organizations, where disciplining is an arduous task.

Knowing how to handle a difficult employee includes knowing how to manage your side of the conversation, particularly the challenging questions that commonly arise during these tense situations. This chapter will help you get ready for the usual ones.

Suppose you've finally arrived at the point where you must call her in to begin the disciplinary process—nothing else has worked. She has figured out by now that her performance hasn't been up to par in your view, so she's going to be edgy when she enters your office and you close the door behind her.

15.1 SO WHAT HAVE I DONE WRONG NOW?

This question comes from your employee with low self-esteem—she's a complainer and a whiner. She definitely is a negatively focused individual with a very large chip on her shoulder. Your employee might be subconsciously hoping you'll reaffirm the low opinion she has of herself. Being a victim has its advantages, because then she can blame the world for all her problems and not have to shoulder responsibility for her life. (Refer to section 3.7 for related comments.)

When we're provoked by a difficult personality, we tend to react in ways that make the situation worse. We take the offense personally and sometimes attack back or belittle her with a biting retort, "You mean what *didn't* you do wrong?" or "With an attitude like that, why should I waste my time?"

Don't agree with negatively focused perception. And don't let her hostile questions draw you into a quarrel over whether all you do is discuss problems.

Bridge back to:

- ❑ Expectations

- ❑ Performance

- ❑ Solutions

- ❑ Measurements

- ❑ Consequences

> "This isn't a conversation either of us wants to have, but we've got to do it. I'd like us to focus on what you've done *right*, and what *you could and must do better*. I've explained many times to you what my expectations are. Let's go over some, and let me get your reaction as to why things have fallen behind."

"It's important to me that you do well in this job, just as I'm sure it's important to you that you keep this job. I'd like us to go over where I feel *your performance should be better,* so that both of us are satisfied with the results."

15.2 ARE YOU GOING TO FIRE ME? IS THAT WHAT THIS IS ABOUT?

With this challenge, your employee has just cut right to the chase—most people are prone to fear the worst. Imagine the feelings that have been racing through her head since you invited her into your closed office: despair, anger, resentment, resignation, doom, and gloom—all reactions to the old bugaboo known as insecurity.

Don't match negative with negative by saying something like, "Do you think I should fire you?" or "Give me one good reason why I shouldn't fire you!" Slow down and think, before you say something you might later regret. Put her at ease, without giving up firm control of the conversation. Lay out your expectations and the consequences of further performance problems. It's important to acknowledge and resolve her initial misgivings before you move on to your points. (Refer to section 1.7 for related comments.)

"If I had given up on you entirely, firing would be the quick way out. *But I haven't.* Even the best employees need guidance and direction occasionally. I'd like to put some effort into making this work, but it's up to you to show me *this is something you can do and want to do well.*"

"No, I didn't call you in here to fire you. I called you in here to see *whether we can bring your performance up to a level we can both be proud of.* If you really care about this job and are willing to improve, you can count on my support to help you be successful. Now let's talk over the problems that are preventing you from achieving your goals."

"I understand that you're probably nervous right now. I'm a bit nervous myself. You may even get upset over some of the things I'm about to say. I want you to know that my intention is not to make things harder for you, *but to see you do your job better—for yourself and the company.* Do you want to work with me on this?"

"After we're done discussing this, I will write up a report that will be a summary of this meeting and a plan for the future. This discussion is private—it won't be shared with other staff, unless you choose to say

---

Tip: Avoid *informal* questions or responses.

None of the questions or responses should be considered **informal** during a disciplinary discussion. This is serious business, and you should prepare (and practice) your responses beforehand. If you aren't ready to handle the likely tough discipline **questions,** you aren't ready for the discipline **discussion.** Your strategy should include noting the employee's questions (without the barbs, of course) and your responses, so that you can write a complete summary afterwards for you and the employee. (Refer to section 1.11 for related comments.)

---

something. I want to look at this as a counseling interview where I clearly state where your performance hasn't met the standards *and what you must do to improve.* We must be completely clear, and that is why I'll prepare a written summary that we'll both need to sign."

15.3 WHAT FACTS DO YOU HAVE TO BACK THIS UP?

Now your employee has posed a direct challenge with this question. She knows you've got to have the facts if the evaluation is to be upheld. Most managers think they have the facts, but often they have only opinions or unsubstantiated judgments. For the purposes of this book, facts are not our judgments, least of all our opinions.

Simply stated, factual words objectively describe what happened—such as what we see or hear directly. Was the report late (time fact)? Were numbers missing or added up incorrectly (observable fact)? Did 30 percent of the products come back with defective parts (measurable fact)?

So, what facts do you have to back up your statement that the employee should be disciplined? Equally important is how you have recorded and preserved those facts. Because if you had the facts but didn't preserve them by documentation, you probably no longer have *the facts* to answer him. Yes, you've got your memory, but how well will that stand up upon appeal of the discipline?

"I didn't decide in haste to take the action. I *reviewed the results of your work* to make sure it was really necessary to correct the deficiencies in your performance."

"I separate facts from my judgment and my opinions. One fact I have is a record that shows *five of seven memos* you wrote were filled with errors. Also, four of the contracts you prepared were *delivered late* by more than two weeks. All of the memos and contracts had *misspelled words. My judgment of these facts* is that your work often has not met the needs and standards of the organization. The discipline I am imposing today is meant to make a point. . . ."

15.4 I'VE NEVER HAD A PROBLEM AT OTHER JOBS. HOW CAN YOU SAY THIS IS MY FAULT? FRANKLY, I THINK IT'S JUST A PERSONALITY CONFLICT BETWEEN YOU AND ME, DON'T YOU?

Here you're faced with a really touchy question: Your employee is using supposedly excellent work elsewhere to imply her work is fine but you aren't. So it's your fault things aren't going well now? You aren't likely to make a dent in her flawless armor of excellence by soft-pedaling the issue. Now direct statements are needed to ensure the points you need to get across are made clearly and firmly. Of course, you can acknowledge that she might have done good work elsewhere, but you still need to switch to the issue at hand, which is her performance here, not at the former job.

> "*Please listen* to what I am saying. Really listen and think about it for a moment. We've got plenty of time to discuss other things you might be thinking about. Your work has not been acceptable *here, and this is where you work now.* I accept that you may have had a fine record elsewhere. But I challenge you to do the same level of work for *this organization.* My responsibility as manager is to see that company standards for productivity are met. If any employee's performance falls short, I have a responsibility to lay it on the line and make it clear that the worker's *performance must improve.*"

> "I'm glad you did well in *other* positions. I don't doubt that you did. However, I am concerned with how you are doing *in this job.* Let me explain to you *what is* and *what is not* acceptable in this position, then we can determine how you can be a success in your work with us."

> "The only experience I can draw from is your performance and behavior *with this organization.* Let me explain to you specifically where I expect improvement in your work. Then I'll expect you to have some suggestions on how you can improve in these areas."

15.5 ALL YOU'VE EVER DONE IS CRITICIZE ME! WHY DON'T YOU EVER APPRECIATE OR DRAW ATTENTION TO THE GOOD THINGS I'VE DONE?

How many times have you heard the phrase "She doesn't take criticism well." Actually, that's a comment that applies to all of us during a certain critical phase of life: birth till death. If you have kids, there's a good chance they occasionally feel you never recognize the good they do, only the bad. Didn't you harbor the same grudge against your own siblings or parents, at some point in your life?

Criticism can be constructive or destructive. Sadly, it's often the latter, which is why so many of us take it so much to heart. Five nice comments can be undone by one negative one. Whether or not you feel you've doled out the praise when it was deserved and tempered the fault finding, her hostile questions say otherwise.

Don't argue, just be clear and firm. Explain calmly what is and is not acceptable. Set limits and measurements in your response and stick with them. If she persists in her argumentative questions, tell yourself to remain calm and repeat your response so there is no misunderstanding of your expectations.

Keep your emotions out of your responses. Don't say, "It's obvious you just don't give a damn." Give facts and present examples. "Your reports were late the last nine out of ten times." Make sure when you give your professional judgment about why the problems are occurring, it is based on facts. Of course, you can't counsel well without giving your judgment, but it must be soundly based, or it will do more harm than good.

"I try to recognize good work, and perhaps I have overlooked something. What do you think you've done well that hasn't been recognized?"

Listen patiently without interruption or debate while she lists her good achievements.

"Your good work in some projects *does not erase the serious performance shortcoming in other assignments*—we need to keep them separate in our discussion here today. We are talking about numerous important assignments that you haven't completed very well."

Tip: To bring closure, be positive and persistent.

Tough as it may be, end your answers on a positive note. Respond by saying you are confident she can do better. Include how you will measure her performance; say how and when. Invite her to occasionally give you feedback on her progress. And when there is progress, make sure it gets noticed. **And then follow up, follow up, follow up.**

"Okay, I agree that you've done some really good work in *some areas*, and I'll try to do a better job of acknowledging above-average performance. But that's not why we're here today. I need to make it clear that you cannot continue this way. And I want to convince you to *produce more of the good work* we both know you are capable of doing. I am giving you a written reprimand. I hope that this will lead to the changes you must make. . . ."

15.6 WHY ARE YOU BLAMING ME FOR OTHER PEOPLE'S MISTAKES?

Your employee has asked a seemingly simple question that is more complex than a three-dimensional chess game. She knows that her individual contribution to a work product is usually just one part of the final result. For example, before the employee wrote a memo by herself, she obtained information from many sources. If the information she was given was incorrect and so then was the memo, whose fault is it? So think once, and then twice, before you plunge forward with, "Oh, I'm not and you know it. You are responsible for your work no matter what."

Another example would be if an employee on an assembly line depends on another worker's products for her work, and the second worker is slow, will you know that? Before answering the preceding question, make sure you're talking to the right person.

At what point does the accuracy of the information or quality of the materials become the responsibility of the worker it is given to? It won't work just to glare menacingly at a worker and say she is responsible (meaning you can blame and then punish later). That doesn't solve anything, but will make morale sink to rock bottom.

If there is a clear assignment of responsibilities *and* there are processes that create the capability for employees to ensure quality, you can respond this way:

> "It's your responsibility to make sure all of the information is correct in your documents. And just as important, we have a *process for you and everyone else to use in checking these things.* I am not blaming you for other people's mistakes. I am, however, saying you could have—and should have—found those mistakes and corrected them before they became your mistakes. This is too serious to ignore. We are taking disciplinary action to ensure this gets your full attention, so it doesn't happen again."

Be prepared to describe clearly at what point the mistakes of other staff contributing to the employee's work become her mistakes. Where are the "hand-off points?" If you can't identify those and describe them clearly, there's almost no chance at this moment that you can illuminate the mind of your angry subordinate.

Moreover, be prepared to remind the subordinate of what process she could and should have used to catch those errors before they become her faulty results. If you aren't prepared to do both of these, you aren't prepared for all these tough questions, and worse, you aren't prepared to deliver discipline that will do any good.

15.7 ARE YOU SAYING THAT I'M REALLY THAT BAD? THAT I'M ONE OF THE GOOF-OFFS?

The employee has asked a question that attempts to get you to overextend your remarks. Under the surface of her question lies a trap. If you agree to place the label of goof-off on the employee, she then will argue your evidence and present her own to show why you are wrong. If you are wrong on the label, or can't substantiate, then your failure to be right will be used to cast doubt on everything else you have said.

To answer this question effectively, you must see the distinction between the person and her behavior—they are not the same. The issue isn't who the employee is, but what she has done—or not done.

"I'm not saying anything about you personally. *My comments are about your work performance.* People can debate all day about *labels* for employees. What counts here is the work you do—how much of it, how fast, and how well. *When standards aren't met* as often as in your case, corrective action must be taken. I share a responsibility to make sure we have an effective organization for everyone's benefit, including yours. My intention is that this corrective discipline is carried out in a positive manner. It is really up to you now."

Tough Questions Worksheet

Create responses to the difficult questions you could face on this chapter's topics, using the formulas below. Use **logic, emotion,** and **ethics** whenever possible. Experiment by answering the same question with different formulas to learn which best fits your natural style. Use pencil so you can erase and refine your answers.

Past, Present, Future:

What happened was:

What's happening now is:

The way we'll prevent it from happening again is by:

Problem to Solution:

*The **problems** we have are:*

*I'd like to go directly to a proposed **solution:***

Problem - Cause - Solution - Timing (PCST):

*The **problems** we have are:*

*They were **caused** by:*

*The **solutions** we may implement are:*

*Our **timing** is:*

Wrong, Right, and What It Means:

*This is an extremely complex area and our track record has **overall** been very good:*

*We do very difficult things and sometimes we have failures. What **happened** is that:*

*What this **means** for us now is:*

Three-Step Explanation:

I understand what you are asking and why it concerns you so much:

Other people who had your experiences probably would feel the same way:

However, I would like to explain a little about this problem:

Other formulas and responses I want to use for tough questions related to this chapter:

16

Facing Difficult Pleas When Firing New Employees

16.1   *I can do better. Can't you give me more time?*

16.2   *I can't believe you're doing this to me! What valid reason could you possibly have?*

16.3   *Some of my work is really good. Doesn't that count?*

16.4   *Will you give me a good job reference? You owe me that, at least, don't you?*

16.5   *Isn't there another job I could do here?*

16.6   *What am I supposed to do now? How am I going to put food on the table and pay the rent if you fire me?*

16.7   *I can show you my work has been good. Can't we talk about how well I've done this year?*

In the business world "fire" is a four-letter word that spells only pain. Whether it's the smart thing to do, or you're dealing with the employee from hell, it's not a task to be taken lightly. It is a decision to cut someone's feet out from under him, and perhaps his family. It's also a decision that exposes an organization to liability. The number of complaints filed with the U.S. Equal Rights Commission has increased 30 percent in just the last 5 years.

In such a moment, a million emotions will likely bubble up in both of you. He appears surprised, hurt, confused, angry, and fearful of his future. You might feel rotten, mean, misunderstood, and angry that you're in such a crummy bind. Making it more difficult, sometimes the new employee desperately pleads for one more chance. But you both know that isn't going to happen—the decision has been made, and you've got to implement it.

At such emotional times, the odds increase that anger will erupt on one or both sides, especially if you are a newer manager and haven't built up a lot of scar tissue. When people are angry they may try to lash back. It's crucial you maintain your composure. You're more likely to do that if you've prepared careful responses based on sound documentation. Think you don't need to prepare? Consider that at risk are the person's self-esteem—and a potential lawsuit.

Few supervisors in mid- or large-sized organizations would be foolish enough to fire someone without consulting the human resources director (and legal counsel). Having made those consultations, make sure you get their approvals before you deliver the document, terminate the employee, and react to his questioning.

Terminate Employment, Not the Employee

Your responses should keep in the mind the sage advice from one veteran human resources director, who said, "Terminate his *employment*, not the *employee*—there's a hell of a difference." Sometimes fearful managers overstate their cases and make the dismissed employee feel he isn't worth anything to anyone. If you keep in mind that you are ending his job at your company, not everything else he is or has been, you will find the right words to distinguish that for both of you when he asks tough questions.

16.1 I CAN DO BETTER. CAN'T YOU GIVE ME MORE TIME?

Your employee is asking for just a little more time He says that maybe he can do better, so you won't have to kick him out onto the street. And you won't have to feel so rotten. Tempting, isn't it? Your heart pulls one way while your brain pushes you in another.

However, there's a crude but true old saying that goes, "Don't cut off the dog's tail an inch at a time." Dragging out a painful process makes it only more painful for everyone. You aren't doing the employee any favors if you give in and keep him a little longer, knowing it probably won't work out anyway. Get it over for both of you. Plan for a short meeting lasting no more than 10 minutes, 15 at the most.

"No, this decision is final. There's no changing it. *Making this process last any longer isn't going to do anyone any good.* We wanted you to succeed from the day you were hired. We believed you had what it takes to make it here. We spent a lot of time and effort to make sure you were trained correctly. But all of the training and coaching and second chances just *haven't produced the results we've got to have.* If you or anyone else isn't able to do the job by now, it isn't going to get much better with time. *I'm sorry, but there won't be any more* extensions. Today will be your last day."

16.2 I CAN'T BELIEVE YOU'RE DOING THIS TO ME! WHAT VALID REASON COULD YOU POSSIBLY HAVE?

The employee's tough question expresses surprise and demands to know what substantial cause you have for dismissal. His query obviously is setting up the foundation for an unpleasant argument. Tensions are running high and hearts are pounding as the confrontation begins.

Despite the difficulty of this scene, if you've done your job (training and counseling) properly, the moment you fire him shouldn't come as a surprise to either of you. Regardless, the employee may still appear shocked when it actually happens.

And what valid reasons do you have? Can you say it in 50 words or less? Can you keep your mind focused so you can get your words out clearly without tripping over your tongue? Don't rely on going over it in your head. You should develop your responses like an organizational position and rehearse it until it becomes memory. That helps when the emotions are churning. (Refer to section 1.10.)

And here's a pretty relevant question you may not be, but perhaps should be considering: Are you about to the join the thousands of supervisors and organizations sued by discharged employees?

When the unpleasant time arrives, it is a wonderful blessing to have a well-documented personnel file, tedious though the process of keeping one may be (i.e., giving warnings, providing remedial training, allowing a reasonable amount of time for correction, etc.). The documentation should be factual, updated as incidents occur, and should show that communication with the employee was direct and timely.

If the justification is violation of work rules or similar canons of behavior, then refer to specific documents in your explanation. You should also remind him of memos in his file documenting prior discussions on poor performance. If you can't do so, you probably don't have a "valid" reason and your personnel department may not allow you to terminate him. The following reasons for termination should be bridged to in your response:

Poor performance (measurable!)	Insubordination
Absenteeism	Work-rule violations
Security breaches	Dishonesty
Theft	Unsafe conduct
Other crimes	Repeated dress code violations

"Yes, there are valid reasons. We don't take these steps lightly. The duties of your position are clearly stated in the job description. The letter I'm going to give you is very specific as to why your employment here is terminated. The letter specifies the duties you were supposed to carry out and the results that were required. After you were provided training and feedback, your performance *still did not produce those results.* Also, you *violated three work rules* after you were given previous oral and written reprimands. *These are valid reasons* for terminating your employment. Each one is explained in this letter."

"There are valid reasons, and they are explained clearly in the memos you were sent. There are copies in your personnel file and *they detail your poor performance and rule violations.* This shouldn't come as a surprise to you based on . . ."

16.3 SOME OF MY WORK IS REALLY GOOD.
DOESN'T THAT COUNT?

Do you admit that some of the employee's work is really good and thereby give him leverage in pleading his lost case even further? You'd like to be honest by saying that, indeed, some of his work has been outstanding. But will he use that against you here, and later in court? Besides, if you don't allow him that, maybe he'll be even more down on himself. And you know the rest of what you have to say will lack credibility, because you weren't honest about the quality of some of his work. You can safely say some of the employee's work was good but it wasn't good enough often enough.

"No one has said that *all* of your performance was unacceptable. Some of your work was good. But please don't let that mislead you— this is important. What I'm saying is that your performance reports reflect that *not nearly enough of your work met the quality necessary to do this job.* This is clearly laid out in the position description and the performance evaluations. Certainly, some of the work was acceptable, but *some is not enough.* That is why your employment is being terminated here today."

If the shoe were on the other foot, would the employee accept having only three of his car's four brakes fixed properly? Would the employee give his mechanic a C and say the repairs were "average" because three brakes were done really well? Would it be okay for a store clerk to return correct change to the employee 95 percent of the times he bought bread and milk? No, so your response can honestly point out that employees are expected to do good work all of the time, not just some or most of the time.

16.4 WILL YOU GIVE ME A GOOD JOB REFERENCE? YOU OWE ME THAT, AT LEAST, DON'T YOU?

Well, finally there's one decent thing you can do for the employee. You can help him get his next job. This must show he's thinking about the future anyway. And it would assuage your guilty feelings if you could fudge a little in a nice but vaguely worded "To whom it may concern" letter. This question is close to the helpless victim issues outlined in section 3.7.

Many managers have learned the hard way that reference letters can come back to haunt them. For this reason, your company may want a policy that allows for *no* exceptions:

Tip: Don't respond with words you don't mean.

Don't give in to the temptation to respond by agreeing to write a nice letter of reference, even a vaguely worded one. Wouldn't that look just great in the hands of the employee's lawyers as they prepare to sue you and your company? Don't respond with nice words you don't mean.

"I understand that anyone who's terminated would want a good reference letter, but that won't be done. We don't write letters one way or the other when an employee is terminated. If anyone calls here about your work, they will be told this organization generally *does not give out references or reasons why an employee left*. I can assure you I *won't say anything that would interfere* with your getting your next job. I really hope it works out better for you in your next position."

16.5 ISN'T THERE ANOTHER JOB I COULD DO HERE?

Like everyone else, the employee knows there are several vacancies. Because he's been around for awhile, he knows some of what it takes to do the various jobs. He claims he is certainly willing to "reapply" himself in another position. He'd have to learn the job, but a transfer would get you off the hook. Any hint in your reply or tone that suggests the dismissal isn't final would cause his hopes to soar high, only to be dashed again. Don't let him, or you cause him unnecessary pain. This is the time to be clear and direct, particularly as you bridge back to your main point: He is terminated.

> "No, this termination is final. If other managers felt you were the right person for those vacancies, you would have been offered them instead of termination. But the fact is your performance has not been what is necessary to work here. There is no position for you, and today is your last day. While you may not want to believe it, I am sorry this hasn't worked out. I hope things go better for you at your next job."

16.6 WHAT AM I SUPPOSED TO DO NOW? HOW AM I GOING TO PUT FOOD ON THE TABLE AND PAY THE RENT IF YOU FIRE ME?

The employee is in a tailspin now. He sees a scary, bleak future without this job—little money for food, rent, car payments, dental bills, heat and light, and clothes for the kids. He's feeling powerless and is putting the responsibility on you. He is slipping into the victim role.

Don't let the "helpless victim" hook you with his troubles. That does not mean you should be cold, indifferent, and ignore his plight. But listening and empathy do not mean letting him put his responsibilities onto you. Have your response gently, yet firmly, return the responsibility to him.

Where you can, point out where he can get information and help, even counseling. That is being helpful.

If you don't agree with this advice, consider whether you want to be responsible for the outcome if you make the employee's decisions for him, but things don't work out. He did what you told him to do—will he blame you? You bet he will. So, today your duty is to terminate his employment and refer him to others who might help. Human resource professionals will tell you that it is vital to urge professional counseling if he gets really desperate and hints at harming himself. It's rare but it can happen—be ready to contact human resources immediately. (Refer to section 3.7 for more on these points.)

> "I'm sorry, *but I don't have answers for those questions.* I won't pretend things aren't going to be difficult, *but you are the only person who can decide what happens from here on out.* Our human resources department has referral information that will tell you where you can get some assistance. You can get more information from the state unemployment office and the county social services department. You might consider checking with your church or temple."

16.7 I CAN SHOW YOU MY WORK HAS BEEN GOOD. CAN'T WE TALK ABOUT HOW WELL I'VE DONE THIS YEAR?

The employee thinks he has evidence showing why this is all a mistake, that you really shouldn't go through with terminating his employment. He's getting ready to cite numerous big and little jobs he's done quite well. He wants you to stop the process and hear him out. That, he says, would only be fair, and you want to be fair, right?

The moment you discharge an employee is not the time to rehash the employee's previous evaluations, and neither is it a good time to begin one. Understandably, the desperate employee's mind will grasp at anything that might forestall the frightful consequence about to happen to him. It is not a kind act to allow him to drag both of you into a retrial of past events. The case is over, a decision has been made, and now the only course is to implement it without starting a futile appeal.

> "The time for that was long ago. We considered your work this year *before we concluded your employment should be terminated here.* No, I won't

agree to go over your work record item by item. That was done during the annual performance evaluation. The best statement I can make today is written very carefully—and clearly—in this letter. It's best if you accept that *this decision is final and go on from there. . . ."*

Unless he is guilty of theft or insubordination, he would have been placed on probation (30, 60, or 90 days) and know full well what the conditions were. You may want to review those in case he has a memory loss. This is all the more reason why you should give the employee a copy of the disciplinary correspondence—and have him sign a copy for the personnel file.

Tough Questions Worksheet

Create responses to the difficult questions you could face on this chapter's topics, using the formulas below. Use **logic, emotion,** and **ethics** whenever possible. Experiment by answering the same question with different formulas to learn which best fits your natural style. Use pencil so you can erase and refine your answers.

Past, Present, Future:

What happened was:

What's happening now is:

The way we'll prevent it from happening again is by:

Problem to Solution:

*The **problems** we have are:*

*I'd like to go directly to a proposed **solution:***

Problem - Cause - Solution - Timing (PCST):

*The **problems** we have are:*

*They were **caused** by:*

*The **solutions** we may implement are:*

*Our **timing** is:*

Wrong, Right, and What It Means:

*This is an extremely complex area and our track record has **overall** been very **good:***

*We do very difficult things and sometimes we have failures. What **happened** is that:*

*What this **means** for us now is:*

Three-Step Explanation:

I understand what you are asking and why it concerns you so much:

Other people who had your experiences probably would feel the same way:

However, I would like to explain a little about this problem:

Other formulas and responses I want to use for tough questions related to this chapter:

17

Survival Responses Amid Nepotism, Cronyism, and Favoritism

17.1   This favoritism stinks, and you know it. What really happened?

17.2   How are the rest of us supposed to get ahead if we don't have political influence or sleep with the boss?

17.3   Why should we bother working hard if it doesn't get us anywhere?

17.4   Why don't you just tell them to go to hell and then hire who you really want?

It happens in every company, from the family-owned business to the publicly traded corporate empire. People get hired, promoted, and favorably treated for reasons other than competence and hard work. As the old joke goes, "Everyone is indeed treated equally, except some people are treated more equally than others."

Powerful people take care of their own: family, friends, supporters, and lovers. Oh yes, it isn't supposed to happen in government, which proudly carries before it the moral shield of treating everyone equally, regardless of race, sex, or political persuasion. But it does, frequently.

When your hard-working employees question the unfairness triumvirate—nepotism-cronyism-favoritism—you're caught between the proverbial rock and a very hard place. You may have your reasons (keeping your job, for example) for not bluntly agreeing with the accusing questions, but pretending it didn't happen knocks you down a few rungs on the ladder of respect.

It's tempting to acknowledge the obvious, but consider this: If your answers confirm the nepotism, cronyism, and favoritism, you won't solve anything but you surely will double your trouble (refer to Chapter 5 for more similar issues.) When you verify the rumor, they then know for sure it's true. Knowing is more powerful than believing. Knowing adds strength to their anger and resentment. You don't have to lie about it, but you don't have to confirm it either. Although it's hard to be certain what the right response should be every time, here are some ideas on how to dance the dance, without stepping on too many toes.

17.1 THIS FAVORITISM STINKS, AND YOU KNOW IT. WHAT REALLY HAPPENED?

Assume a common scenario—a recent hiring smacks of one of the big three: nepotism, cronyism, or favoritism. You were pressured to hire a friend of the CEO. The hired person is obviously much less qualified than some of the other employees who applied for the plum job.

The other staff are red-hot with anger. They've been loyal and hard working for years and were ignored in the hiring process because of favoritism. And now they're nailing you with tough questions, demanding to know why you didn't take a stand against the biased hiring.

You have to decide whether to ignore, downplay, justify, or find another way of responding. If you admit to the unfairness of the situation, your confirmation will be amplified through the rumor mill until it reaches the ears of your superiors.

On the other hand, if you decide to at least hint at your dissatisfaction to maintain the respect of your employees but not say anything self-destructive, here are some suggestions.

> "What really happened is that *I did my job. Some decisions are beyond my control*—regardless of whether I agree with them. I've learned when to fight battles *and when to accept* the fact I may not know everything. Let's just hope it works out in the long run. We have pretty good jobs and fairly decent pay, which are still important things we can appreciate."

> "There are lots of things that I don't necessarily agree with or understand. What I've learned, mainly through my own mistakes, is that *I don't always have to approve of everything that goes on. I am not going to fall on my sword for every decision I might not like.* Sometimes it turns out that they were good decisions, and it's best to let things work themselves out. Other opportunities will come along, and I hope you go for them."

"I've put my foot in my mouth enough times to know that I much prefer the taste of patience and prudence. *I don't presume to understand or agree with everything* that happens around here, but I do know that over the long run, things have a way of working themselves out, *and I will concentrate on helping that happen.*"

"We both have our own thoughts about why this happened, and let's leave them unsaid. You know *I always do my best* to see that you and other employees here get every chance to advance. *There is nothing useful I can do about this situation* but I want you to know that there will be other opportunities for you and I'm still behind you 100 percent."

Yes, those responses dance around the question—they don't say much directly. But they make a subtle point or two while they protect you from being quoted. They hint to your employees that the hiring may be one of those things you don't agree with. They also say you've learned through experience not to mess with the inevitable. The comments suggest they should do the same.

But this may be cold comfort to the employee who believes she should have gotten the job. The next comment places the burden of responding back on the questioner.

"If you were in my shoes, what would you have done? Tell me why, and what good would have come from it?"

Using Rhetorical Questions Carefully Can Help

Posing rhetorical questions in response to hostile questions usually is not a good tactic because you can easily lose control or open yourself up for another blast before you've had time to recover from the first one. However, when you believe that you have most of the logic and rationale on your side, you can reverse the momentum of tough questions. Throw the inquiry back onto the inquisitor. When she answers your question, you can use your knowledge to defeat her attempt to attack you.

17.2 HOW ARE THE REST OF US SUPPOSED TO GET AHEAD IF WE DON'T HAVE POLITICAL INFLUENCE OR SLEEP WITH THE BOSS?

Your employee implies she believes the gossip about how the new employee got the job. She's heard that the newly hired person is good-looking and has political ties to upper management. You have heard it, too, and

---

Tip: Honorable evasion has respectable benefit.

The myth of legends and movie heroes is that evading or retreating is cowardly. We love the idea of John Wayne going straight at the enemy and beating them all. But that is only a story that is quite foolish in real life. Any good chess player or military general knows **tactical evasion and retreats are sometimes wiser** and often healthier. So, too, in hostile questions.

Don't worry about what others might think of you, because they would do the same thing. But if **they** wouldn't, well, then **they** are not smart enough to do the job.

---

you think it might be true, but you really don't know (which is the case in most such circumstances).

It's "private stuff," and when it finds its way into the workplace where most of us spend the majority of our waking moments, it's demoralizing. It's hard to target, hard to prove, hard to talk about. Even when it's glaringly apparent to you and everyone else, it's darn hard to discuss openly.

The possibility that the allegation may be true makes the hostile inquiry even tougher to handle. Consider these responses if you want to quell the discussion:

> "I think I understand what you're saying. I've said many times that *I value your work, and I think your raises and reviews reflect that.* I'll be happy to discuss your performance, and we can talk about other opportunities for you in this organization. *I won't, however, discuss the motivations behind the hiring of other people.*"

> "I know you're upset, and I wish I could do something to change the circumstances for you, *but I can't—not this time.* It's better that you focus on what you want and what's attainable. In this division I evaluate employees by the work they do, not by what they think they know about other people. You do your work very well, *and I'll do my best to find ways to reward you for that.* But it's best you *accept the fact someone else got the job,* and neither of us can change that."

17.3 WHY SHOULD WE BOTHER WORKING HARD IF IT DOESN'T GET US ANYWHERE?

Now your employee poses a difficult question that could have immediate impact on morale and productivity. Her rhetorical query demonstrates how quickly favoritism can send morale down the tubes. Nevertheless, as the manager you can't let your employees dwell on the bitterness displayed by their questioning accusations. The real bottom line is that all of you still have to work hard—you have jobs to do for which you get paychecks.

Use your responses as an opportunity to acknowledge their concerns while you also help them get used to the idea that the hiring is over and done with. Bridge to where you intend to lead: The decision was made, and everyone should get used to that fact for their own emotional sakes. (Refer to sections 1.5 and 1.7 for related comments.)

> "The way *most people* get ahead in this company is through hard work, experience, and dedication. I can see that you're upset about this, but I'm not going to compare people or justify why some get the positions they do. If someone came to me and complained that you got the job because you were a man, or my friend, or whatever, I'd say the same thing. I value your work and your commitment to this company. *Don't let this sour your outlook—you're too good for that.* I hope you'll trust me that when there is *an opportunity that matches your skills and interests, I will do everything I can to help you.*"

> "I think I am an example of where hard work and good performance made a difference. *I certainly wasn't promoted because of nepotism or any other kind of favoritism.* There are plenty of others like me here. You need to settle your feelings about the hiring and let it go; otherwise you will just keep reliving it and make yourself unhappy. *Let's keep working toward the kind of opportunity that I have earned;* it does work sometimes."

> "One way to get ahead in my department, and in most companies, is not to dwell on malicious rumors or get angry when other people are promoted or hired. It doesn't do any good *but it sure can make a person feel unhappy a lot longer. Things happen, and you and I don't always know why.* I've learned to focus on my job and not second-guess other people. *I intend to adjust to the hiring and find ways to make it work the best for me, and I hope you'll do the same for yourself.*"

17.4 WHY DON'T YOU JUST TELL THEM TO GO TO HELL AND THEN HIRE WHO YOU REALLY WANT?

During these antagonizing questions from your angry staff, you can't help but feel a little heat under your collar. Your staff knows darn well why you don't spout off and say stupid things that would get you fired. Use your

---

Tip: Some favoritism can be "fair."

When the promotion goes to the owner's son, daughter, or favorite relative, is that unfair favoritism? Or is the owner exercising a right to groom a successor, a perfectly legitimate process in smaller companies. If so, you might be able to turn the angry staff's perspective on the question by having your response cast the issue as one involving the need to **develop successors** and the **proper right** of the owner to give her business to whomever she wants.

---

self-talk to control the urge to throw it back in their faces (i.e., Well, if you're so brave, why don't you go up there and tell 'em off? Let's see you put your money where your mouth is!)

Tell yourself to hang on a little longer while you respond tactfully: Don't make up stories either. Not telling the truth in your replies would be remembered for years. Although you probably don't want to say much substantively, make sure it is true no matter what. (Refer to section 1.9.)

> "I can't tell you how many times *other people have gotten jobs that I felt I should have gotten.* It's caused a lot of sleepless nights, ruined dinners, and created a lot of stomach acid. Sometimes I still feel that way. It weighs on me a little more heavily now that I'm a supervisor, because I know the decisions I make affect other people and their families. I just want you to know there are *things that happen I have some control over, and things I have little or no control over.* I wish I had the luxury of pointing them out, but I don't. I know that someday, if I have anything to do with it, and I hope to, you will get to experience these same wonderful challenges and guilt trips."

Tough Questions Worksheet

Create responses to the difficult questions you could face on this chapter's topics, using the formulas below. Use **logic, emotion,** and **ethics** whenever possible. Experiment by answering the same question with different formulas to learn which best fits your natural style. Use pencil so you can erase and refine your answers.

Past, Present, Future:

What happened was:

What's happening now is:

The way we'll prevent it from happening again is by:

Problem to Solution:

*The **problems** we have are:*

*I'd like to go directly to a proposed **solution:***

Problem - Cause - Solution - Timing (PCST):

*The **problems** we have are:*

*They were **caused** by:*

*The **solutions** we may implement are:*

*Our **timing** is:*

Wrong, Right, and What It Means:

*This is an extremely complex area and our track record has **overall** been very **good:***

*We do very difficult things and sometimes we have failures. What **happened** is that:*

*What this **means** for us now is:*

Three-Step Explanation:

I understand what you are asking and why it concerns you so much:

Other people who had your experiences probably would feel the same way:

However, I would like to explain a little about this problem:

Other formulas and responses I want to use for tough questions related to this chapter:

18

Holding Firm While Insisting on Alcohol/Drug-Abuse Help

18.1   Why are you picking on me? I'm not the only one here who drinks!

18.2   You're not a doctor! What makes you qualified to judge my health?

18.3   I've seen you drink at parties. Are you going to get treatment too?

18.4   I've seen you do your share of pot. How can you be such a hypocrite and tell me to get treatment?

18.5   Who told you that crap? Have you been spying on me?

18.6   I do my work, so what business is it of yours what I do on my personal time?

18.7   You're going to ruin my work record. Do you realize what you're doing to me?

18.8   Come on, give me a break! This is the first time in four months that I've come in a little hung over!

18.9   I tested negative—you're going to be talking to my lawyer! Why didn't you believe me when I told you I wasn't a druggie?

18.10   I didn't knock the scaffolding down on purpose. What's the big deal if I'm the only person who got hurt?

18.11   You better watch your backside! Do you honestly think you can hurt me like that and not pay for it someday?

Drug and alcohol abuse is one of the most serious problems facing employers today. The costs are staggering. According to the federal government, drug/alcohol abuse causes more than $100 billion a year in accidents, lost productivity, and related problems.

For small businesses in particular, the costs can be devastating. All it takes is one accident by an employee to cause major financial and public relations nightmares.

But directing an employee to get help for a suspected drug or alcohol problem is no easy task. People under the influence often don't see how their abuse affects every facet of the employer/employee relationship: attendance, punctuality, dependability, safety, security, trust, self-esteem, work quality, relationships, and more.

Because of the legal implications alone, it's important that you realize that in no way are you an expert in working with drug-affected people. Before confronting your employee, it's important that you first consult with your human resources (HR) director, and with a representative of the Employee Assistance Program (EAP), if you have one. You should specifically discuss what you should say and what you shouldn't. Be prepared for denial and accusations from the employee.

18.1 WHY ARE YOU PICKING ON ME? I'M NOT THE ONLY ONE HERE WHO DRINKS!

If everyone does it, well, it can't be that bad, right? Or at least she isn't worse than the others. Your employee has the common subconscious misunderstanding many people use as a rule of thumb for deciding right or wrong: Does everyone else do it? She mixes the illogical moral concept to paint a picture of normalcy—she's just like a lot of folks here, who aren't so bad. So isn't she okay?

Focus on Observable Behavior

For any suspected drug- or alcohol-abuse-intervention interview, experts will tell you it's important to focus on observable behavior and performance declines you can document. What did you see, hear, or smell? The information you use in your response must be observable and convincing to others in management, as well as to the employee.

Professional counselors will tell you to be alert to warning signs such as legal or severe family problems, excessive feelings or none at all, lying or blaming others, complaints from others, expressions of mood that are inappropriate for the situation, such as laughing at serious requests or taking safety risks that result in injury.

Additionally, you need to document declines in appearance or health. Does your employee frequently look sick or injured? Do you note a sudden weight gain or loss, tremors, punctures or bruises, inappropriate use of sunglasses, or a decline in agility?

Your responses need to incorporate succinct facts, ethics or standards, and some examples, if possible, to be powerful persuaders. (See sections 1.4 and 23.6 for related comments.) Your replies must reflect these documented behavioral or performance problems.

"My role isn't to be judgmental about you or anyone else. We both know that I am not a counselor. I'm not trying to be your big brother or sister. I think you already know what this kind of problem can mean to a family and a job. I am just focusing on the facts of what I see and hear. *This interview is not about whether you drink. It's about a documented decline in performance and behavior.*"

"You are *not being treated any differently* from any other employee in your situation. My instructions aren't related to the disagreement we had last month, and I don't play favorites. *I have documented a decline in your work that needs to stop.* We have evidence that something is very wrong. *This is an intervention interview—it's part of a process with professionals to determine if you have a problem.* If they determine you do, then treatment may be needed so you can return to being a productive employee again."

"Yes, you are being singled out because your problem has shown up at work. What others do off the job is their business *until it comes into the workplace.* If it shows up here I will deal with it the same way I am dealing with you. *I'm concerned about your performance here in the shop.*"

"*Right now we are talking about you and you only, not other employees.* Regardless of what they tell you, you don't know whether I have given the same instruction to them as well. We're here to talk about what is happening to you. I have seen and heard enough to be convinced you need to be evaluated by a professional. If the counselor decides you need treatment, you must do that in order to keep your job here. You can do excellent work and we really want you to stay. Whether it seems like it or not, we care about you and your family. *The evaluation is mandatory.* Will you accept that?"

"This isn't a case of 'everybody's doing it so why not me.' I'm sure other employees drink, but they still manage to do their jobs well. *I am concerned that your work, as documented in this file, has become shoddy, and you've taken risks that have caused injury to others. Your appearance has also caused a lot of concern.* We are having this intervention interview because you *may* have a problem that is causing serious problems on the job."

"I am sorry if it seems as if I'm doing a diagnosis. But I'm not. *There are many things that make me think something may be very wrong.* You've had excessive absenteeism, increased work errors, and you've left early many times. You've been short-tempered lately, which you never were before. You have lost a lot of weight, and your eyes are often blood-shot—sometimes you seem to stagger when you walk. *I am not an expert on drug problems, but I have seen enough to be sure you've got to be examined by a professional.*"

No matter how much information you think you have, keep telling yourself you don't really know for sure. Otherwise, your certainty may slip into your responses, much to your regret later.

18.2 YOU'RE NOT A DOCTOR! WHAT MAKES YOU QUALIFIED TO JUDGE MY HEALTH?

It is important to remind yourself that you are not a doctor. Many things can cause an employee to suddenly perform in an uncharacteristic manner. Did she go home last week to find her husband had packed up their children and left? Has she taken on the responsibility of caring for a parent with cancer in her home? Did she have to take on a night job to keep her son in college? Did her doctor change her high-blood-pressure medicine to a different dosage?

When a subordinate might be abusing drugs, including the most abused substance—alcohol—there is no risk-free way to respond to her questions. If you take the easy way out and back down, you may be avoiding the risk of a blow-up now and possible legal action from her later.

But while you avoid those risks, your response opens you up to blow-ups from other staff. They will know you failed to resolve the problem.

Tip: For effective responses, first seek advice from experts.

Before you think you are ready to give responses during the intervention interview, **contact experts** including human resource directors, employee assistance program coordinators, local hospitals, county mental health centers, or your state attorney's office. They can provide a list of testing/counseling centers in your area. You will want to ask what services they provide. For example, do they test only for chemicals or do they also interview and perform a physical? **They can also assist you** in preparing for the employee's difficult questions.

Moreover, you may still be sued if the drug-affected employee harms herself or another employee. They will contend you failed to act when you could and should have.

"I'm not qualified to judge your health, *but as your manager I am qualified to judge how you perform your job.* I know something must be wrong because I have seen your work in the past and it has been very good. I do not want to lose you, but I can't keep asking others to do your job. There has been a serious change for the worse in your work, your appearance, and your behavior. *Has something happened that could explain these problems?"*

"No, I'm not a doctor. But when personal problems affect work performance, it's my job to *get that performance back up to where it should be.* I realize that most people go through personal crises at some point in their lives. We suffer and try to deal with them. But sometimes we aren't able to overcome them alone and we need support and help. *I'm not saying you do need counseling, but I am clearly saying you must be evaluated.* I will leave the conclusions to the medical professionals."

18.3 I'VE SEEN YOU DRINK AT PARTIES. ARE YOU GOING TO GET TREATMENT TOO?

The desperate employee senses your ability to exercise managerial authority might be weakened if you are somehow pictured in the same damning scene in which she is portrayed. She intuitively applies the biblical lesson: If you are not without sin, how can you cast the first stone?

Human resource experts will tell you that you are under no obligation to discuss your personal situation. Even if the employee knew you were being treated for substance abuse, your responses should still remain focused on the employee's performance.

> "Whatever I drink or don't drink has no bearing on whether your performance is suffering and *whether you need to be evaluated*. If my work did deteriorate, I would hope my boss would intervene with help, just as I'm doing here. This interview is *about your work* and not mine."

> "We are here to talk about *your work only*. I picked up some literature from the employee assistance program that I want you to read. *I am still not saying I know for sure you have a drinking problem, but I am saying you need to be evaluated*."

> "Even if I were in a treatment program, we wouldn't be talking about it here—*the point of this intervention interview is not my behavior but your work performance*. If I had a similar problem and my boss held an interview like this, it would be *confidential just as this will be for you*. Let's get back to discussing your work and the medical evaluation you must accept."

18.4 I'VE SEEN YOU DO YOUR SHARE OF POT. HOW CAN YOU BE SUCH A HYPOCRITE AND TELL ME TO GET TREATMENT?

You and a few employees had a few joints together back in the good old days when you first started at the company. Like many young adults, you trailed off and kept away from the stuff in recent years. You were promoted, and now you are her manager. But your party days have come back to haunt you.

Your credibility is weakened because she has seen you use illegal drugs. If you have no choice but to be the one who must order her to accept evaluation, you will just have to keep returning the conversation back to her performance and your instructions.

Obviously, this is a good reason not to get into a situation like this in the first place, but how many of us are so wise we can make decisions with such accurate foresight?

> "I'm not going to get into what I've done in the past. *Even if I did something tonight that would get me fired tomorrow, it wouldn't change your situation at all*. Your work has gone downhill as I said before, and you've got to accept the medical evaluation."

If you find yourself in such a situation, consider turning the documentation over to another supervisor for intervention. Of course, that could be very difficult, because you would have to explain why to your administrator and human resources director. Get specific outside advice from drug treatment professionals on how to handle your predicament and the likely touchy questions.

In addition, you need to consider your future. Are you one of the gang or the boss? It is never wise to get drunk or stoned in front of your employees. This can and will come back to haunt you.

18.5 WHO TOLD YOU THAT CRAP?
HAVE YOU BEEN SPYING ON ME?

The employee knows you are not around her work station all the time. Consequently, she thinks you must be spying on her or getting tips from co-workers about her behavior. Since all you had is eyewitness accounts of her behavior, reliable though they may be, a verbal warning was your logical first step (after consulting with HR/EAP professionals). She, however, takes the discussion toward the diversionary issue of how you could know such private information.

> "I really believe in privacy. I would not consider using my time or asking someone else to spy on you. *What I have here is evidence obtained through normal channels.* These complaint letters from our customers and your declining sales calls are signs of trouble. *If I didn't have solid information to raise this subject with you, I wouldn't risk calling such a meeting.* At this point I'm not going to place anything in your permanent file, but I am giving you a verbal warning that these complaints had better stop."

> "*I've got several complaints here where you embarrassed our company.* Your behavior represents our behavior. I understand the necessity to entertain our customers, but you supposedly were not in control of yourself. The rep from the Jackson Mill said he had to drive you home, and the rep from RFT complained you were falling into their engineers' laps. *While your sales numbers are up, this threat to our company image is not acceptable.* I can't ignore these complaints, and I've written a warning to be placed in your permanent record. But I'm not going to turn it in unless you don't improve. Why don't you tell me what's been going on so we can work out a solution?"

Tip: Lessen denial with documentation.

As you reply, remember that **denial plays an immense role in addiction.** Denial sometimes can be overcome by your sound documentation; your records could help the employee realize her problem. For example, if you have received a call from a customer complaining about the employee's alleged drunkenness at a social function, you could ask for a written note describing the situation. If the customer does not want to write the note, you can write your own. Either of these notes could be used (with the customer's permission) to tactfully resolve the employee's denial.

Your responses should also emphasize that maintaining the company image is vital. Once again, consult with human resource and employee assistance coordinators before stepping into the intervention meeting. They can help you to prepare and practice your answers to potentially troublesome questions.

Listen to Hearsay, but Act Only on Observation

If you brought that employee in for an intervention interview with no more than hearsay, you could indeed be courting a libel suit. While co-workers may be the first people to witness a problem, your lawyer will probably tell you it's vital that you and other managers observe and document the behavior too.

Is this a one-time occurrence or a pattern? Is this woman sick Monday morning because she's pregnant? Is the concerned clerical worker coming to you because she had an argument with the employee?

If, however, the complaints are just the straw that broke the camel's back and you have your own observations and documentation to rely on as well, here is a stronger response:

> "I know that you and Ellen have your differences, but I have not called you in here based on her observation alone. Your supervisor provided me with your time cards for the past six months. You rarely make it to your desk on time on Mondays. I have other data to show your typing errors increase dramatically the beginning of each week. It's Monday. You arrived an hour late; you say you feel sick again, and you do look ill. *I feel I have given you performance documentation that backs up my need to send you for immediate testing.*"

18.6 I DO MY WORK, SO WHAT BUSINESS IS IT OF YOURS WHAT I DO ON MY PERSONAL TIME?

Your employee's last probe reveals that she knows your authority is generally limited to the work site. In this challenge, she attempts to sever the circumstances of her outside life from the authority of company management. As an independent adult, she fully understands that she has a legal right to live and associate as she chooses. Her challenge here attempts to push you off balance.

Among the most tricky challenges to answer is when do you have a right to meddle in an employee's off-hours use of alcohol or other drugs? Experts in this field say your personal dislike for such things, legal or not, is generally not enough for action in the work place.

For example, if your employee was charged but not convicted for drug possession on her personal time in a manner that does not affect or implicate your company, you may have little recourse. At the risk of overemphasis, see your lawyer and HR director before you use documentation to support why you are ordering the employee to be evaluated. And then practice a lot before the meeting starts. (Refer to sections 1.10 and 1.11.)

"You are correct that in most cases a supervisor does not have the right to meddle in an employee's personal life. *That is true, unless it has some connection to the workplace.* As I said before in detail, your behavior and *your work is being affected* by something. I don't know for sure, *but we must find out,* and you must accept the test and evaluation."

"Yes, it was your personal time, but three of our customers are on your baseball team. They paid to bail you out of jail on the drug possession charges. Your work performance is acceptable, *but what you are doing on your private time has created concern about how it reflects on this company.* We feel this Monday-morning testing for cause is in order."

"I saw the Sunday paper. We let you take the van home because you are on call at times. That photo shows our company name on the truck and the headline says a drunk driver ran the car off the road and into a tree. Okay, you didn't damage the truck, but *you damaged our business reputation* in the community. *Your behavior on your own time equals lost business on work time.*"

18.7 YOU'RE GOING TO RUIN MY WORK RECORD. DO YOU REALIZE WHAT YOU'RE DOING TO ME?

Okay, so now the employee seems to admit that there might be a little truth to the alleged substance abuse. But she feels that's no reason for you to damage her reputation. She points out you have a choice and really do not have to order this embarrassing evaluation. She claims it will ruin her work record, not to mention what everyone else at the company will say about her. Her question has put the onus on you. You need to put it back where it belongs. (Refer to section 3.7 for related comments.)

The fact that she is concerned about her work record gives you an entry. Emphasize her worth to your organization and your concern that down the road her positive path will end if this obstacle is not overcome.

Put the responsibility to act back on her shoulders where it belongs. Don't let her pretend that no one but the two of you suspect her problem. While you will keep your information confidential, it is nearly impossible for others not to at least suspect (given her absences, behavior, and physical appearance). Make it clear that it is only she who can choose which path to take.

> "I'm not ruining your career, I'm trying to save it. We feel that in the past you have had the dedication and performance we desire. This is an obstacle that could end your good record. If you want to get back on track, I insist you accept intervention."

> "The only thing that makes this intervention meeting necessary is your performance. If our concerns are shown to be unfounded by the test and evaluation, that would be great. You are not being made a victim by anyone here. There's no power in being a victim, so let's talk about what you can do for yourself and who might help you do that."

> "The only person who has the power to ruin your work record is you. Your work record will be made or broken by what you do. Your behavior at work has been noticed by almost everyone, so this evaluation may help rebuild your reputation. If you don't choose to beat the problem we are talking about, you will let it beat you. Will you please accept the test and evaluation?"

> "Getting help doesn't mean you can't have a good work record, or that you're weak or whatever. You have a lot to offer that we need. Remember when we found we were in over our heads on laptop computers? You were

the one who said 'Let's not waste time trying to learn how to cure problems. Let's get the experts in here *to help us tackle this.*' I'm telling you now, it's time to bring the experts in to help you tackle this."

"Over the years, we've developed a good personal relationship. I realize you have an impressive career and work record, but it's now overshadowed by the fact that your performance has dropped. If it continues, it may wreck your career. I can't just cover for you on this. *It wouldn't do you any good, and it could do a lot of harm. Our friendship can't affect this one way or the other.* I don't want to sound as if I'm arguing with you or threatening you. *But you must make a choice* about accepting the evaluation if you want to continue working here."

18.8 COME ON, GIVE ME A BREAK! THIS IS THE FIRST TIME IN FOUR MONTHS THAT I'VE COME IN A LITTLE HUNG OVER!

A repeat offender had been diagnosed and was in a treatment program. But she has fallen "off the wagon" while still on the treatment probationary period. As she arrives at your office, you are ready to spell out the conditions under which she can remain a part of your organization.

Your original expression of concern, however, does not mean you will support this person through the long term if she does not keep her end of the bargain. This question is another version of the helpless victim pattern demonstrated in section 18.7 and in section 3.7. Make sure you keep the responsibility to act on the employee.

"I am not a social worker or therapist. I fulfilled my responsibilities by documenting the original problem, getting you intervention and treatment for your problem. *I do not have an obligation to make this a long-term roller-coaster relationship.* I am not going to be an *enabler* who helps you wreck your job and endanger this company. If you fail the requirements again, you will be terminated immediately."

"When you returned to work after your first treatment we held a back-to-work conference. It included you, me, the treatment counselor, and your union representative. I promised you we would help you all we could, *but treatment is not an excuse for continuing bad performance. I put in writing what the consequences would be if the abuse problem surfaced again.* And that's what's happening now. This is your last chance—you *must stick with the treatment and stay off drugs* or you won't be employed here anymore."

"I gave you a break four months ago. I said then it was the *only break I would give you.* You had that in writing as part of our agreement for you to return to work. I kept my part of the bargain. The company paid for your treatment and let you come back. *You knew what the deal was to be. You signed it. You didn't do your part,* and I'm letting you go."

You and your organization should consider a program in which, if an employee tests positive, he or she is given one chance to enter a treatment program in your community. The refusal to be tested or enrolled in a treatment program may be grounds for dismissal. This is now a standard in business and you would be following a precedent—but see your lawyer and HR/EAP professional first.

Have any employee who tests positive and cooperates with treatment sign a "Last Chance" document that states if she fails again, she will be terminated.

Don't Open Yourself Up to Potential ADA Trouble

Experts who study the Americans with Disabilities Act (ADA) of 1990 say the legislation views drug and alcohol addictions as treatable diseases under certain circumstances. Before you tangle with the allegedly drug-affected employee, make certain you do not leave yourself open for a discrimination lawsuit. People who are rehabilitated or enrolled in a program may be considered protected under ADA.

At the same time, as a manager, you are allowed to control and ban drug use in your workplace. You are also expected to control situations where impaired performance poses a danger. Keep in mind that ADA and related interpretations are very complex legislation, so consult with a specialist who is current with recent interpretations and applications for further information *before* you are in a position where you must respond to the employee.

18.9 I TESTED NEGATIVE—YOU'RE GOING TO BE TALKING TO MY LAWYER! WHY DIDN'T YOU BELIEVE ME WHEN I TOLD YOU I WASN'T A DRUGGIE?

The employee who showed all the signs of substance abuse comes back with a negative test result. She has been evaluated and no alcohol/drug abuse was found. She is really self-righteous and indignant. Tiptoe lightly here, and stick to your documentation. Whatever she asks, bridge back to your documentation.

> *"Your lawyer may contact the company attorney* to discuss the issue, if that's what you choose to do. Whether you believe it or not, I'm glad that you tested negative. As I said when you were required to take the test, we want you to keep working here. *We didn't make this referral lightly.* We did our homework and have the necessary documentation and observations. *The evaluation is a method for determining if there is a problem and then plotting a course to fix it.* I don't diagnose the problem, I just observe the problem and get professional help. I am mostly concerned with performance, and I'm willing to discuss how you can be productive again."

> *"As I remember, I never said you were a drug addict. The driving force behind my insistence on your evaluation was your behavior.* The company's attorney will be happy to provide your lawyer with statements from witnesses who watched your temper outbursts become increasingly more violent. The evaluation has led me and others to recommend counseling."

> *"As we discussed when I first set up your appointment for evaluation, everything we do here is strictly confidential.* Do you understand that none of your colleagues are aware of what transpired? Do you also understand that the clinic we use for evaluation follows legal procedures for sample handling that are admissible in court? *They, too, follow strict confidentiality rules."*

Lawyers will tell you that not only is documentation important, so is your track record of confidentiality and your use of a system that provides a chain of evidence. It could be difficult for the employee to sue for defamation of character if no one knows of the intervention.

18.10 I DIDN'T KNOCK THE SCAFFOLDING DOWN ON PURPOSE. WHAT'S THE BIG DEAL IF I'M THE ONLY PERSON WHO GOT HURT?

The only person who got hurt was herself? If she hurts just herself, isn't that her problem and not yours? Can't she take whatever risks she wants? It's clear that she does not seem to see (or want to see) the danger to other employees.

Of course, the potential for direct and indirect victims is startling, and with this last straw, your files strongly support drug intervention for her.

Answer this question quickly and act swiftly. Whatever else you may have on your to-do list, it can wait. In your response, let the employee know immediately how serious the situation is and that your answer requires her prompt compliance. If this employee is under the influence, you may have to repeat it several times to make sure she understands.

"It is a big deal. *An injury to any employee is a concern.* The fact that you hurt only yourself makes me ask you, 'What if your assistant painter had not been on break? What if he was up on that scaffold?' *I need to know why you are wobbly, as you describe yourself.*"

"Even if you don't care about getting hurt, we do. And we also are concerned about someone else getting hurt here—if not this time maybe next time. *You don't have a right to endanger yourself or anyone else like that.* From what you said and from what I can see, something seems to be wrong, and I am instructing you to accept an evaluation."

"I never accused you of knocking the scaffolding down intentionally, but I'm not just going to ignore this as a minor mistake. I see by your attitude that you don't seem to understand the cost of the damage you created both for the equipment and yourself. *This is a serious accident that could have hurt others, and I observed that you may not have been in control of yourself.*"

"You don't have a pattern of unusual behavior or abuse, *but this accident is so potentially dangerous that it warrants 'just cause' testing.* You've had an on-site accident that could have killed two other workers, and

---

Tip: Watch those contracts to avoid trouble.

Depending on your industry, there may be legal requirements as to the handling of on-the-job "for cause" accidents. If you have a grant or contract with the federal government, the monetary value may specify notification and sanction requirements. If your employees fall under DOT (Department of Transportation) guidelines, for example, drug testing of employees in sensitive positions is required. State and local statutes may also control "for cause" workplace testing. Consult with your local legal experts as these **regulations change often, sometimes yearly.**

you too. When you say, 'It's no big deal' I wonder if your reasoning skills are impaired. You admit feeling unstable yet pass it off as not important. *This is too serious not to require immediate testing that is legally permitted both by statutes and company rules."*

Your risk manager will probably want you to instruct the employee to take the test as soon as possible, because some drugs and alcohol can move quickly out of the body.

18.11 YOU BETTER WATCH YOUR BACKSIDE! DO YOU HONESTLY THINK YOU CAN HURT ME LIKE THAT AND NOT PAY FOR IT SOMEDAY?

It should be made very clear to the angry employee that any threat of retribution will be grounds for dismissal. As a manager, this can be a real concern, as you worry about when and what form this revenge might take. Will she come after me or my family physically or will she spread career-damaging rumors about me? If you decide to back down and take no further intervention action with this employee, what have you gained? Maybe it would be better to say, what will you lose?

You have a suspected drug addict who now knows she can control you with threats. Is that how you want to manage your staff? You have your documentation. You are correct in acting on it.

Every person reacts differently to being confronted. Some cry, and some act with rage. You must remain in control and not react. Preparation is key. You have known this person for a period of time. How might she respond? How will you maintain control? Regardless, don't be intimidated by emotional responses. Focus on your goals (see section 1.5) and the documentation. Hold employees accountable for their performance and conduct.

> "First, let me emphasize that your threats can be grounds for dismissal. I am not 'ratting on you,' *I am telling you that I have observed and documented your poor performance.* It's that performance that is threatening your job, not I. If you plan to continue here, you will need *to work with me to get to the root of your decline.* If you choose to avoid your problems by threatening me, then you will not have a job here."

"Your threats are not acceptable. We have brought you in for this intervention meeting to start a process we hope will end your performance drop. Any retribution you attempt will be dealt with harshly by
the team. Before you go any further with this line of reasoning, let me
inform you that I have asked Security to have an officer wait by the el-
evators should we require his assistance."

When dealing with a bully, it's important for you to be in control. If
you feel you are in physical danger, invite another manager to be with you
at the intervention meeting. Feel free to have a company security officer or
a local police officer nearby where they can be summoned if necessary. Remember, though, you have rules of confidentiality to uphold. It would not
look good to have this employee brought into your office in front of his colleagues and then post a guard at the door.

Tough Questions Worksheet

Create responses to the difficult questions you could face on this chapter's topics, using the formulas below. Use **logic, emotion,** and **ethics** whenever possible. Experiment by answering the same question with different formulas to learn which best fits your natural style. Use pencil so you can erase and refine your answers.

Past, Present, Future:

What happened was:

What's happening now is:

The way we'll prevent it from happening again is by:

Problem to Solution:

*The **problems** we have are:*

*I'd like to go directly to a proposed **solution:***

Problem - Cause - Solution - Timing (PCST):

*The **problems** we have are:*

*They were **caused** by:*

*The **solutions** we may implement are:*

*Our **timing** is:*

Wrong, Right, and What It Means:

*This is an extremely complex area and our track record has **overall** been very **good:***

*We do very difficult things and sometimes we have failures. What **happened** is that:*

*What this **means** for us now is:*

Three-Step Explanation:

I understand what you are asking and why it concerns you so much:

Other people who had your experiences probably would feel the same way:

However, I would like to explain a little about this problem:

Other formulas and responses I want to use for tough questions related to this chapter:

19

Successfully Rebutting Dress-Code Queries

19.1 *Dress code! Come on, who cares about how we dress as long as it's clean and neat?*

19.2 *If we can dress casually on Fridays, why not every day?*

19.3 *If I do my job well, what difference does it make how much jewelry I wear?*

19.4 *Why should I have to compromise my principles about what I want to wear just to please a few narrow-minded people?*

We wear clothes to say something about ourselves. More important, we interpret the dress of others to be a statement (intended or not) about themselves. Even when the 1960s flower people preached that clothes did not mean a thing, they adorned themselves with the antiestablishment uniform of long hair, sandals, love beads, hip-hugging jeans for women, and bib overalls for men. You were not "hip" without the uniform nonuniform.

But today we complain when some executive proclaims a dress code for the office. What about our rights under the First Amendment! Dress code? Didn't that go out with the 'sixties? Get off it. What's your hang up? No one will stand (or sit) for it.

19.1 DRESS CODE! COME ON, WHO CARES ABOUT HOW WE DRESS AS LONG AS IT'S CLEAN AND NEAT?

Year by year your staff have grown used to a new norm in office dress. More casual each year, few ties, even fewer skirts, many more slacks. Soon after casual Fridays began, designer jeans gave way to traditional blue jeans, and then came a few strategically placed, factory-installed rips and tears. Sweat pants slipped in the back door while maroon shorts and orange tank tops came in the front. So far no Speedo swimsuits or neon halter tops.

Now you have been told by senior management to enforce the old dress code. If you start out your response by referring to the upset employee's clothes in particular, your reply will cause an emotional barrier. All of us are sensitive about what others say regarding our clothes. Moreover, such comments are taken as remarks about the kind of person we are. As you formulate your response, consider beginning with a depersonalized style as detailed in section 1.8 and also demonstrated in the following quotes.

> *"When people choose their jobs, they enter a set of expectations.* Somebody joining the Marines knows full well he or she will be wearing certain types of clothing—same with a police officer or nurse. When employees are hired, they join a company whose customers and vendors have certain expectations. *The clothes say something to the customers, and we need that to be a positive statement about us.* Let's discuss which clothing says good things about us and which does not."

> "If we think about it, we expect other people to dress within some accepted norms. We expect waiters and waitresses at nice restaurants to dress neatly. We don't like to see sloppy-looking clerks at the shopping mall. Our customers and vendors have expectations of us, too. *These expectations have changed, but some of the clothing worn here lately has gone beyond what I think our customers expect.* We need to get closer to that range."

> "We need to think this through. I like to be able to choose what I wear, but I also realize that what I wear says something about our company. *To a lot of people, what we wear says a lot about us individually.* We have an old dress code that I've got to bring up to date, and then we'll need to follow it. I would rather do this *with your help,* so please cooperate by suggesting what kinds of clothing we should include and exclude. *The test will be what our customers expect from us and what the president will agree to.*"

Free thinkers and casual dressers may proclaim that dress codes are middle-class taboos that should have been shed during the 1960s' social revolution. But that doesn't pass muster logically. Things outside the norm of any group are unacceptable; in other words, they are taboo.

In your response to dress-code protesters, you could ask if they would accept a co-worker wearing flannel pajamas every day? That certainly is taboo in our society. Your staff will probably argue that the pajama example is too extreme to be relevant. Counter by saying, no, it makes your point—we all can agree that some things are too far outside the norm to be acceptable to customers you want to please. The next logical step is to define where the limits have moved to. Define them in a revised dress code.

19.2 IF WE CAN DRESS CASUALLY ON FRIDAYS, WHY NOT EVERY DAY?

The company allows employees to dress casually on Fridays to boost morale and to accommodate concerns about the expense of wearing business attire every work day. Most customers seem to accept the end-of-the-week relaxed atmosphere that casual-wear fosters. Now, however, a few employees ask why they can't wear jeans and colorful shirts every day. If it's logical and good business on Friday, why not other work days? You have given an inch, but they want to take a mile.

There were reasons for the old everyday dress code, and there are reasons for the one-day exception. Even though you might be nearing the end of your patience, this is no time to say, "That is company policy." (Refer to section 4.4 for more points on handling pushy "have to" statements.) Give the sound reasons behind the policy; don't just recite the policy.

"Our customers have accepted casual dress on Fridays, but many would not accept it all week long. *We can't change any faster than our customers will accept*, or we risk losing a lot of them."

"If our customers see us relaxing our dress standards too much, *some of them may think we are getting too casual about them and their business*. We need all our customers. Wearing business attire only four days a week won't keep them away, but five casual days is taking too great a risk."

"I realize that in a few parts of the country some businesses are allowing casual dress more often. That may work well in those locations, *but our customer base here still expects traditional business clothing* for most business occasions. Not only that, but we have customers from across the nation and sometimes from other countries, and they would be put off by too much casual attire."

> **Tip: Make the first impression create a common ground.**
>
> Underdressing or overdressing creates a barrier to potential customers as much as other things such as smoking, unusually long or short hair, and even certain beards. While casual dress or other customer-offending appearances do not mean your employee cannot render good service, she will first have to overcome the bad impressions before she can gain the customer's trust. The old adage that the first impression is a lasting one applies to business clothing. Your company spends a lot of time and money attracting new customers, so you can't afford to lose them merely because of appearances.

19.3 IF I DO MY JOB WELL, WHAT DIFFERENCE DOES IT MAKE HOW MUCH JEWELRY I WEAR?

Your employee loves to wear lots of colorful jewelry—silver rings on six fingers, two necklaces, extra big earrings, and noisy bracelets that clunk on desks and countertops. She says it's artful; you think it's gaudy. She says many customers praise her assortments, so why can't she wear her various collections?

At first glance she seems to have customers' approval and an ethical standard on her side (self-expression). Although her statements reflect her perception, they don't match the reality of the workplace. While a few customers may have complimented her, either sincerely or just to be nice, there are far more who keep their thoughts to themselves. As to her right to self-expression, your reply could acknowledge it while also saying that all personal rights become limited when they start to infringe upon the rights of others.

"A sales representative's appearance can create a common ground between her and the customer, or the appearance can make sure that doesn't happen. *If something makes the customer uncomfortable, the sales rep isn't going to get anywhere, and no sale will take place.* Why wear more and put that barrier in your way? One ring on each hand along with a matching pendant or bracelet would still look quite nice."

"I'm not saying that no one has complimented you. I am saying that by being excessive with your jewelry, you risk offending clients who feel otherwise *but are too polite to say anything.*"

19.4 WHY SHOULD I HAVE TO COMPROMISE MY PRINCIPLES ABOUT WHAT I WANT TO WEAR JUST TO PLEASE A FEW NARROW-MINDED PEOPLE?

The employee has touched the timeless issue of how people judge others by superficial aspects such as clothing. She insists her work and service is excellent, even if she isn't in a business suit. She feels the more strict dress code is an unneeded, outdated infringement on her personal rights.

Instead of letting her know how wrong you think she is, your response should offer her another choice in how she could view the dress code. If you are not sure how to get started, try the feel-felt-found formula. (Refer to section 2.2 for related comments.) This formula works only if you and the questioner have had similar experiences. Common experiences will increase your credibility and therefore the persuasiveness of your reply.

> "I used to *feel* the same way you do. I didn't understand why I needed to wear business suits that made me uncomfortable. I *felt* it was unfair. But after thinking about it a lot, I *found* I could choose to see it as an intrusion on my personal liberties or as just another thing I do to please customers. I do a lot of things to please customers, so why not this?"

> "I understand how you *feel* and I admit I *felt* the same way. However, *I have found* that when I am a customer I am not comfortable with a person whose clothes don't match his role. If I expect that of the people who serve me as a customer, *then it is not unfair for me to do the same for my customers.*"

> "Some clients who prefer traditional business attire want to know we respect them and take their business seriously. *If we meet them in casual clothes, they may think we don't respect them,* or they might think we are too casual toward their serious needs."

> "When flight attendants, hotel clerks, and bank officers put on their work clothes, they are not compromising themselves. They are putting on clothes *that signify that they are stepping into their roles.* The clothes say 'I am on the job and ready to serve you.'"

> "*There is nothing phony or insincere about wearing the kinds of clothes that please customers.* It's like the pleasant face we put on when we are determined to please those we care about. Even when we are troubled by

outside concerns, we summon that special part of our personality to create a pleasant environment for the short time we are with a customer or with anyone else we want to please. *We do that out of choice, and we can do the same with the clothes we choose."*

"The first impression makes the sale a lot easier or a lot tougher. *Why make it harder on yourself?* If that's the way people are, you are not going to change them overnight, and you risk losing a lot of customers in the meantime. You are not right or wrong in what you think and neither are they; it's just a matter of preferences and *who wants to please whom."*

Tough Questions Worksheet

Create responses to the difficult questions you could face on this chapter's topics, using the formulas below. Use **logic, emotion,** and **ethics** whenever possible. Experiment by answering the same question with different formulas to learn which best fits your natural style. Use pencil so you can erase and refine your answers.

Past, Present, Future:

What happened was:

What's happening now is:

The way we'll prevent it from happening again is by:

Problem to Solution:

*The **problems** we have are:*

*I'd like to go directly to a proposed **solution**:*

Problem - Cause - Solution - Timing (PCST):

*The **problems** we have are:*

*They were **caused** by:*

*The **solutions** we may implement are:*

*Our **timing** is:*

Wrong, Right, and What It Means:

*This is an extremely complex area and our track record has **overall** been very good:*

*We do very difficult things and sometimes we have failures. What **happened** is that:*

*What this **means** for us now is:*

Three-Step Explanation:

I understand what you are asking and why it concerns you so much:

Other people who had your experiences probably would feel the same way:

However, I would like to explain a little about this problem:

Other formulas and responses I want to use for tough questions related to this chapter:

20

Handling Customers Who Grill You About Employees' Mistakes

20.1   *What are you going to do about that rude employee?*

20.2   *Don't you believe me? Are you going to take his word over mine?*

20.3   *How can you stay in business with such incompetence? Haven't you trained these people to do anything right?*

When a customer grills you about what's going to be done about your employees' real or perceived mistake, you are faced with a perplexing situation. What do you say to stay in the customer's good graces but without destroying the morale of employees?

Losing a customer can cost a bundle. Consider the impact it will have on other potential customers: business colleagues, friends, family, relatives, and so on. Moreover, how much will it cost you to recruit a new customer to replace the one you lost? On the other hand, if you rebuke your employees wrongly to placate customers, what will it cost to replace workers who walk off the job after you have spent months and great expense training them?

The following model responses demonstrate how you can gracefully walk the fine line between placating the customer and undermining your employee.

20.1 WHAT ARE YOU GOING TO DO ABOUT THAT RUDE EMPLOYEE?

Picture yourself on the phone with an irate customer who is ranting and raving about the alleged rudeness of your lead worker, who you know is the last person who'd be impolite to anyone. You didn't hear the conversation, but nevertheless you must respond.

From experience, however, you know some people add claims of "rudeness" to spice up their main complaint. And you also know that complainants often feel if they can allege two wrongs (rudeness and their main charge), they may have greater leverage for getting the satisfaction they demand.

At the same time, everyone has a bad day once in a while and maybe your best employee has just made his first mistake.

At this point, it really doesn't matter who was at fault. You are being interrogated by an angry customer who demands retribution. Your objective is to regain the customer's confidence and goodwill, without being unfair to your excellent employee.

> "I'm really sorry this happened—*this is not the impression we want to give.* We really try to meet—and exceed—our customers' expectations. I will look into this right away, and I'll have a talk with our employee. Your business is important to us, and I promise that *this will never happen again."*

> "If that's how you feel you were treated, *then we certainly haven't done our job properly.* We value your business, and we want you to know that. So there are no future misunderstandings, from now on please feel free to talk directly with me about your account."

The customer can be right without your staff being wrong. Without saying the employee was at fault, you can honestly apologize that this happened. Even if the customer is mistaken, you are still sorry the incident occurred, no matter what or who caused it.

Furthermore, you can sincerely say your organization strives to give a good impression and that the company's goal is to surpass customers' expectations. Without a doubt, you can assure the complainant you'll look into the concern and will talk with the employee. Moreover, you can genuinely proclaim the customer's business is of utmost importance. (Refer to section 1.3 for related comments.)

If your customer gets the idea you are just going through the motions she will be further incensed. Your attitude and your answer should reflect total concern—"How do we get back in your good graces?"

Finally, you can promise this will not happen again. How? Whether or not you believe the worker was rude, you can talk with him and make it clear that the next time the customer calls, the employee will have to do extra duty to please her. You can empathize with the worker by acknowledging how difficult it can be to deal with "problem" customers. Offer coaching on how to handle these situations smoothly.

Notice how the second preceding response goes directly to winning the customer over. This approach "elevates" the customer's status by inviting her to deal directly with you. Do you think that's beneath your responsibilities? Ask yourself, how much do you want to please this customer keep her future business? The cost of making this extra effort will probably be a lot less than what it'll cost you to find a new customer (who just may be difficult to handle).

20.2 DON'T YOU BELIEVE ME?
ARE YOU GOING TO TAKE HIS WORD OVER MINE?

This customer senses that you may not believe her claims about your employee's mistakes or rudeness. Now you feel that if you don't promise to beat the tar out of your staff, she will press you further for a punishment commitment. She may do it by insisting that you accept her word as conclusive evidence. Your mental alarm should go off instantly, sending out this message: "This is a trap. Don't walk into it."

Don't let the customer trap you with the hidden premise of these types of questions. The question tries to create a reality that there are only two choices: the customer's word or your employee's word. It just begs for an argument. (Section 3.6 offers related comments.) Some people have a deep emotional need to dominate others—and situations. You will regret any attempt to show such people how wrong they are about your wonderful subordinate. Their self-esteem is too low to afford being wrong again.

You need to control the focus of the discussion or you will lose any chance of changing its direction. Understand there may be many layers to the customer's feelings: the original customer-service problem, her subsequent anger, and her possible need to dominate.

Know what you want to talk about (the service or product problem) and maneuver away from futile areas (i.e., who's right or wrong, who's good or bad, and so on.) For example, don't get into a discussion about who is more credible. How could you possibly win? Sidestep and parry with one of these responses:

"There is no question that you have been offended, and this can only mean *we haven't done our job of providing you with the service and courtesy we strive to provide everyone.* Please trust me to do what is right in the way of follow-up action. Believe me, I am as concerned as you are about the situation."

"Ms. Anderson, *I believe that you have been offended. I don't doubt that at all.* I'm going to look into this as soon as we're done talking here. And I promise that this will never happen again."

If she persists, try to gently but firmly shut off discussion by saying:

"Ms. Anderson, I have assured you that we'll review this quickly. *But we are not permitted to discuss internal actions* such as the exact treatment of employees. Please believe that this won't happen again."

It is a costly mistake to falsely tell the complainant that, yes, she was right, and pretend that you will immediately tar and feather the subordinate. Rumors and bad news are like water; they go where they want, and you can't stop them most of the time. Your little convenient lie will probably get back to the subordinate, who may be quite displeased because you didn't stand up to the rude customer. The employee will be angry, because you know him and his professionalism while you may know nothing about the customer. Picking sides helps create a demoralized employee who may actually be rude to future customers.

20.3 HOW CAN YOU STAY IN BUSINESS WITH SUCH INCOMPETENCE? HAVEN'T YOU TRAINED THESE PEOPLE TO DO ANYTHING RIGHT?

In these two hostile questions and others like them, an angry customer implies something went wrong and your employees' incompetence is the cause. You recognize this isn't the ideal time to expound on how well your company trains employees. You have been around long enough to know that those aren't the real issues anyway.

These barbs are attack and false-premise questions. If you respond to them head-on, you'll have two quarrels: the original customer-service problem and a useless fight over the secondary issue of relative competence (the false premise).

Tip: You absolutely cannot calm them down.

If the customer is filled with raging emotions, she can't listen effectively. But don't think that you can calm her down. **You can't reach into her mind and flip a switch to shut off heated emotions.** She will calm down when she has vented her feelings. Not before. You can help, though, by not provoking her with aggravating retorts. Furthermore, you can lead her to calm **herself** by using your own questions to regain control of the situation. Redirect it with a response formula (see Chapter 3 for other examples).

Sometimes a delay is all that is needed. Judge whether it should be an hour or a day. Explain that you need a little time to check a few things, then schedule a time to call back. Keep the appointment no matter what. (Refer to Chapter 4 for related word choices.)

Pick a method that will allow the customer to vent while you find out what the real issues are behind the nasty comments. Keep the focus there.

Here is a specialized application of an all-purpose response formula called past-present-future.

You ask the complainant "What happened?" (Listen without interrupting or correcting.)

Then "What's the situation now?" (Still listen.)

Last, "What would you like done?" (Listen some more.)

After all that listening, determine whether you can do something immediately to please the unhappy customer, or if you will need to check further and get back to her. (Refer to section 2.3 for more on the past-present-future formula.)

Tough Questions Worksheet

Create responses to the difficult questions you could face on this chapter's topics, using the formulas below. Use **logic, emotion,** and **ethics** whenever possible. Experiment by answering the same question with different formulas to learn which best fits your natural style. Use pencil so you can erase and refine your answers.

Past, Present, Future:

What happened was:

What's happening now is:

The way we'll prevent it from happening again is by:

Problem to Solution:

*The **problems** we have are:*

*I'd like to go directly to a proposed **solution:***

Problem - Cause - Solution - Timing (PCST):

*The **problems** we have are:*

*They were **caused** by:*

*The **solutions** we may implement are:*

*Our **timing** is:*

Wrong, Right, and What It Means:

*This is an extremely complex area and our track record has **overall** been very good:*

*We do very difficult things and sometimes we have failures. What **happened** is that:*

*What this **means** for us now is:*

Three-Step Explanation:

I understand what you are asking and why it concerns you so much:

Other people who had your experiences probably would feel the same way:

However, I would like to explain a little about this problem:

Other formulas and responses I want to use for tough questions related to this chapter:

21

Serving Well Even When Accused of Being "The Big Bad Bureaucrat"

21.1 Aren't you supposed to serve the public?

21.2 Are you saying I don't know what I'm talking about?

21.3 I've known the governor a long time. Do you want me to tell him how badly you treat the public?

21.4 Don't you care at all what happens to me? How can I do my job (feed my family, pay the rent . . .) if you don't do more to help me?

Being a bureaucrat is a thankless job at times. Few people know that government managers are a lot like their private-sector counterparts. They have about the same proportion of hardworking, concerned managers frequently used as pincushions for angry customers. Although some government managers are striving diligently to invigorate their agencies, the bureaucrat stereotype lives on.

The stereotype leads some citizens to be abusive in their questions, which often are really personal attacks. The worst fall into several predictable personality patterns. Once you learn to recognize them, you're well on your way to knowing the best strategy for responding.

21.1 AREN'T YOU SUPPOSED TO SERVE THE PUBLIC?

The Abusive Ramrod. The abusive ramrod asks insulting questions like this. He often gets his way in life by using boorish behavior so offensive that we often give in just to get rid of him. When we do so, however, we reinforce his bullying tactics, ensuring it will be worse the next time. He might also throw some of these hostile questions in rapid fire:

Don't you think it's damn rude of you to suggest that?

When have you done an honest day's work?

Do you get your jollies playing God?

Have you forgotten that my tax dollars are paying your salary?

How come you government loafers don't give a damn about the rest of us?

Now your favorite abusive ramrod is back at your office counter, and you have said no to his latest demand. He switches on his offensive personality and fires attack questions at you, one after another.

Don't answer attack questions. Don't explain how you "serve" the public; that you are serving him the right way; that you aren't a loafer; that you do care about him; that you always put in an honest day's work, and that you don't play God. Answering gives him more to argue about.

Since you realize he won't go away as a bad dream would, wait for a momentary pause in his stream of hot air, and say something like:

Step one: "If you don't mind, I would like to get a clearer idea of what we are dealing with. Tell me again *what happened?*" (Then you listen while he summarizes, but interrupt politely after a minute for step two.)

Step two: "Okay, I've got a pretty good idea about what happened. What is *happening now?*" (You listen for a minute, and then interrupt for step three.)

Step three: "I understand what happened and what's happening now, so what would you *want done next?*"

If the abusive ramrod won't follow your lead, you might use the next response until he blows off enough steam to calm down.

"Okay, I'm ready to take notes. Please go ahead and tell me again. . . ."

There are generally two subspecies of abusive ramrods: the first are temporarily afflicted with this personality disorder.

The temporarily afflicted attacks you with nonstop questions and insults until he vents his frustration. After realizing another approach would have been wiser, he's capable of offering a sincere apology, although usually much later.

The foregoing response is from the past-present-future formula, which works exceptionally well with the temporarily afflicted ramrod. The past-present-future formula obtains real information, sets up a venting strategy, and enables you to control the discussion and direct it to the end point.

Past-present-future succeeds in confrontations on the phone and in face-to-face meetings. You actually save time with this response formula by preventing him from wandering all over the map in his ramblings. (Refer to sections 1.1 through 1.3 and sections 2.3 and 3.9 for related insights.)

The permanently afflicted abusive ramrod is less common but exceedingly difficult to handle. A permanently afflicted ramrod does not intend to stop asking, demanding, badgering, and criticizing until you give in. He knows exactly what he's doing and why.

Brace yourself for the task of standing firm in the face of belligerence, assault questions, and personal criticisms. You can't take control of the conversation unless you keep your cool. Tell yourself: "I'm not going to let him get to me. . . . He wins if I get sarcastic. . . . I'm just going to keep returning to the same choices and information, no matter what he says or asks. . . . This will be over in a few minutes. . . ."

People under attack from abusive ramrods make their worst mistakes when they don't prepare themselves psychologically. Remember, these aren't rational questions. They are attacks by someone playing by different rules, or no rules at all.

If the ramrod has called you on the phone, you have the advantage of putting him on hold while you clear you head, regain your composure, and then return to the line, ready to stand firm. Using your best actor's voice, say something like:

"I would like to help you if I can, but talking like that won't make it any easier. *Will you let me try to help you?*"

He pauses, or you repeat the first line if he hasn't. Then:

"Thank you. Let me be as clear as I can be. I understand your request and I have compared it to the guidelines I am required to follow. I believe you when you say how difficult your situation is and that you don't agree with this decision. While I cannot change the decision, *the help I can offer is information about your choices and how you could appeal.* The choices you have are . . . you can appeal the decision in this agency by . . . or by . . ."

When he objects to the repeated answer, just keep giving the same answer until he tires of it.

"I understand you would like a different answer, but this is *the only one I have for you.* Your choices are to . . . you can appeal by . . ."

Stand Firm, But Don't Engage *His* Fight

The response immediately above stakes out your position and also lets him know what his options are. Once you have made it clear your decision will not change, stick to it.

Sometimes the abusive ramrod will interrupt your responses when they are not going his way. Try to keep control by asking, "May I finish answering your question?" If he won't allow that, let him babble on while you remain silent. You can't stuff a sock in his mouth, so let him spew forth while your silence tells him his words are going nowhere.

Often, the silence will cause the abusive ramrod to attempt to engage you again by saying something like, "Are you listening to me?" or, "You don't give a damn what I say, do you?" Don't answer those taunts; instead, jump back in and immediately repeat the choices, "The choices you have are . . . you can appeal by. . . ."

If you slip and engage his tirade, the abusive character will keep insulting and demanding until he finds a debatable issue he can use to argue about all over again. He will keep probing until you get confused or lose your temper, thereby allowing him to switch to the victim role. He'll then demand special consideration because he was wronged by you, the abusive bureaucrat.

Erect a Sanity Barrier to Stay Calm

If your abusive ramrod is on the phone, as most are, there's a simple bureaucratic maneuver you can occasionally use to put an end to the bullying. This is only for when you are sure you have done all you possibly can to solve his problem and you have double-checked everything to be certain. The step involves switching your communication method from phone to letter.

> **Tip: Restore yourself to be ready for the next one.**
>
> After dealing with an abusive ramrod, do yourself a favor and take a break. After the call, do some stress-reduction breathing-and-thinking exercises. You've been on an emotional roller coaster; **you need to regain your emotional balance.** Otherwise, you'll carry that stirred-up feeling into your next call, meeting, and so forth.
>
> You don't have ten minutes? Then take at least one full minute: breath deeply through your nose, exhale through your mouth, close your eyes, and tell yourself you have survived this before and you can again. Lunch or quitting time is only a few hours away, so keep the lid on until you can let it out later. Make sure you do let it out later; otherwise, you may become an abusive ramrod with someone else at any moment. Moreover, your ability to handle tough questions decreases in proportion to the stress you let stay built up inside you.

By switching to written communication, you intentionally erect a useful barrier between yourself and the abusive ramrod. Of course, we shouldn't push away most citizen-customers as shown here, even the ones who occasionally blow their tops, as we all do sometimes.

But once the abusive ramrod goes past rational discussion to begin a war of attrition on your emotions, the issue is no longer "good service." The issue is reasonable self-protection and saving time so you can help someone who can and wants to be helped. Switching to letters to push away an abusive ramrod may not be nice, but it may be necessary.

"I will agree to review this one more time. I will recheck everything and *send you a letter.* That way *you'll have it in writing.* Then there won't be any doubt about what was said. If you have something important you want to add, please jot it down—longhand is fine—and mail it to me quickly. I know you want this reviewed right away, so *I will begin as soon as I get off the phone with you.*"

21.2 ARE YOU SAYING I DON'T KNOW WHAT I'M TALKING ABOUT?

The Professor. The professor talks as though he's an expert on everything. He claims to know all the important laws and court cases. Better yet, the professor seems to possess a detailed knowledge of *your* job. In addition to this classic taunt, the professor may hit you with other attack questions like the following:

Don't you know what you are doing is illegal?

How can you do that when it's unconstitutional?

Doesn't the state statute say . . .?

Do you want me to tell you what you should be doing?

You obviously don't know your own rules, do you?

If you're faced with any of these questions, it should be an instant tip-off that your citizen-customer is the professor. In support of his difficult demands and questions, he'll cite articles, books, and public names. The professor often misuses language.

The professor will bluntly tell you what the problem is and uses pedantic language while explaining what you should decide. He wonders how you could possibly reach any other conclusion, because he has thoroughly researched it, of course. He won't accept the possibility that you may know more than he does.

In your response, don't tell the professor that he doesn't know what he's talking about, or that he's got everything all mixed up. Generally ignore his contentions, unless there is serious misinformation that needs to be corrected for his later benefit. (Refer to section 3.3 for related suggestions.) Merely give him the correct information about your authority and the appropriate rules or accepted interpretations.

"I understand what you are saying, that's how a lot of *people* interpret the regulations. However, it isn't quite that simple. *I'd like to explain* a few things I am familiar with from dealing with this every day. I would like to provide the latest information we have. . . ."

"I am not in a position to know what others may have told you. *And I'm not questioning what you know or don't know.* But I would like to offer you the best information I have and the limits of my authority. I can tell you what I'm *allowed to do* and what I am *not permitted to do.* Maybe that will help you better understand the basis for my decision. . . ."

The know-everything professor probably has very low self-esteem and, consequently, can't live with being wrong. If your response threatens his self-esteem, he'll fight all the harder to be right. Make sure you serve him with the correct information but don't make him wrong or you'll have twice the argument.

21.3 I'VE KNOWN THE GOVERNOR A LONG TIME. DO YOU WANT ME TO TELL HIM HOW BADLY YOU TREAT THE PUBLIC?

The Politically Connected. The politically connected toss out names faster than a used-car salesman tosses out deals. She personally knows the governor, the senator, the company president, chairman of the board, everybody and anybody in a position to get you fired—today. Then she threatens you by asking if she should expose your poor service by telling her powerful friends.

"Hey, it's still a free country, so talk to whomever you wish, but nothing's going to change in this office." That's the essence of your response, but dress it up with diplomatic language as follows. Gently acknowledge her right to involve anyone she wants, but otherwise don't comment about the alleged political connection.

Don't say you're impressed or that you couldn't care less. Don't make the alleged connection an additional issue to quarrel about. Keep bridging back to issues, ignoring the threats and self-serving delusions of grandeur. Assure the complainant that you are giving her the same level of treatment you would give everyone else.

> "You certainly have the right to share your concerns with whomever you feel it's appropriate. *I'd be happy to explain this information to anyone you designate.* In any case, I would like to explain again that the reason for my decision is . . ."

> "We do our best to treat everyone the same. In fact, the governor insists that we respond equally to all constituents. Let me reiterate what we can do for you. . . ."

The few people who actually do have pull with a governor or company president usually are smart enough not to be so blatant in throwing their weight around. But just in case she really does know the governor or the company president, alert your boss.

21.4 DON'T YOU CARE AT ALL WHAT HAPPENS TO ME? HOW CAN I DO MY JOB (FEED MY FAMILY, PAY THE RENT . . .) IF YOU DON'T DO MORE TO HELP ME?

The Helpless Victim. Nearly all angry or desperate people eventually reach for the helpless victim role. If they can't get you to do what they want by request, threat, or bribery, then they instinctively appeal to your social conscience. They quickly disempower themselves by saying only you, the powerful bureaucrat, can change their circumstances. Simultaneously, they throw their responsibilities onto your shoulders, attempting to make you blamable for what happens to them.

Let's assume you are a manager at a social services agency that has done all it can for this individual. You've informed him of other programs available that might offer help, and you've encouraged him to look into these (church, food pantry, etc.). After explaining this, he's now playing the helpless victim role to the hilt. He'd rather make the problem yours. He's avoiding any responsibility for his predicament and blames everyone and everything else. (Refer to section 3.7 for related points.)

Despite your misgivings about where the conversation is headed, make certain you have a good understanding of his frustration and whether you've done all you can for him. Use a question that will encourage him to pinpoint his exact circumstances and needs.

> "I can't decide for you what you should or shouldn't do. *Those are questions only you can answer.* I will meet my responsibility to provide you with as much help as I legally can. But you are responsible for making the best of your circumstances. What would you like to see done? *Please share with me your specific concerns and needs* and then together we can address them."

Avoid Advice; It Falls on Deaf Ears

Look for the choices, albeit difficult, he can make. Focus your response on them. For example, what time or resources do you have to serve that person . . . and what are the limits that you and the "victim" must accept? Instead of giving advice on how this person should run his or her life, respond by saying what you can do and what you cannot do.

Always return to the bottom line that the choices are his, and only his.

"I can list the options available to you and what the results might be. *But only you can decide* whether to pursue them after that."

"I can see you're very frustrated, but please believe me that we've done all that we're allowed to do for you. Why don't you tell me specifically what your needs are, and once again I can explain what help is available here and where you might get other assistance. *I can't, however, seek those opportunities for you.*"

Although it's difficult to respond to questions about hardships, avoid the hook of paternalism, which helpless victims play to the hilt. He really doesn't want you to decide what's best for him anyway, so don't fall into the trap of telling him what he should or shouldn't do. List options and possible outcomes.

Tough Questions Worksheet

Create responses to the difficult questions you could face on this chapter's topics, using the formulas below. Use **logic, emotion,** and **ethics** whenever possible. Experiment by answering the same question with different formulas to learn which best fits your natural style. Use pencil so you can erase and refine your answers.

Past, Present, Future:

What happened was:

What's happening now is:

The way we'll prevent it from happening again is by:

Problem to Solution:

*The **problems** we have are:*

*I'd like to go directly to a proposed **solution:***

Problem - Cause - Solution - Timing (PCST):

*The **problems** we have are:*

*They were **caused** by:*

*The **solutions** we may implement are:*

*Our **timing** is:*

Wrong, Right, and What It Means:

*This is an extremely complex area and our track record has **overall** been very **good:***

*We do very difficult things and sometimes we have failures. What **happened** is that:*

*What this **means** for us now is:*

Three-Step Explanation:

I understand what you are asking and why it concerns you so much:

Other people who had your experiences probably would feel the same way:

However, I would like to explain a little about this problem:

Other formulas and responses I want to use for tough questions related to this chapter:

22

Dodging Stings and Barbs
When You Must Change Your Mind

22.1   *Where has your head been? Why didn't you think of this in the first place?*

22.2   *Why do you flip-flop all the time?*

22.3   *How do I know you aren't going to change your mind—again?*

22.4   *What else are you forgetting to tell us?*

22.5   *Are you going to take the blame for the wasted time and money?*

The look. If you've ever had to change your mind midway through a project, you know the look. When you try and explain your presumed flip-flop, your staff's faces go blank, except for the creases between their narrowing eyebrows. Their body language silently shouts in frustration "Not again, not now, you idiot."

Humble, leery. Those are charitable words that describe how we sometimes feel when a surprise development requires another change in a tardy project, causing more wasted time and money.

The pressure of an approaching deadline along with a hectic pace creates extra stress. Tension climbs, patience vanishes, and tempers flare. You wonder why you took this job in the first place.

You worry about the rhetorical barbs your staff will likely throw, and you fantasize about being invisible for a month. But then you brace yourself and deliver the bad news.

22.1 WHERE HAS YOUR HEAD BEEN?
WHY DIDN'T YOU THINK OF THIS IN THE FIRST PLACE?

Unfair! That is what you tell yourself when this question is hurled at you by unsupportive staff. Can't they see that you're overworked? Don't they realize that if you had discovered the problem earlier, of course you would have said something sooner.

Despite your unintentional oversight, and their unjust observations, you recognize that engaging in verbal combat would only increase the casualties, so you opt to take the arrows. (Refer to section 1.6 for related comments.)

Be Sorry, Be Patient, Be Ready

Even if you are the boss, you can't expect people not to react with frustration and a feeling of futility when you announce jarring changes midway through a project. This is especially true when changes waste precious time and double the pressure on everyone to meet an unforgiving deadline. Being openly sorry is fine but it isn't enough, not yet anyway. Allow them to absorb your apology and go through the natural process of venting.

As you let them vent, be patient. And be ready to encourage everyone to come up with better ideas and strategies for corrective action.

> *"I'm very sorry and I sincerely apologize to you.* I wish I had found the problem sooner—but I didn't and I can't undo that. You've got every right to be angry with me. I'm the only one to blame. I hate losing all this time just as much as you do. *If you can think of a better way to solve the situation we have today, I would love to hear it."*

> *"I know this is my fault, and you've got good reason to be angry with me.* I am very sorry, yet I know that doesn't get back the time we've lost. This is the best solution I can think of today. I'm open to any alternatives you can come up with to get us back on track as soon as possible. *I'll do whatever I can to help."*

> "The truth is that I didn't think of this problem when we began—it just didn't occur to me. I went through a checklist but it never came up. *Yes, it's my responsibility,* and I wish I had seen it from the start. *I've learned a tough lesson here,* but that doesn't help us today. We've got to make this change or come up with an alternative as soon as possible."

If they fall silent (out of fear of you?), you may want to instigate the venting of their emotions by asking how they really feel. Unless they get rid of their frustrations, they may not be listening or participating very well at the time when you need all the guidance and help you can get. So put your "authority" in your back pocket while you take your verbal lumps—deserved or not.

22.2 WHY DO YOU FLIP-FLOP ALL THE TIME?

By this question, your staff implies that you frequently change direction, depending on which way the wind is blowing. They see your changes as a sign of indecision or poor planning. Now you realize the cost of not taking time from your horrendous schedule to keep them more informed.

People hold firmly to what they think they observed, and it's difficult to convince them that their perceptions are inaccurate or unfair. If they say you flip-flop all the time, it's futile to debate whether they have judged you fairly.

It is a perception that for the most part is meaningless, because in most instances it has no important consequence on the new change you must make to the project. So why waste the precious few minutes you have of their attention?

Imagine spending the first ten minutes arguing about whether you have a tendency to flip-flop? What would emotions be like then? Would they still be listening? How much more cooperation (or less) would you expect to get?

"Well, I can't argue with how it looks to you. It does show me that I could be doing a much better job of communicating the 'why' behind these changes. Believe me, I don't believe in making *change for the sake of change* and I've said *no* on many occasions. That's a lot easier to say than to do. We've got to make this change, and we can't take time today to go over the past. But I promise we will discuss this, so I can be more consistent—and explain things better in the future."

"I can understand why these changes look like flip-flopping to you. *Everything around us keeps changing, and I've had to be flexible and adapt when we need to.* I can't promise this isn't going to happen again, *because nearly everything we do in today's world is being affected by rapid changes going on everywhere.* We can do some good planning beforehand to minimize the flip-flops, but I can't honestly tell you it isn't going to happen again. I can only hope it won't be often."

Commit to keeping them better informed so that in the future they may be more supportive when inevitable changes become necessary. In this era of hyper change (where new changes overlap on recent changes before the latter are played out), managers can expect employees to second-guess their "about-face" directives. Only by your preparing them beforehand with frequent briefings can the employees know enough to be supportive instead of resistant.

22.3 HOW DO I KNOW YOU AREN'T GOING TO CHANGE YOUR MIND—AGAIN?

Any man or woman who hasn't changed his or her mind a few times doesn't have one. That's a clever saying with a ring of truth to it, but this is not the time for philosophizing. Your staff is treating you more coolly, and they seem to have lost enthusiasm for the work, at least for the moment.

Your staff is not really asking if you would ever change your mind again. Lord help them if you never did. The real issue embedded in their question is about the integrity of your commitment—do you keep your promises? Are you going to meet your responsibility to foresee the foreseeable and stick by your words? (Refer to section 3.1 for related comments.)

To answer this type of future-pledge question, do not predict the future (i.e., you will never change you mind again—a guaranteed trap). Instead, acknowledge your responsibility and restate your commitment to show integrity by living up to your word as much as humanly possible.

"You can believe I don't want to go through this again. I'm going to check the project from one end to the other *to make certain there's nothing else foreseeable that might trip us up.* In fact, each person here should rethink it through so we have the *best chance* of avoiding any more big changes. Let me know by 3 o'clock tomorrow if you think of anything, and I'll do the same."

"The question is whether I would change my mind again. The answer is no, *not unless I absolutely have to and can't avoid it no matter what.* This isn't fun for me either. I'd be a lot happier with myself today if we didn't have to stop and change things. I sure hope we don't ever have to do this again. But I can't sit here and guarantee it can't happen to me or to any of you. I do guarantee that *we won't switch directions again if I can do something to prevent it.*"

22.4 WHAT ELSE ARE YOU FORGETTING TO TELL US?

By this time, your staff is coming closer to making you pay enough penance, but not quite yet. They toss out this extra question, which appears more like another verbal jab at you. Maybe it's time to tell them who is boss or what you really think of their comments. Or, maybe you can hold your patience a little longer. You have a change that must be implemented and you want their assistance.

Only on television did the Lone Ranger handle everything himself (actually he wasn't alone; he had the culturally challenged Tonto and an extensive TV crew). When your staff asks what you might be forgetting, skip the Lone Ranger role and enlist them in your posse to track down anything else that needs to be found. Deputize them one by one by asking them individually to question you.

> "I am not planning to forget anything. I've checked and rechecked everything I can think of. *But help me here. What can you think of that I might not have?* What do we need to do to make this work without additional changes?"

> "Just as the cliché says, I'm glad you asked that question. Help me make sure I'm not forgetting anything. What do you think I could be overlooking? *Let's go around the table one by one, so each of you can ask me what you think should be checked before we make this change.* Then we can discuss how we are going to implement it."

Yes, it could be embarrassing if they ask about something you still haven't planned for, but wouldn't that be more pleasant than another "surprise" change next month?

22.5 ARE YOU GOING TO TAKE THE BLAME FOR THE WASTED TIME AND MONEY?

Now your staff is down to the final phase of your penance for the transgression of frustrating them with surprise changes to the project. Now they want you to carry modern-day sackcloth and ashes— blame. They don't want the blame, so shouldn't you take it?

If you have failed in some responsibility that has affected others, both you and they will feel better about the situation if you apologize for the error and seek forgiveness. So, if you have wronged people and refuse to recognize the blame hanging above your head, it may follow you the rest of your career (guilty conscience, less respect from colleagues, and so on).

Within the context of saying who is going to volunteer to take the blame, you can make the meaningless question vanish by "taking" the blame and not arguing about it. If you are going to be blamed, it will be done with or without your acceptance. Just "take it" to settle the issue and thereby avoid arguing over an empty abstraction.

> "As I said before, I'm sorry to ask you to make this change. I know it's aggravating and frustrating. *If anyone wants to blame someone, they can point to me.* I'm more concerned about how we can make the shift as soon as possible and get on with the project."

> "If it will make people feel better by placing blame somewhere, they can blame me. I won't argue with that. *I'm not ducking anything, but let's get past that* and get on with fixing the problem today."

Tough Questions Worksheet

Create responses to the difficult questions you could face on this chapter's topics, using the formulas below. Use **logic, emotion,** and **ethics** whenever possible. Experiment by answering the same question with different formulas to learn which best fits your natural style. Use pencil so you can erase and refine your answers.

Past, Present, Future:

What happened was:

What's happening now is:

The way we'll prevent it from happening again is by:

Problem to Solution:

*The **problems** we have are:*

*I'd like to go directly to a proposed **solution:***

Problem - Cause - Solution - Timing (PCST):

*The **problems** we have are:*

*They were **caused** by:*

*The **solutions** we may implement are:*

*Our **timing** is:*

Wrong, Right, and What It Means:

*This is an extremely complex area and our track record has **overall** been very good:*

*We do very difficult things and sometimes we have failures. What **happened** is that:*

*What this **means** for us now is:*

Three-Step Explanation:

I understand what you are asking and why it concerns you so much:

Other people who had your experiences probably would feel the same way:

However, I would like to explain a little about this problem:

Other formulas and responses I want to use for tough questions related to this chapter:

23

Defending Change and the Chaos It Creates

23.1   *If it isn't broken, why do you insist on fixing it?*

23.2   *Am I supposed to train him so you can replace me later?*

23.3   *You promised me this schedule, so why change it now?*

23.4   *How come we weren't consulted before you changed our procedures?*

23.5   *Why do you insist on making people here so unhappy?*

23.6   *Why is the company killing this town by transferring us out of state?*

23.7   *Why is the company moving us to Human Resources after we've been a part of Marketing for decades?*

23.8   *I love working on this project. How can you take me off now when we're so close to the launch date?*

23.9   *I worked hard to get the same perks as men before me, but now because of some fad the company thinks it can put me out with the greenhorns in open offices. What's your explanation?*

Change is stressful.

Change is exciting.

Change is frightening.

No one likes to have his comfort zone disrupted, not you and not your employees. The comfort zone is safe. You know how people will act and react. The comfort zone provides guidelines. Everyone knows the rules, and they know how to follow, challenge, or tweak them safely.

To change your employees' comfort zone is to create fear. Who's getting more power? Who's losing it? Are you still an ally or are you now the enemy? Are their past accomplishments now worthless? They fear getting hurt some way, somehow.

You know your decision will cause controversy; you've decided to change the status quo. You hope to help your employees see the gray areas rather than only a black-and-white crisis.

You know your employees need to understand the pressures that now force your group down a new path. You want to stop any possible morale decline, which will result in a productivity decline that will hurt your bottom line. The fearful employees are asking hostile questions, but will they listen to your answers?

23.1 IF IT ISN'T BROKEN, WHY DO YOU INSIST ON FIXING IT?

Workers in your department don't see the big picture—things are working fine now. But can you wait until they are broken? You know you need to demonstrate cause and effect and help them see this is not change for the sake of change. For example, your advertising department has been creating high-quality sales brochures for years. The staff has received a lot of praise from the higher-ups.

Suddenly, with the popularity of PC-based desktop publishing, your competitor is printing brochures on the office laser printers faster and at a fraction of your cost. You understand this threatens your department's existence if everyone ignores the competition. Your staff stubbornly says their work is of far superior quality (which it is). They argue that the competitors' amateurish work will surely disappear.

But you recognize the new need to get brochures to customers faster, so you plan a new advertising service that will offer both the high-quality, high-cost brochure and the desktop version. The staff will need to learn the new PC software, which will be yet another task in an overbooked production schedule. You know (or at least believe) it will get easier as the staff becomes more comfortable with this new way of creating an old service.

This doesn't change the fact that they are threatened and upset. And they want to know why you insist on fixing things that aren't broken. You opt to use a past-present-future response formula to settle some fears and direct their attention to the inevitable change.

"When we were the only game in town, *we could set our own rules* and our own standards. But *now we have a competitor* in the market. It isn't 'broken' but it needs new paint *to stay ahead*, to still be something special when everyone is copying us."

"While there *was nothing wrong* with how we've created the sales brochures in the past, management received a tip that our competitor *is releasing* faster and cheaper sales materials starting this fall. They've upgraded their in-house technology. If we don't change procedures, our sales force *will be eating their dust.*"

"I'm happy with your *past performance*, but the market *is different* from last year. I'm not changing; I'm modifying our marketing services."

"We have turned out top-notch work, but did you notice *demand seems to be down* from last year? I've discovered that it's not the economy, but our outside printer *can't offer the fast turnaround* that desktop publishing can. We need to add desktop service for those critical sales needs that can't wait for the high-end literature. To keep clients, *we need a fresh and faster approach.*"

When introducing change, it's important that your responses emphasize you haven't been unhappy with your staff's work historically. Reassure them that you appreciate their past efforts, but that something in the work environment has changed, which now means "we" must change.

You will face fewer hostile questions if you get more "buy-in" by making employees part of the process from the beginning. It is not "if" you will make more major changes, it is only "when" and "how." The same goes for the concomitant tough questions.

Answer Change Questions *Before* They're Asked

Have your employees develop customer survey questions, gather data, and create change proposals based on the results of the survey. You will have a team dedicated to continuous improvement, not to the status quo. They will have firsthand knowledge of customer issues and play a vital part in addressing them, rather than being fear-filled, suspicious, and resistant to your every move.

Done fairly, openly, and honestly, a customer satisfaction survey is not a negative tool to point blame at past performance, but a method of finding and meeting customer needs as they change and change and change again. It takes the threat off your employees' attitude: "Why are you fixing me?" and makes it more service driven: "What can we do to meet customer requirements better?"

23.2 AM I SUPPOSED TO TRAIN HIM SO YOU CAN REPLACE ME LATER?

Job security is shaky at your company, so employees try to make themselves indispensable. The secrets they keep about their procedures and contacts have caused you problems during vacations, sudden medical leaves, and when a key employee suddenly resigned.

Then there is your veteran professional who trained the young men and women fresh out of college, only to see them promoted while she, devoting years of service, remains behind. Why should she share her knowledge and expertise again for you when there is no benefit for her?

Your company has cut its work force to a dangerously lean staff of specialists, no two jobs alike. Everyone is holding on to their own piece of the action, sharing information on a need-to-know basis. They all know they're doing the job of a staff that was twice as large only a few years back, many of them taking on the tasks of two or three people.

You know you are vulnerable. You have no back-up personnel. When people are out, you've had to hire temporary help to perform key jobs just to keep the department functioning. Few employees share information on how they perform their jobs, so you've had a difficult time team building. You've called this meeting to introduce cross-training, but your staff feel threatened.

They, in turn, ask a question with a false premise you can't afford to let go unanswered.

> "Learning how to do the more critical aspects of each other's job *is not my attempt to downsize or fire anyone.* I value the specialized expertise you all offer, *but we can no longer operate like individual islands.* Bringing in temporary help when one of you is absent is disruptive. We waste a lot of effort bringing a stranger up to speed only for her to leave. We need to work together, and the way to do this is to *be more interchangeable when conditions demand it.*"

> "No, I'm not asking you to train him so he can replace you. If we walk in our colleague's shoes, there will be more teamwork and fewer 'yours and

mine' territorial battles. Cross-training will help everyone see the job demands and requirements of other department members. We can be working together *instead of against one another."*

"At this point, *I don't feel we can lose one more member* of this staff. We are operating too lean already. I have no plans to replace anyone, but we need to have some knowledge of one another's job duties *so production doesn't slow to a snail's pace* just because someone takes a week's vacation."

"Over the past year I know many jobs have been combined into the positions you now hold. In some cases we are duplicating one another. By training others to do some of your job tasks, we can find out new ways *to be more efficient around here.* We might even *take away some of the stress* from long hours we may be spending unnecessarily."

"I accept that many of you are *the* specialist in your specific area. By sharing your job knowledge with a colleague who returns the same favor, *both of you will have a back-up.* If you're heavily involved in a project, you will have *someone to turn to for help* who understands your procedures. Likewise, when he gets in a time bind, you can offer help based on your expertise and the knowledge you gained about his job."

Notice that all of these responses directly or indirectly attempt to neutralize the false premise on which the question is built. The first two quotes knock down faulty assumptions immediately and then bridge to why there is mutual self-interest in the cross-training. The other responses use indirect approaches for when subtlety is likely to be most effective. (Refer to sections 1.4 and 3.4 for related advice.)

23.3 YOU PROMISED ME THIS SCHEDULE, SO WHY CHANGE IT NOW?

Decades ago, an employee at your organization who worked hard could count on having a job for many years, possibly for life. The typical employee never openly questioned demands made upon him, because the job came first and most everything else in life second. The company took care of him.

But as his job security declined, so did his dedication.

Today the typical employee gives the same return on investment that your organization gives him. As a manager representing the company, you can't guarantee him a job for a decade, much less for life. He does not completely dedicate his waking hours to you and has filled all those free moments that surround his workday with everything from community involvement and classes at the junior college to second jobs and car pooling commitments.

Historically, it was the female employee who fought job changes because of her family needs. No longer. Now male employees are turning down promotions and transfers that create problems in their personal lives. Your workplace is no longer their only top priority.

As the manager of a small packaging company, you are suddenly elated to find that business is booming. Several new contracts have pushed you to make changes in the workplace to meet new production demands. Packaging orders will have to be shipped out twice a day, instead of on the morning truck your employees have loaded for decades.

However, your enthusiasm is not shared by the work force, who see this as a major disruption to their busy and entangled hours away from work. Long ago you both had mutually agreed to the current schedule. But now you know that the only practical way to meet work demands is to disrupt his life by changing the schedules.

Your response to tough questions such as section 23.3 should demonstrate your compassion for the staff while explaining the forces that make the changes imperative. (See section 1.7 for more on this approach.)

> "When you were hired, your schedule was *based on the work we were doing at that time.* No one can guarantee a schedule *forever.* This business boom may cause you temporary hardships as you change your personal commitments, but in the long run *it gives you more job security than I could offer before.*"

> "If this turns out to be a temporary boom, I will make all efforts to get everyone back on the hours they had before. Until then, you need to help us out during the time the second truck is here. If you run into a *personal conflict* you need help with, please come to my office and *let's work it out.* I'm on your side and I need you to be on mine; I really need to have experienced people like you on the dock at night."

> "I know the hour change throws a monkey wrench in your personal life, *but everyone is affected.* We can try to offset some of the impacts. Maybe we can use the bulletin board as a message center for folks who need help, like a new car pool or child-care site."

In explaining why you must change work schedule, always give yourself an out. Is that sneaky or cowardly? Not at all. Since you are not

God, your vision of the future isn't totally precise, so you can't be completely sure you know what will happen. You can promise in your responses to do the best you can, and you can make yourself keep that promise honorably. But also bridge to the point that no one should be expected to make absolute assurances that lead to absurd results.

You'll have fewer hostile questions about sudden schedule changes if you keep your employees informed. While good times mean extra hours, bad times may mean reduced hours. If your business is or has become volatile, don't keep employees in the dark. A company newsletter, a bulletin board, or a quarterly report let everyone know how your business is doing, both good and bad. Good communication like this is something you should start long before you need it.

23.4 HOW COME WE WEREN'T CONSULTED BEFORE YOU CHANGED *OUR* PROCEDURES?

Many executives talk about giving employees "ownership" of their jobs, some sort of control and decision-making power. This usually positive experience increases productivity. It can, however, backfire if the group is rudderless. If they go off on their own and in circles, they stop contributing to your business as a whole. It's as if a separate little company has formed within the bigger one.

You were just appointed to manage the Engineering department. The previous head recently retired after years of chronic illness. He had let the department manage itself over the past five years and the prima donnas took over. You personally have experienced some of their poorly thought-out planning, which cost your previous department plenty in time spent redoing Engineering work.

Past experience by you and other managers found that these people were not willing to compromise or entertain other opinions. This department has a bad reputation, and you know you need to change it rapidly.

When they ask why you made them an exception and unilaterally changed their work procedures, consider this rejoinder.

"I will respond to your question, but *you probably won't like the answer.* Employees and managers throughout the company have said your work procedures have caused *a crisis that had to be dealt with swiftly.* I understand this may surprise you, but I did what had to be done immediately. I will respect your *abilities and good work,* and I hope you will respect *my commitment* to do a good job for everyone in and outside this department."

If the firm yet diplomatic phrasing of the preceding response does not get the message across, then stronger terms may be necessary.

"I am going to make some *very frank remarks here.* I realize that Jack's illness left you guys on your own for a long time, and you were allowed to work independently. I and most other managers here believe *you have become too independent,* and that there is *'no way but your way.'* You are one part of this plant, not a company on your own. We are going to go through a rigorous self-examination to rediscover what and who we are. When I see an effort *to work as a team* with other departments, you will be *consulted as a team* for future changes."

It's not easy to take over an existing team, especially if it's drifted off on its own and grown too independent from the main organization. Before you get into the hostile-question situation, make sure you have solid back-up from top management and other line management too. Cultivate a manager who's been around for awhile and whom the staff respects. Invite her to your next meeting as a contributor to the agenda. Have her let the staff know how the new changes can help their department. The endorsement solidifies your action and may moderate the hostility. (Refer to sections 1.9 and 1.11 for related suggestions.)

Tip: Cushion surprises to reduce hostility.

When delivering bad news, you can lessen hostile reactions by cushioning the impact of surprise. Before you begin the substance of your remarks, let them know you are **about to say something they "probably won't like."** That gives them a moment to brace themselves for the emotional impact. The few seconds won't make the bad news "good" but maybe less shocking.

You increase the power and persuasiveness of your statements by **referring to other qualified observers.** For example, the preceding responses say that other managers and departments have the same observation you have. That demonstrates it isn't your view alone. Even if the team wishes to think there is something wrong with your thinking, the attribution to other observers can help keep the issue from becoming too personal.

23.5 WHY DO YOU INSIST ON MAKING PEOPLE HERE SO UNHAPPY?

Formerly loyal employees now unhappy with radical changes either booby-trap the workplace, spread malicious gossip about you, or quit. None of these is good for you or your business.

The chaos created by change makes you wonder why you decided to "screw with the status quo." But you know your course of action is sound, and your next goal is to smooth hurt feelings. Some managers might say "If you don't like it, then quit." You know better. You spent a lot of time hiring and training just the right people and you want them to stay.

When you began working here, the first employees became part of your family. With each new person, your department has grown through the years into a close-knit group of a dozen. Everyone lived through your secretary's on-and-off relationship with the budget manager and finally celebrated at their wedding. The whole company hurt when the shipping clerk's son was killed in a car wreck. Like a family, your employees feel one another's joys and sorrows.

So it was not an easy decision to make when you and the other managers agreed to move the business to the suburbs. It meant long commutes for people who used to walk to work. It meant that one single mother had to hire a sitter to be home for her children after school. There is a lot of unhappiness, but management's decision to move closer to the customers has paid off.

Now it's time to comfort the "family" and help them face yet another challenge they need to join together to overcome. In responding to the question of section 23.5, don't attempt to explain that you are not intentionally making people unhappy. Ignore the literal question but go directly to the underlying issue causing the distress. (See section 3.9 for more on that approach.)

> *"I'm sorry you are unhappy because of these changes.* We made the move for the long-term health of the company and our jobs. Whether it seems like it or not, I do value your contributions here and I am going to need your help in the future. *While changes won't be reversed, I want to help you succeed here.* Tell me what isn't working for you, and let's try to resolve it together."

> "Leaving the old building on Second Street *was difficult for everyone.* I know this move has made many people sad or frustrated or just stressed out. We have to remember, though, *that we are a business.* This

move has meant financial security for all of us. I will do whatever I can *to accommodate each of you."*

Making radical changes like moving a business to a new location can cause long-lasting disruption and damage to any organization. But it doesn't have to be. How you respond to your employees' tough questions will be a factor in how much or how little time it takes to regain normalcy.

What can you do to accelerate their acclimation and inversely shorten their period of resistance? In the example of moving the company, you could help them feel more comfortable at the new setting by scouting new service businesses. On your bulletin board, you could add the business card of the dry cleaner two blocks away, the day care with openings, the deli that offers carry-out at lunch, the flyer from the hair salon with late hours, or the coupons from the convenience store down the street. The hassle of a new commute is lessened if you know the services near your new job location.

What changes are you contemplating? What could you do to make it easier on everyone? How many fewer hostile questions (and therefore fewer hostile feelings) would you face if you anticipated and resolved these concerns before you made the big changes?

23.6 WHY IS THE COMPANY KILLING THIS TOWN BY TRANSFERRING US OUT OF STATE?

The history of America is made up of towns that sprang up overnight because of an industry and died just as fast when that industry disappeared. Out West in the former "Gold Rush" territory they're called ghost towns. Most of us know of a bustling little village that boarded up its downtown when a major highway passed around it. It's one thing to make changes in your workplace that make the day uncomfortable for employees. It's quite another thing when your decisions cause catastrophic ramifications through their homes and out into the community.

You are one of the managers at the Bloom manufacturing plant. Not too many years ago, the town threw a weekend festival celebrating your company's 75-year anniversary. As one of the community's major employers, many other businesses in town survive by supporting either the plant directly or its work force.

Your management's decision to move the entire operation to another state was made after years of personal anguish about how to save Bloom and what this will do to your town.

While your product is superior to the competition's, the cost of transporting raw materials by truck long distances destroyed your competitive edge. Geography prevents the use of rail or air cargo, which the competition uses heavily to beat your turnaround time by 80 percent. The plant has been operating in the red for two years. When a competing community courted your company with tax-free land next to a major airport and rail service, your management knew it was the only way to save the company from ruin.

Now you and many other managers face both employees and your own family's pain as you prepare to move away from your current town for an unknown future. Even though you as a midlevel manager didn't make the decision, you nonetheless must respond to difficult questions.

No glib phrases can eliminate the pain that everyone will feel to some degree. So there are no painless responses you can give. But some of your remarks may evoke less pain and may help people start down the path of acceptance and accommodation, instead of keeping angry feelings alive and burning. (Refer to sections 1.4 and 1.5 for related comments.)

Use All Three Persuasion Factors: Logic, Emotions, Standards

The loss of a major employer is an emotional event for a small town. Treat it like the death of a family member and allow your employees the space to grieve. The preceding responses seek to weave together emotion, logic, and a reasonable standard of behavior. Each of these three factors owes its power to a response to make its influence grow. They build upon each other to multiply their total impact when used in combination.

Just saying you feel the same is not enough, but citing the cold hard facts sounds cruel and unfeeling. And referencing a standard of behavior without including the logic of why it applies to your action will sound irrelevant. But weaving all three into one short message can move listeners one step closer to understanding and accepting the big change. Don't expect them to stand up and cheer when they hear your responses—acceptance and cooperation would be major achievements at this point.

The past-present-future formula (section 2.3) can help you outline the new perspective.

"I realize this move will mean economic hardship for this town. *It's been my home too.* Yet, our responsibility is to keep the business alive. If we don't do that, we'd be *throwing away jobs we could have saved* by making this move. If we stay and go under here, that *won't help this town, and it sure would hurt all of our employees in the near future.*"

"In the past, the loyalty between this company and our community has been a resource we treasured. It worked well in those days *but the world economy is not the same.* We need to implement this change now if we want to have jobs next year and ten years from now. There's no reason our traditions will not continue at our new facility. *You and your children can find a home at our new location as you and your parents did here.*"

"*We had few options.* To keep the plant open here would mean the inevitable would occur within the next few years . . . we shut the doors for good. By moving out of state now, we stay alive as a business and save jobs, even though they won't be here. No one likes dislocation like this, but this move is *the best and only realistic option we have for the future.*"

"Our plant is not the same place it was in your grandparents' day. Then, resources came to us down the river by barge. Today we need the *speed of rail and air, which is not available at this location.*"

"My folks will be staying here. They're retired and this is home, so we'll be back for visits. *It's not easy for us either.* My daughter's a junior and you know how hard it can be to switch high schools midstream. What will ease the transition for her is knowing she's not alone . . . a lot of other employees' kids will be at the new location too. *Your family won't be going through this alone.*"

For extreme changes like moves or other radical disruptions, be prepared to bridge to the extra steps your company is taking to assist employees being relocated or laid off. For example, outside counseling help, both financial and personal, is not only humane but also may be well worth the expense to honestly smooth over hard feelings.

In your efforts to save and move your own company, you made national industry connections. A well-appreciated public relations tool is to link town officials with firms that may take over your abandoned facility. You want to sell this property in any event to help your bottom line. Being part of the future solution helps preserve your history in a better light. By all means, bridge to those points in your responses.

23.7 WHY IS THE COMPANY MOVING US TO HUMAN RESOURCES AFTER WE'VE BEEN A PART OF MARKETING FOR DECADES?

Company politics is fun. Right? The company management chart on paper does not reflect the true power flow. The wrong leadership makes a difference all the way to the bottom.

Through retirement, your corporation has lost not only several board members, but also the CEO this year. The presiding philosophy from the past 30 years is gone now that new blood is in charge. New executives have been hired from the outside bringing in fresh ideas about corporate structure.

Even though it was not your decision to move your unit, you again must answer for management. It's a new ball game and you have already found that restructuring has rattled employees corporation-wide. Within your group, you find the training department now fits better under a different division from yours, considering the new corporate direction. Your employees feel you have thrown them away.

In preparing for the anticipated difficult questions, you remember what you learned from a wise psychologist/management consultant who demonstrated one day how we can use our responses to create either negative or positive feelings from the same situation. She led a discussion group of you and other worried business managers who faced collapsing markets and wrenching decisions.

After your group listed all your severe problems, she led the group in a discussion of what business opportunities it could possibly create next, despite the irrevocable problems you faced. In response to her questions, the group listed dozens of possibilities, some of which could be achieved with the same hard work and brain power used to win past successes.

At the end of the long meeting, you and other managers expressed surprise at how good you all felt compared to two days earlier. *The facts of your situation had not changed a bit, but your group once again had some hope, and you couldn't help but feel better* (not great but better). Conversely, when the group had focused only on the serious problems two days earlier, you all consequently could not help but feel despair.

With that recollection in mind, use your responses to bridge to authentic opportunities that are plausible for worried employees. It won't be a cure-all, but as one manager said, "When I have hope, I can't help but feel good, even though nothing has changed yet." Most employees will experience positive feelings that will supplant some of the negative feelings, if your replies help lead them to discover those positive possibilities.

> "While financial profit on paper certainly is what drives our corporation, we consider people a resource, too. Your position in this company hasn't diminished, *but it is refocused.* Every experience is a means to an end, and your new department will broaden your experiences. It's better to be the person *with many experiences over 25 years* instead of the person with 25 years of *one experience.*"

> "Whether you see it or not, you have empowerment, not because your group has been put under a new VP, but because *you have a successful track record* that gives us the confidence to let you innovate and create. Yes, there is a philosophical difference between the perceived "hard" skills of outside sales and the "soft" skills of inside people handling. Yet, if you think about it, your communication programs *are tailored for either of them.*"

23.8 I LOVE WORKING ON THIS PROJECT. HOW CAN YOU TAKE ME OFF NOW WHEN WE'RE SO CLOSE TO THE LAUNCH DATE?

You are the supervisor of a small job shop where there is too much work and too few people to do it. The questioner is a dedicated employee who has lost sight of other priorities, but you realize that you don't want to discourage the eager beaver.

She is a very talented employee who, when she finds a job she really loves, devotes every moment to completing it to perfection. Unfortunately, you have a lot of work that other customers also want done. If it does not fall under one of her pet projects, it sits. You know it is time to set priorities and take control.

This could be the time to use the PCST formula, problem-cause-solution-timing (see section 2.5 for additional information). Your PCST response can help the employee realize that it's time to let go. But don't be abrupt. A somewhat slower response structured around PCST can help the employee step back and see the reason for your decision. It would also provide her with a rationale her ego could accept.

> "I realize how important this project has become to you. However, the *problem* is that the project is taking up more of your time than we can

afford. This was *caused* by the difficulty of getting it started and fully developed. The *solution* to this problem is to let other members of the team put the final touches on this. The hard work is done, and I need your talents on other projects *next week for sure.* Don't worry, the team will do good work, and I'll make sure you still get full credit. Everyone knows you are the creator of this project."

The comments express your gratitude for those extra hours away from her family but they also give direction, not discipline. However, if she persists with challenging questions, and you feel it's time for a stronger response, then consider a more direct reply.

"I'm not saying you wasted your time over the past year, but *you didn't manage your time as well as we need you to.* There are other projects you've let slide in favor of this one. *One perfect program isn't worth the cost if we have three incomplete assignments.* It's too late to go back and capture lost time, so let's chalk this up to a lesson learned. You're a good worker but we've got to stay closer together on where you are putting most of your time."

23.9 I WORKED HARD TO GET THE SAME PERKS AS THE MEN BEFORE ME, BUT NOW BECAUSE OF SOME FAD THE COMPANY THINKS IT CAN PUT ME OUT WITH THE GREENHORNS IN OPEN OFFICES. WHAT'S YOUR EXPLANATION?

A few years ago a national fast-food chain headquartered in Florida typified your American conservative corporation with the mahogany-paneled executive suite. It took a hurricane, which severely damaged the corporate headquarters, to provide the opportunity to change the culture to a more informal environment.

New leadership at the top found that clothing, office trappings, and the view from an office window had little to do with communication and productivity. In fact, while temporarily located in multiple sites around Miami as the headquarters was rebuilt, informality opened up lines of communication restricted by the former caste system. The new headquarters likewise featured an open office environment that offered far less physical separation between management and employees. Longtime executives who were destined for the mahogany suite were distressed to find it missing. The carrot was blown away by the weather.

What if you were a top manager? What would you say to your colleagues who fought their way to supervisor and manager positions only to find some perks are being pulled away? You know that, overall, the cultural change has triggered fresh internal ideas, and new concepts are revitalizing your company's market hold. The new cross-discipline access has creative juices flowing again.

But you know also that you need to get your older supervisors and fellow managers to buy in to the new culture and not be threatened. Your subordinate supervisor's question is built upon a false premise that you need to correct. It will block her commitment as long as she believes the changes are merely a fad, not a long-term and well-reasoned new approach. (Refer to Chapter 3 for more on false-premise questions.) The change has been so well received that you know you can justify (with financial numbers) how it is for the better and will now become permanent.

"This isn't a fad. It's our new culture. It's here to stay. *You're not alone in the way you feel, though.* But be careful; it will hurt your career more if you fight this than if you embrace it. I know there were many times in our careers when we had to shift gears and head in a new direction. It was usually for the good of the company, *and for employees in the long run.*"

"You won't be sitting in a 'peon' area. That's the wrong attitude. *This move is about accessibility.* Your staff, and you, now have better opportunities to share ideas. The former executive suite *was intimidating* for employees. You were cut off from a lot of good ideas because people were afraid to enter the seat of power."

"You haven't lost any of the awards for long service; you've gained new ones such as employees who no longer see the brick wall of status *that bred morale and productivity problems.*"

"This 'fad,' as you call it, has also been adopted by three of our competitors. *We were losing our best people* who saw a more open, free, and creative environment on the other side of the fence. *Now they may stay here.*"

Tough Questions Worksheet

Create responses to the difficult questions you could face on this chapter's topics, using the formulas below. Use **logic, emotion,** and **ethics** whenever possible. Experiment by answering the same question with different formulas to learn which best fits your natural style. Use pencil so you can erase and refine your answers.

Past, Present, Future:

What happened was:

What's happening now is:

The way we'll prevent it from happening again is by:

Problem to Solution:

*The **problems** we have are:*

*I'd like to go directly to a proposed **solution:***

Problem - Cause - Solution - Timing (PCST):

*The **problems** we have are:*

*They were **caused** by:*

*The **solutions** we may implement are:*

*Our **timing** is:*

Wrong, Right, and What It Means:

*This is an extremely complex area and our track record has **overall** been very **good:***

*We do very difficult things and sometimes we have failures. What **happened** is that:*

*What this **means** for us now is:*

Three-Step Explanation:

I understand what you are asking and why it concerns you so much:

Other people who had your experiences probably would feel the same way:

However, I would like to explain a little about this problem:

Other formulas and responses I want to use for tough questions related to this chapter:

24

Rebutting Tough Questions to Keep Control of Unruly Meetings

24.1   *I'm not involved in this issue. Why do I have to be here?*

24.2   *Is this meeting going to be a waste of my time like all the others?*

24.3   *What's the use committing to anything when nothing ever happens afterward?*

24.4   *No one listens to us anyway, so why should we bother to meet and develop recommendations?*

24.5   *Why meet on a plan they'll never approve?*

24.6   *Can I have more time so I can give my full explanation?*

Among any manager's greatest challenges is holding a meeting of the unwilling, the uninterested, and the unwanted. Although you prepared a fine agenda, you can sense as the grumbling staff and other managers enter the meeting room that it's going to be a struggle today to keep things on track and get something done.

You long for the good ol' days, for meetings you didn't chair. Then you were concerned about only your own little part, presenting your report. If somebody got out of hand, you didn't have to confront him. If a long-winded staffer asked for more time, you didn't have to be the one to say no. But now you are in charge of this communication beast. The success of the gathering is based on your ability to control it, including responding to undermining questions from staff, who act as you once did. The kind of hostile questions posed in this chapter are typical in meetings conducted by unsure, inexperienced managers.

24.1 I'M NOT INVOLVED IN THIS ISSUE. WHY DO I HAVE TO BE HERE?

Staff feel they're drowning in meetings, both in the workplace and at home in their community. Meeting after meeting has become a sea of notes and activities and obligations and deadlines and lost time.

And now one fellow manager agrees with a veteran employee and says the agenda for *your* meeting doesn't contain topics that interest or involve them. So why are you asking them to attend? Make sure you know why before you call the meeting. Consider the following suggested responses. They don't preach to reluctant participants that they ought to want to attend as good girls and boys should. Instead, the responses tie themselves to the self-interest among attendees.

"You may not have a direct assignment today for any of these topics, but the purpose of these discussions is to expand *your general knowledge* of how this organization operates. And that will help all of us work better together. I hope you will listen and participate in a way that gets *value for your time.* I promise you this meeting will not run one minute longer than it needs to."

"I know you are having a problem justifying your time here each week. This is a large organization, and sometimes it gets filled with cliques. *One of the purposes of these meetings is to give you a chance to put*

Tip: Get rid of those you don't need before trouble starts.

If you take a hard look at what you are doing, sometimes there are people who really should not be part of your meeting. They are not actually needed even though it seemed initially they would be. If their contribution will not add to your goals, **dismiss them before they hit you with embarrassing questions.** If their departments' needs can be filled with a written report or with minutes, do that.

If you find a person is having difficulty attending your meetings, allow him or her the opportunity to resign or appoint an alternate. By giving members this out, you can trim membership from those who want to end their involvement to people intrigued by the issues enough to want to get more involved. And you lessen the risk of taunting questions making it tougher on the group to get something done.

---

some faces with names and establish relationships. If nothing else, you're gaining contacts: people in other areas whom you may need to call for information someday."

24.2 IS THIS MEETING GOING TO BE A WASTE OF MY TIME LIKE ALL THE OTHERS?

Because of millions of poorly run meetings, most people feel they are wasteful alternatives to work. Staff members who ask a loaded-premise question such as this obviously have that opinion. Not much will get done at your meeting if you let the question stand.

This would be a perfect place to use the Problem-Solution formula in a direct fashion along with a question they can't ignore. (See section 2.4 for related comments.) If they don't like the meetings, make them come forward with ideas on how they can be made better.

> "I get the point, *so let's meet this straight on.* You don't want to waste your time, and neither do I. We're here to do something worthwhile— to share information and then solve some problems. *Let's get to a solution then.* What can we do to make these meetings worth your time?

> "The *problem* is that this meeting will be a waste of time if each of us lets that happen, or it will be as productive as each person makes it. *The solution is to make it better.* What do you want done here today, and what don't you want?

> *"I won't waste your time if you won't let me.* What's behind your question? Did I let people socialize too much last time? Do you believe too little was accomplished? Do you feel your opinions were ignored? Are the goals of today's meeting unclear? *How can we make this meeting better?* Let's be candid."

> "Is anyone here feeling as frustrated as I am? The *problem* is that we seem to be spinning our wheels. Let's break from the agenda to review *what we've accomplished and where we're heading.* Let's go around the table and toss out some ideas on how we can increase our productivity in these meetings. *What do you see as our biggest obstacle?"*

Don't let them drag you into the past by discussing how bad the meetings have been. If they start complaining about past meetings, say something like:

"Okay, that's in the *past and it's over*. How can we make the meetings better today and next time? *Let's stick to something we can do something about.*"

Releasing the Brain Brakes so You Can Move Ahead

When participants come in mumbling about wasting time, understand that you can't move forward on the agenda until they release their brain brakes. Draw them out with a few questions about their concerns. Get the issues out in the open and resolve them one by one (not all at once). Keep control of what may turn into a complaint session by stating how you will ensure an effective meeting.

Don't criticize the person who asked taunting questions. He did you a favor by speaking aloud what others are probably thinking. His grumbling tipped you off to a problem you probably didn't know you had but needed to fix pronto. If you can, genuinely thank him for getting the complaints out in the open where you can see and resolve them. Thank him for helping you improve your meetings.

24.3 WHAT'S THE USE COMMITTING TO ANYTHING WHEN NOTHING EVER HAPPENS AFTERWARD?

A committee member contends nothing ever gets done and challenges you on why she should commit to making an effort. Her claim is similar to that of committee members everywhere. She has not seen (nor recognized) results from previous gatherings. You can't afford to let her negative thinking become general despair among the committee members. Everyone has participated in meetings where big ideas were put forth but nothing was accomplished later. Given that common experience, you could use the feel-felt-found response formula very effectively.

"I know *how you feel* about going to meetings that don't seem to lead to anything once the meeting's over. *I have felt the same way myself.* However, *I have found* that it doesn't have to be that way. If we can agree today on how we can ensure that assignments get done, we can make our meetings more productive than ever. Who has some suggestions on follow-up?

Getting Them Engaged Again

The next response uses the Problem-Solution formula. Most of the emphasis is on eliciting solutions from committee members. You could state just how the meetings and follow-up will be improved, but that won't get your passive committee members engaged in your meetings.

There is nothing tricky or dishonest about using these formulas; they are simply structures for your comments. All comments need structure of some type, or they will be gibberish. By using a formula, you knowingly guide yourself to where you want to go.

> "We may not agree on what got done at past meetings or afterwards, *but let's start right now to clear this up.* What do we need to settle at this meeting? What do we need to follow up on after today to make sure assignments are done? Do we need a tickler file for reminders? *Let's do a round robin and each person here gives answers to these questions.* This way we'll all know what is going to be done, by whom, and when. Mary, what are your suggestions . . . ?"

Buy in Now to Save Later

If you want the heralded "buy-in" of teamwork you must start now, when such an undermining question is posed in front of others. Don't deftly sidestep it, yet don't meet it head-on with proof about how well you've run past meetings and how much you've accomplished. Grab the momentum of the question and use its power to push your agenda along.

Ask participants what should be done and solicit "volunteers," one way or another, to take on assignments, including follow-up. That's one way to make certain the work of your meeting continues after you adjourn.

This swift response, which converts a tough question into an action plan, will cause members to feel the connection between a meeting and subsequent results. They will see their time isn't being wasted.

In your response, mention that you plan to call and ask each person how he or she is doing on the respective assignments. It gently reminds them they have a role coming up. It also gives you the opportunity to handle problems before they are presented in front of the group. Furthermore, a response with clear action statements demonstrates to meeting participants that you are serious about making your meetings productive.

24.4 NO ONE LISTENS TO US ANYWAY, SO WHY SHOULD WE BOTHER TO MEET AND DEVELOP RECOMMENDATIONS?

Your group feels powerless. They've assembled at your request to gather information on a problem, brainstorm solutions, and develop recommendations. Like most committees, they lack authority to implement their recommendations, of which upper management may or may not approve.

Their past frustrations block your drive to whip up enthusiasm among committee members. They perceive that in reality no one will listen to them. Bridging, as illustrated throughout Chapter 2, creates a new reality that could empower them.

> "If we don't make recommendations, I promise you *nothing will be improved the way we think it should.* If we don't tell anyone what we think should be done, that guarantees it won't happen. I can't say for sure our recommendations will be approved, but I'd rather offer our finest ideas and hope for the best, *instead of giving up and not trying at all.*"

> "We can really disempower ourselves by telling one another that nothing we say matters. I know we don't have as much authority as we need to get things improved, but let's use whatever influence we do have. We have *the power of what we know,* the power to make recommendations, and the power to ask for senior management's attention. Let's use what we have the best way we can."

> "If we don't make proposals, someone else might. And I doubt any group can come up with better ideas than we can. In fact, someone else might propose some pretty screwy recommendations. We could be stuck with them. If senior management is going to consider anyone's ideas, it's better for us that we make sure the proposals are ours and not someone else's."

> "Just because senior management hasn't approved much of what we proposed in the past *doesn't mean there's absolutely no chance for these new ideas.* I would rather ask and be turned down, because at least I'd be satisfied that I tried."

Point out that although senior management's past decisions may help predict future decisions, they do not dictate for certain what top management will approve in the future. Furthermore, note that it's far better that senior management review your group's recommendations instead of the

---

Tip: Get results by focusing on what power they do have.

As the meeting leader, use your responses to **help them focus on the power they *do have*,** not the power they don't have. In nearly every organization, lower-level staff don't have the authority to implement their recommendations while upper management often lacks firsthand information about what's really going on. Hence the age-old clash between suggestions from street-wise staff and decisions from insulated upper management. Nevertheless, use their disempowering questions to reempower the committee members. **Emphasize what you *can do* and emphasize why it's better than doing nothing.**

---

harebrained ideas of other people, whose suggestions you could be stuck with for a long, long time.

24.5 WHY MEET ON A PLAN THEY'LL NEVER APPROVE?

The natural human tendency to guess how other people will act, based on their known habits and personality, often guides you and your fellow committee members in what to plan for senior management's consideration. Like most people, your group is right often enough in those guesses that they fall victim to self-defeating beliefs. You all think you really do know what will or what won't be acceptable.

Ever notice how hypothetical and speculative questions tend to be based on negative perceptions of the future? The fatalistic guess of the inevitable can become real and can create despair in the minds of everyone present. As with any hypothetical question, the weakness in the preceding one is that the future can't be predicted with absolute certainty. (See sections 3.1 and 3.2 for related comments.)

You are just as free to imagine positive results as participants dream up all kinds of reasons to give up entirely.

> "Yes, senior management might say no, but *let's not decide for them by not even putting the question to them.* If nothing else, they'll know what we think. They might learn important information that may be helpful to us later on related issues."

"If we *don't even ask* for approval of this plan, we will be the ones who make sure *the answer is no.* I don't want always to wonder what could have been possible if we just would've asked, so let's give it our best shot."

"If we think our plan is *feasible,* then let's not decide whether to recommend it on whether it's *probable* that senior management will approve it. We should do our job the best we can and let them do theirs, however they will do it."

Your staff and co-workers might have a very good basis for their beliefs, but they won't really know until they ask. A surprise decision is one that is unexpected. How many surprises have you seen in life so far? Show your negative-thinking group that if their plan is practically feasible, they shouldn't hold back just because they guess it isn't probable. If you don't ask, you don't get. And most ideas start out as unpopular ideas.

24.6 CAN I HAVE MORE TIME SO I CAN GIVE MY FULL EXPLANATION?

Does "full point of view" mean this fellow manager should get permission to do another endless monologue? You know that this is one of the biggest complaints of your meeting participants: They feel you let a windbag talk forever.

Your long-winded colleague does not understand the difference between a conversation and a presentation. He doesn't allow for any input, questions, or disagreement. Yet he insists that you all listen to *his* detailed explanations and opinions.

So how do you respond when he asks for more time while the clock is ticking and the participants seem ready to explode?

When the windy fellow asks for more time, say no (or yes, but just for a *few minutes*). Get ready to enforce your decision by another interruption. Interrupting is easy once you learn the art—just keep saying, "Excuse me, wait a second, I need to interrupt, Joe, excuse me . . ." until he stops.

"We agree that your information is important, but we also need to balance it with the *time we have left. There are other important issues* that committee members have prepared. If you could *summarize the rest* of your information in one or two minutes, that would leave the others time to give their information or ask questions. Go ahead with one *final* comment, but please keep it to *under two more minutes.*"

"Let's give Joe the chance to *finish his comments* before we jump in and add our thoughts. Okay, Joe, please *wrap it up in one or two sentences of 25 words or less* so we can ask a few questions. That's all the time we have for now."

"Joe, excuse me, . . . ah, Joe, please hold up a second. I don't mean to be impolite, but we really *can't afford to spend more time on this item* at today's meeting. I know it's important, but we have other issues scheduled for today. If you want to put this on another agenda, or maybe bring it up again *after we have covered all the other topics,* let me know. Thanks for your information, but *let's move on now to Lillie's report."*

"Joe, I appreciate your willingness to give us more information, but how about holding up on that for awhile, so we can *call on some of the people who have been silent.* Some of us, and I'm one of them, tend to not give others a chance to contribute. *We won't learn anything unless we listen to them.* Brigitte, you've been quiet so far, what's your comment? Do you agree or disagree with Joe's proposal?

If you fail to control the flow of ideas at your meeting, the know-it-all will silence all input but his own. Therefore, being "nice" to a blowhard by failing to stop him is actually being rude to other meeting participants, who suffer in silence. Some of your group's best solutions might come from that quiet, thoughtful member who has digested all the information and now waits for the chance to spell out her strategy without interference.

No matter what it takes, don't let the windbag get started again. Break eye contact with him and look at the person you intend to call on (and ignore Joe's waving hand). In a continuous flow of words, cut off Joe and call on the next person. If Joe interrupts your interruption, say "I'm sorry, Joe, but I need to be firm on where we spend the rest of our time. Brigitte, okay, please go ahead."

Tough Questions Worksheet

Create responses to the difficult questions you could face on this chapter's topics, using the formulas below. Use **logic, emotion, and ethics** whenever possible. Experiment by answering the same question with different formulas to learn which best fits your natural style. Use pencil so you can erase and refine your answers.

Past, Present, Future:

What happened was:

What's happening now is:

The way we'll prevent it from happening again is by:

Problem to Solution:

*The **problems** we have are:*

*I'd like to go directly to a proposed **solution:***

Problem - Cause - Solution - Timing (PCST):

*The **problems** we have are:*

*They were **caused** by:*

*The **solutions** we may implement are:*

*Our **timing** is:*

Wrong, Right, and What It Means:

*This is an extremely complex area and our track record has **overall** been very **good:***

*We do very difficult things and sometimes we have failures. What **happened** is that:*

*What this **means** for us now is:*

Three-Step Explanation:

I understand what you are asking and why it concerns you so much:

Other people who had your experiences probably would feel the same way:

However, I would like to explain a little about this problem:

Other formulas and responses I want to use for tough questions related to this chapter:

25

Turning Around Taunts About Total Quality Improvement

25.1   *Isn't QI just another management fad?*

25.2   *The Japanese are conformist and we're individualists. How can QI work here?*

25.3   *Doesn't QI mean "do more with less" while the big shots keep doing the same old things?*

25.4   *Why are we being forced to improve quality here when others aren't?*

25.5   *I haven't got enough time to do my work as it is! Where am I going to find extra time to do this QI thing?*

25.6   *What's this baloney about teamwork? Are you saying we don't work well together?*

25.7   *This is a "service" company. Don't you think QI is for factories?*

25.8   *Why don't you managers go play your QI games by yourselves and let us get some work done?*

25.9   *Why should we make quality suggestions when you never listen to us?*

25.10 *If I gather data about the problems in my job, how do I know you won't use this against me in my performance review?*

Deming, Juran, Crosby—managers who have been fortunate to learn from these great men of the Quality Improvement (QI) movement are sometimes called upon to respond to taunting questions from doubters. In order to respond effectively to these very difficult but also very important questions, a manager needs to know some of the history of Total Quality Improvement.

After World War II, statistician W. Edwards Deming's ideas to improve industry were ignored in the United States. So he helped show a recovering postwar Japan how to go from producing junk to manufacturing some of the most technologically advanced products in the world. Today, around the globe, business follows his philosophy that productivity improves as variability decreases, that is, Statistical Process Control or SPC.

Joseph Juran, who also helped postwar Japan, was a professor who felt the technical aspects of QI were being handled but the management side was being ignored. He emphasized the human side of the movement, including vendors and customers as part of improvement teams.

A corporate Quality director, Philip Crosby started his own consulting firm and introduced the concept of Zero Defects as a goal. He teaches that everyone's concept of high or poor quality is different. You need a common language called conformance to mutually agree upon requirements.

Unless they are associated with a larger corporation, many Americans have not heard of this trilogy of American Quality philosophers . . . until their company or agency decides to sell globally or bid on a contract to supply the auto, chemical, paper, steel, or oil industry. Or they find their contracts in jeopardy unless they supply SPC charts and become ISO 9000 certified, and show evidence of internal customer satisfaction surveys and Quality Action and Corrective Action teams, and so forth. "Whoa! What's going on? What is all this jargon? Why do we have to change, not them?" your employees ask.

When management makes the decision to adopt one or all of the Quality philosophies (often to remain competitive and keep existing business), it means a dramatic culture change for the work force. It means a new way of doing an old thing. Status lines need to be broken down and employees across disciplines and hierarchy need to communicate in new ways. Suddenly, a boiler operator may have more clout in changing work procedures than his far-removed vice president does at headquarters two states away. The agency director may serve on a corrective action team with his secretary and with the president of a local manufacturing firm.

Some in the work force see this as just another management fad. Managers who think otherwise face taunts from doubters. Critics claim that nothing else has worked yet and nothing else will ever work except good old-fashioned, hard-nosed authority.

25.1 ISN'T QI JUST ANOTHER MANAGEMENT FAD?

Employees who have been around for 15 years or more are probably familiar with Management by Objective and Management by Results. There was also a perversion known as Management by Stretch, which didn't last long because the stress it caused had a tendency to kill people by causing heart attacks. So now the company has adopted Quality Improvement.

Who can blame employees for being just a little hesitant to embrace QI? Why should they invest several more years of hard work learning what could be gone before they even get to use it; just like what happened to MBO and MBR? Your assignment is to introduce and develop QI in your work unit despite the cynicism. Showing understanding, as explained further in section 1.7, can gain credibility for your responses.

> *"Everyone here has good reason to be skeptical about another new management method.* None of us wants to waste a lot of time on something that won't stick around for long. *I had the same doubts when I first heard about QI, but I really believe in it now.* They say QI takes a long time to develop, and that's good in my view. I don't believe there are any magic bullets that can solve every problem instantly. But we've got to have some method, and if QI works half as well as they say it will, *I think it's worth a try."*

> *"No, it's not a fad.* Quality Improvement transformed Japan and other countries over the last 40 years. Japan went from making junk to producing some of the best products in the world. *With competition as fierce as it is, we need QI to make improved products at lower cost. If we want to stay in business, we can't afford to do any less.* I intend to use it in my area to show all of you how it can work to our advantage here."

Tip: Be powerful by your example.

Even the great Svengali, using words alone, couldn't persuade skeptics to immediately jump and cheer about QI after they had been pummeled by management's quick fixes time after time. Considering that QI has been extremely effective in Japanese corporations and throughout the world, it obviously isn't a passing fad. If you cite the experience of corporations worldwide and then show your commitment, **you can lead and persuade by example.**

---

25. 2 THE JAPANESE ARE CONFORMIST
AND WE'RE INDIVIDUALISTS. HOW CAN QI WORK HERE?

Many people wrongly perceive QI as a contest between Japan and the United States. They also say QI works for the Japanese because they are conformist unlike the "rugged individualist" Americans. They think the Japanese easily submit to authority, peer group pressure, male controls, and the example of their Emperor. When you ask them to voluntarily adopt QI, they may think you want them to become submissive. The SIA (Simplify, Illuminate, Advance) formula will help here by conveying a concise explanation of a complex philosophy and a concomitant methodology. (Section 2.6 explains this further.)

> "I don't know what the Japanese people are actually like. They probably don't know us very well either. *But Quality Improvement doesn't depend on conformism. A lot of tough, independent-minded Americans are making it work very well.* It's being used *worldwide* in everything from automobile plants to government agencies. A lot of unions have gotten behind QI because their members get to use their brains and not just their hands. We can adapt QI here just as America has successfully adapted so many things from other countries and vice versa. *That doesn't mean we have to become like them.*"

Question 25.2 has a false premise that must be corrected if you are to succeed in paving the way for Quality Improvement. The response's first two sentences neutralize the critic's assumption by implying no one knows what the Japanese are really like. The third sentence further refutes the critic's premise in which he contends QI depends on conformism. The fourth sentence undermines the premise by saying other tough-guy Americans have incorporated QI. (Refer to section 1.4 for related suggestions.)

Your responses can be more powerful if you note that QI may actually lead to more independence for most workers. When QI is properly and completely implemented, all workers have the necessary authority to do whatever needs to be done—from shutting down an assembly line to learning about corporate finances. As an example, the Corning Plant in Virginia has eliminated all management positions. They have only a plant manager and work teams, and the teams are almost completely autonomous.

25.3 DOESN'T QI MEAN "DO MORE WITH LESS" WHILE THE BIG SHOTS KEEP DOING THE SAME OLD THINGS?

Too often employees have been on the receiving end of "do more with less" (while more work was piled on). To them, QI sounds like some insincere exhortation to do better work because management said so. Amid the bloody "downsizing" (which is also producing lean and efficient companies to compete worldwide) anything new and different may look more like staff cuts and increased work. And now here you are asking them to open their minds one more time.

> "QI doesn't have anything to do with whether staff should be increased or reduced. *Hirings or layoffs could happen with or without QI.* I think we have a better chance of not having to 'do more with less' if we can make QI work here. *Quality Improvement gives all workers at all levels the means to build quality into every step of our processes.* With continuous improvement, we will be able to keep more customers—and more jobs here."

> "QI is not a window dressing or a quick fix. It requires a real and lasting commitment from top management. *It requires top management to relinquish some of their control and authority.* This has to come first, because

---

Tip: Fear from reasonable people gives you insights.

Nowadays employees who are normally rational have **good reason to be paranoiac about strange offerings that are supposed to "help them."** And when some QI enthusiasts elevate principles of Deming, Juran, and Crosby to nearly divine status, it is no wonder that lower-level employees and supervisors react with skepticism.

As companies and governments gut their organizations in the name of efficiency, QI can appear to be a way to reinvent yourself out of a job instead of what it really is—a great way to protect jobs through customer satisfaction and efficiency. QI also offers individuals the opportunity to be directly involved in the decision-making process, to achieve recognition, and to reduce job tension and boredom. **Don't dismiss your staff's worried questions as irrational and unfounded.** If you do, it's you who is being irrational by not recognizing the reality on which their fears are based.

---

otherwise we don't expect employees to buy into it. *So you see, it won't be business as usual, and the big shots won't be calling all the shots.* You'll be calling the ones that relate to how you fit into the picture."

25.4 WHY ARE WE BEING FORCED TO IMPROVE QUALITY HERE WHEN OTHERS AREN'T?

You staff is like most groups of employees who believe, "We always do better than people in other divisions." They think their work is average to good. They resent hearing praise about Total Quality Improvement when they think other divisions are much worse and are not being asked to improve. While the staff can easily see that others are falling short of preferred quality (advertising, production, sales, or engineering), they don't see their mistakes as patterns of poor quality. Your responses need to correct their misunderstanding of TQI while also bridging to a simple explanation that might appeal to them.

> "This isn't about who does or doesn't need to be fixed. *QI is about looking very objectively at how we can do a million little things, every step of the way, to add quality to our products.* It's also about making some big things come about, such as a suggestion leading to a major systems change. *QI is not another form of product inspection so we can find out who's to blame.* We want to fix the quality, not the blame. Everyone here is being asked to join in, including us and all other divisions."

25.5 I HAVEN'T GOT ENOUGH TIME TO DO MY WORK AS IT IS! WHERE AM I GOING TO FIND EXTRA TIME TO DO THIS QI THING?

Even if your employees are willing to give QI an honest try, they may be skeptical about how they're going to find the time. After all, they barely have time to do their work as it is. Once again they misunderstand the fundamental concept of Total Quality Improvement, and it's your job to correct that in your reply. You must first correct the false premise before they will accept your explanation.

> "QI isn't something we do in place of work, like going to a meeting. Quality Improvement is *how* we do our work. We're going to be pro-

ducing the same products, but with *more participation, quality, and efficiency.* All of that is up to you, because QI relies heavily on what *you know and what you can see happening,* not what top-level executives think they know about your work."

25.6 WHAT'S THIS BALONEY ABOUT TEAMWORK? ARE YOU SAYING WE DON'T WORK WELL TOGETHER?

Your staff says that while there are some differences, it's nothing that upper management should get excited about. They don't think you need to tell them about teams and all that camaraderie stuff. They feel the company wastes a lot of money on consultants who come in and preach about teamwork. Your employees do their own work and get along with co-workers, so bug off. But your staff has asked a question that misquotes what you have been trying to say. Instead of arguing whether they were listening or taking things the wrong way, turn the misquote into a chance to restate your views. (Refer to section 3.3 for more on mastering misquotes.)

"No one is saying anything about how you get along with others. *If that's how this is coming across, I haven't explained it very well.* We're not pointing fingers at anyone. I recognize that teamwork means different

---

Tip: Creating new meanings can be done, if . . .

Most veteran workers have seen the treachery and back stabbing that goes on in almost every workplace. Experienced employees know also that once in awhile some idealistic manager attempts to smooth things over by exhorting the troops about the joys of "teamwork." **Hence veteran employees initially hear "teamwork" as an accusation of infighting** (or being hitched to a heavy load—harnessed along with the other beasts of burden).

Make sure your responses draw a clear picture of what you mean by teamwork in contrast to what they have seen before. If you really mean QI teamwork, **you need to prove it by deeds.** Promise them that your teamwork centers around honesty, openness, factual information—not on management by intimidation and punishment. Some tyrannical administrators mouth the words of QI but their punitive methods speak much louder. **So your QI deeds must match your QI words.**

things to different people. Teamwork to me doesn't mean everyone acts nice and they pat one another on the back. This kind of teamwork means we really take an honest look to find ways we can support one another. That may sound trite—but it isn't. All of us can benefit from an honest review of *how we work together.*"

25. 7 THIS IS A "SERVICE" COMPANY. DON'T YOU THINK QI IS FOR FACTORIES?

To some of your employees, QI is tied solely to statistics and measurable results. But service organizations such as insurance companies and government agencies are not manufacturers of concrete products that are easily quantified. Your staff demands to know how you can objectively measure and count the number of flaws in service quality as though they were scratches in painted fenders. Their doubting questions give you an opportunity to once again drive home the main points you want to get across.

These broad questions cover so many issues that they are like multiple-part questions, that allow you to pick where you want to concentrate your response (see section 3.8 for more on multipart questions).

> "We can *measure* how well people say they were *satisfied.* We can *count* how many customers *come back again.* It also gives you and me a lot of leeway in what we can invent for ourselves to measure our company's effectiveness."

Tip: Continuous improvement equals continuous invention.

Deming himself said he was never satisfied with his famous 14 principles and methods. He felt he had not stopped learning and improving, and neither should we. When you answer these doubting questions, say that **there will always be change.** Continuous changes means a constant need to **improve methods and products** to keep us competitive in the world marketplace.

When skeptics point out that QI originated in manufacturing, tell them that QI is a continuous and evolving process that can be applied to every aspect and every level of an organization. It doesn't measure everything, **just the important indicators.** Invite them to take part. If they were truly given the freedom to come up with new measurements, imagine how inventive they might be.

"You are right. We can't measure every little detail the way manufacturing can, but if we're creative enough, *we can develop ways to measure what we need to know.* QI could very easily have started in the service industries, and then manufacturing would have had the same challenge. It's been proven time and again that *the most important quality principles are easily transferred* from one discipline to another, from making bolts to making decisions."

25.8 WHY DON'T YOU MANAGERS GO PLAY YOUR QI GAMES BY YOURSELVES AND LET US GET SOME WORK DONE?

Your employees have heard the phrase Total Quality "Management" and see that as a way to opt out of this stuff. "Management" must refer to higher-level executives, not them—so they shouldn't have to be bothered with this foolishness.

Like many lower-level employees, they probably don't think managers do real work anyway, hence only managers have time for QI and other "games." Thus far you have not gotten across to them that QI is not just something management does or that workers do separately from managers. You decide to acknowledge their concerns while you plan to bridge a better explanation. So you smile, take a deep breath, and say something like:

> "*Even though this may sound like a cliché,* I do believe that the most valuable asset of any company is its people. You folks are the ones who produce the product, maintain the inventory, answer customer calls, and deliver the goods, day in and day out. *Without your involvement,* there couldn't be a Total Quality program to produce any product of any sort."

> "Why are we bothering you with this? *Because we can't do it alone.* QI means building quality improvements from the *beginning to the end,* from the bottom to the top. If there are layers in QI, it doesn't work."

> "We can't afford to leave you out of this because *we don't know as much as you know about your work.* No person can know everything the next person knows. *You understand things about your job that we don't.* We all have a better chance of making lasting improvements if we get ideas from the people closest to the work. *We need you because you know so much . . . no joke.*"

> ### Tip: You benefit by seeing how *little* you really know.
>
> No matter how smart you are, you can never know or see all that your staff does—never, ever. Because you must rely on their efforts and cooperation, you need the best they have to offer. It is important that everyone realize QI can work only as a joint venture of management and labor. Let your staff know they are **imperative** to quality improvement and that you value them highly because of their knowledge and ability.

25.9 WHY SHOULD WE MAKE QUALITY SUGGESTIONS WHEN YOU NEVER LISTEN TO US?

Your staff remember suggesting all kinds of things to higher management, but "no one listened." Together they join the chorus and chime in about past slights from "aloof" superiors. Surely you jest—you want these folks to get creative and put their thinking caps on again? This is the kind of false-premise question with an attack that isn't worth combating. Sidestep the allegation that you haven't listened in the past and bridge directly to what you will do in the future. (See sections 1.1, 3.3, and 3.9 for more on handling personal attacks.)

> "Look at it this way, if you believe I haven't been receptive to your suggestions in the past, the QI program will solve that for you. *Because I'm going to be doing more listening and less talking.* What's the old saying? 'You can't learn a thing when you are the one doing the talking.'"

> *"If that's what it seemed like to you before, I'm sorry.* I didn't mean to come across that way, and I apologize if that's how it seemed to you. I've learned something right now that I wish I had known long ago. I promise to not only be open to your comments about me—good and bad—*but I will go out of my way to ask for your input.* If it looks as if I'm not listening again, call me on it. *I want—no—I need to know that."*

What good would it do to "prove" that you were listening in the past? You would be right and the staff would be wrong, and the gulf between you and them would be wider than ever. It is their perception that you have been closed-minded and that's all that counts.

You regain control of the discussion by expressing your regret that they feel that way. It doesn't mean you or they were wrong about anything; it does mean you thereby sidestep a useless debate. Then you move on to the real point: open and honest communications as the basis of QI. And you must be sincere in what you say. Talk is cheap and you will lose the confidence of your people if you are the least bit insincere.

25.10 IF I GATHER DATA ABOUT THE PROBLEMS IN MY JOB, HOW DO I KNOW YOU WON'T USE THIS AGAINST ME IN MY PERFORMANCE REVIEW?

No one wants to provide his boss with documentation of problems that could be perceived as failures. When QI enthusiasts propose comprehensive data collection, some of your workers in the trenches get nervous. They have seen information used against them by other managers, so they are leery of gathering data that could be the bullets for another attack. As the current manager, you realize that without adequate data, QI programs would revert back to the traditional guesswork. But what do you say to leery skeptics?

Many of your employees haven't learned that the cornerstone of the Quality movement is to not assign blame but to find the root cause of a problem. Your responses should remove the personal threat to employees. Because all organizations of any size have pecking orders, your comments should assure people farther down the order that the Quality process empowers them. Their opinions and documentation now mean something because they carry greater weight in the decision-maker process.

> "What we're asking you to do is called charting. Charting is merely documenting *nonconformance*, things that don't fit. Your data will be added to data collected from employees charting in other groups. The team—*not I*—will then look for methods of correcting problems, and they may seek your advice. *There's no threat to you.* They'll welcome your input."

> "Quality is not a witch-hunt. You are closest to your issues and work processes, and that *makes you the local expert on problems.* A performance review is personal. Quality Improvement is company-wide. Your documentation of the ups and downs of the process reflects on the company's attempts to improve. You will be seen as a player."

Tough Questions Worksheet

Create responses to the difficult questions you could face on this chapter's topics, using the formulas below. Use **logic, emotion,** and **ethics** whenever possible. Experiment by answering the same question with different formulas to learn which best fits your natural style. Use pencil so you can erase
and refine your answers.

Past, Present, Future:

What happened was:

What's happening now is:

The way we'll prevent it from happening again is by:

Problem to Solution:

*The **problems** we have are:*

*I'd like to go directly to a proposed **solution:***

Problem - Cause - Solution - Timing (PCST):

*The **problems** we have are:*

*They were **caused** by:*

*The **solutions** we may implement are:*

*Our **timing** is:*

Wrong, Right, and What It Means:

This is an extremely complex area and our track record has **overall** *been very* **good:**

We do very difficult things and sometimes we have failures. What **happened** *is that:*

What this **means** *for us now is:*

Three-Step Explanation:

I understand what you are asking and why it concerns you so much:

Other people who had your experiences probably would feel the same way:

However, I would like to explain a little about this problem:

Other formulas and responses I want to use for tough questions related to this chapter:

26

Reducing the Agony from Painful Layoff Questions

We now live in a world where job security is becoming a rare privilege. Business is more global and competitive, forcing many companies to take strategic measures to stay afloat. Firings, layoffs—severe cutbacks of people and resources—are the commonplace casualties of doing business in today's unpredictable and often cutthroat markets.

Unfortunately, very few organizations take the necessary time and effort to prepare employees for such a traumatic event. This is unfortunate indeed, for layoffs disrupt careers and families. Not only can they threaten an employee's own self-esteem, but often they cause chaos and shatter morale inside the organization as well.

If your organization has not taken steps to allay the fears and anxieties of employees before the layoff is called, you can expect to face anger, bitterness, and some mighty tough questions from your stunned workers. In this situation, it's not a matter of batting 300, it's more a matter of damage control and doing what you can to lessen the trauma on everyone.

The responses in this chapter assume that impending layoffs are not a knee-jerk reaction to a cyclical business slump, but a painful, well-thought-out, and difficult decision that is mindful of the human trauma it causes. If not, the organization may rightfully come across as callous and unstable.

26.1 HOW CAN THE COMPANY BE SO CALLOUS TOWARD PEOPLE WHO HAVE GIVEN SO MUCH TO IT?

Most workers still put all their emotional eggs into one job basket. So when the layoff news hits, it hits hard, and hostile questions like this one come quickly.

Assume your company missed the boat and kept employees out of the communication loop. Now it's going to be darn near impossible for them to rationally accept the sudden announcement. However, you are one of the managers and must face the angry questions from distraught employees.

It is naturally very difficult for us to accept that our job isn't important enough to save. If my job isn't important, am I? If your employee is being laid off for reasons that have nothing to do with him or his performance, you can cushion the blow by focusing on that reality. (Refer to section 1.7 for related comments.) Here are some ideas on how to respond as positively as possible:

> "If I were in your position, I'd probably be *thinking the same thing*. I'm very sorry we have to let you go. It has absolutely nothing to do with you personally. You're a fine employee, and you're right—you've given a lot to this company, and please know that *we recognize that.* In fact, I've written a letter to that effect. I hope that you'll make use of our counseling program and *let us help you with your job search.* Ann will take you down to Human Resources now where they'll explain things further."

> "This would have happened to anyone who was in your position. It had absolutely nothing to do with you. I have a letter here from the company president expressing that and thanking you for your fine

---

Tip: Cushion the blow to reduce harm to employees.

It'll be a less stressful situation for both of you if the company can cushion the blow by offering departing employees help in finding another job. The three biggest needs are emotional, financial, and career assistance. Some good assistance programs include providing on-site counseling for workers who are overly stressed. Offer employees help in writing resumes, conducting job interviews, and managing finances. This could include providing them with phones for long-distance calls and the use of computers, fax machines, and copiers. **It's a small price to pay, and it helps with morale for remaining employees who carry the task of rebuilding the organization.**

---

work here. Let me describe to you why we made the decision to eliminate the position. It may *help you explain what happened to potential employers.* We intend to do all we can to help you find another position. Let's go over to Human Resources and they can talk with you about our outplacement program."

"It may be hard for you to believe, but this has nothing to do with you personally. The reduction of positions required *some reorganization and reallocations of duties.* In order to be as lean and efficient as possible, we kept and consolidated the most crucial functions. The positions that were eliminated *were important, but not imperative* to the future operation of this company."

People often react to news of their being terminated with denial and shock, followed by hostility (later may come feelings of self-doubt and grief). Let employees vent their anger without your being drawn into an argumentative or defensive posture. Just listen until they are ready to listen.

26.2 WHY DIDN'T THE COMPANY HAVE THE DECENCY TO TELL PEOPLE BEFOREHAND SO THEY COULD LOOK FOR OTHER JOBS?

Your company's top management waited until the final hour to communicate the truth to employees. The senior executives, caught up in the turmoil of change, didn't recognize that they weren't communicating with their most vital resource—not their clients but their own employees. They kept up the guise until the very end, despite heavy rumors to the opposite.

As a middle-level manager, you were not pleased with senior management's approach, yet you still believe there was good reason for the timing of the announcement. And your employee is waiting for your response.

> "We didn't have that much advance information ourselves. We didn't speak sooner because *our information was uncertain.* Had we made the announcement earlier, without knowing the true extent of our troubles, *we may have lost clients and had to lay off even more people as a result.*"

> "We wish we could have shared this information sooner with all of our co-workers. We had to *balance* their legitimate *desire to know* earlier with the concern that premature statements could create stress and unfounded rumors. That would have caused a lot of *unnecessary worry* for employees whose jobs will remain here."

> "Whenever a person's information is uncertain, *it's irresponsible to cause fear* by speaking out before you really know the information is solid and that layoffs can't be avoided. *We acted as quickly as we could once we had solid information* and discovered there was *no alternative left.*"

> "I really wish life were that simple; that we could tell everyone everything. The reality is that life sometimes presents harsh dilemmas like the imperative need to cut costs drastically to survive. Blurting things out without careful consideration of all ramifications would have been *irresponsible and reckless.* The timing of tough decisions and announcements can have major consequences to the entire organization and all of its employees. *We must be responsible and do the best we can for everyone involved.*"

Even if you could clearly explain why you didn't give further advance notice, your answer is unlikely to gain immediate acceptance with your employees. They are being hurt financially and emotionally. Some will want to strike back by making you "bad and wrong" for making their plight worse.

Your answer won't change the circumstances, so satisfy their questions as much as possible while you brace for the inevitable emotional stages caused by the shock of losing one's livelihood. If they won't respect the result, your response might get them to respect the process you used.

26.3 CAN'T THIS BE DELAYED UNTIL WE'VE HAD AN OPPORTUNITY TO GET OUR LIVES IN ORDER AND FIND OTHER JOBS?

Losing their jobs is hitting everyone very hard—it's almost as traumatic as the death of a loved one. A few are outwardly going through natural stages of emotional reaction, and one man is pleading for his job. You may hear questions such as "How am I going to feed my family?" It's painful for any manager to hear an employee beg for his job. As a manager, you find your compassion in conflict with your responsibility to serve and preserve the company.

Postponing the layoff after the announcement could make it worse. There needs to be closure so that employees can get to the stage of acceptance. This is where your replies need to help them see that they need to be seriously pursuing other opportunities.

> "We have already waited as long as we possibly could while *we explored every possible alternative*. There just isn't any other option. We can't delay any longer. Dragging this thing out won't make the situation any better. It would only prolong and *increase the stress on everyone*."

> "We have attempted to achieve staffing cuts over the past several months through attrition, placement of employees with other companies, and through early retirement packages offered to long-term employees. We have reached the point where our *only remaining recourse is layoff*. If we were to wait longer, we would be *endangering* the health of the company and everyone's job."

26.4 COULDN'T THE COMPANY HAVE CUT OTHER COSTS?

The people in your department who are losing their jobs (a.k.a., paychecks, financial security, health insurance, and maybe careers) are understandably desperate persons. They are asking if there isn't some other cost cutting you could recommend to senior management.

You decide to accept their question at face value and prepare a clear, brief answer that says management has cut everywhere else first, and now layoffs are unavoidable. At this point acknowledging their concerns and showing understanding (see section 1.7) is imperative, as is the art of bridging. Your responses for questions such as this must sincerely acknowledge their worries and next bridge back to the logic, rationale, and ethics used in the company decision.

> "That's a fair question, and you deserve a straight answer. I know this isn't going to be easy for you, and you've earned the right to know whether we really could have avoided this. We have been searching out and implementing every practical cost reduction. That did provide some savings. But we have to recognize that our largest expense, by far, is salaries and fringe benefits. *The only remaining avenue open* to us is to undertake reductions in staffing to bring costs into line."

> "A few years ago we entered the era of rapid change, but now *we're in hyper change.* Like it or not, the tough reality is that every organization *must adjust or disappear* from this planet. Hyper change means frequent adaptations, including hiring and, unfortunately, layoffs too. If we don't adapt, *everyone* here will be out of a job."

26.5 HOW CAN THE COMPANY JUSTIFY LETTING PEOPLE GO WHEN IT SHOWS A PROFIT?

How can your company's employees comprehend losing their jobs when the company has posted profits again? That's a difficult concept for them to grasp much less accept when they feel so threatened. Aren't companies supposed to cut-back when they're *losing* money?

In hard times, it's popular to portray the "money" executives as loving profits more than people. It makes for great movies when the good guys nearly always win over the evil corporate management scum. But profits can be put in human terms too. Profits mean jobs now and in the future. Profits mean the economy still operates. Without a profit, the company simply can't survive. Although your replies are not likely to be accepted easily, your comments nevertheless should include the economic realities built into the decisions to continue the drive toward economic efficiency and increased productivity.

> "*It is not unusual for a company to lay off workers when it still shows a profit.* We're not unlike many industries that have laid off workers as a result of deregulation or declining profits. If we were to wait until profits disappeared entirely, we would likely jeopardize the future of the company and all of the jobs here. This would be an abandonment of

our primary responsibility to shareholders and our employees. Only those companies that maintain a *competitive edge* in the marketplace will survive."

26.6 FACING THE NEWS MEDIA'S TOUGH QUESTIONS

Your strategy for managing a layoff should include a plan for dealing with the news media's tough questions. Layoffs affect entire communities and are almost always covered by the media. Reporters frequently look for someone to blame (usually the company), and stories usually contain accusations by angry employees. You may be accused of being "cold-hearted," "ruthless," and "uncaring" of the individual, her family, and the entire community.

How you respond to the media can affect the morale of existing employees, the confidence of your customers or clients, and thus your ability to survive this traumatic crisis.

The following responses contain excellent examples of how to weave emotion, ethics, and facts into a response. In the first one, the human element is captured in the CEO's reference to the friends he has had to lay off, and what it meant for him personally. The logic of wanting to focus on taking care of the remaining 11,000 workers (fact) is both poignant (emotion) and reasonable (ethic or standard). (Refer to section 1.4 for related comments.)

This sort of response is rarely seen in the news media, mainly because organizations undergoing the trauma of a layoff tend to develop a siege mentality and avoid the press at all costs. This is a big mistake. It doesn't mean the story won't get done, but it does mean that the company's good intentions won't get covered. History has shown that in an information vacuum, people will believe what they want to believe, and that's usually the worst, especially after rumors take over.

> "*We recognize the impact* on our employees, their families, and the communities we live and work in and we will try to *minimize the effects.* I have people who were *close friends whom I have had to let go.* It's one of the toughest things I have ever had to do. On the other hand, there are *11,000 people* who need a secure future. I have to think about them too."

> "We have to do this in order to stay in business, period. By tightening our belts, improving efficiency, and cutting costs, we can provide jobs

to the greatest number of people. *We simply can't afford to maintain positions for everyone.* If we tried to do that, soon no one would have a job."

"We did not do this because we wanted to. We did it because we had to. *This layoff is not a first resort.* It is a last and only resort. We've exhausted all other possibilities. And though we are all distressed by this action, it will enable our company *to survive, to compete, and to continue to provide good jobs* for the majority of our employees."

"We believe this action will make the remaining organization and its employees more competitive in a rapidly changing market. *As we become more competitive* and gain more business, *we intend to expand* this company and add more jobs in this community."

When you feel yourself getting defensive at a reporter's questions, be mindful that nowadays layoffs can be shown to be a positive sign that a company is taking aggressive action to remain competitive in the marketplace. Witness AT&T, Ford, GM, and Merck. This should be stressed, as it is often the reason behind a layoff.

Tough Questions Worksheet

Create responses to the difficult questions you could face on this chapter's topics, using the formulas below. Use **logic, emotion,** and **ethics** whenever possible. Experiment by answering the same question with different formulas to learn which best fits your natural style. Use pencil so you can erase and refine your answers.

Past, Present, Future:

What happened was:

What's happening now is:

The way we'll prevent it from happening again is by:

Problem to Solution:

*The **problems** we have are:*

*I'd like to go directly to a proposed **solution:***

Problem - Cause - Solution - Timing (PCST):

*The **problems** we have are:*

*They were **caused** by:*

*The **solutions** we may implement are:*

*Our **timing** is:*

Wrong, Right, and What It Means:

This is an extremely complex area and our track record has **overall** *been very* **good:**

We do very difficult things and sometimes we have failures. What **happened** *is that:*

What this **means** *for us now is:*

Three-Step Explanation:

I understand what you are asking and why it concerns you so much:

Other people who had your experiences probably would feel the same way:

However, I would like to explain a little about this problem:

Other formulas and responses I want to use for tough questions related to this chapter:

27

Forthright Replies to Calm Distrust After Layoffs

There are a lot of buzzwords to describe what happens when a company lays off employees. It's called downsizing, it's called rightsizing, it's called reengineering, but the result is the same. People are "down-right" fired.

Amidst all the unpleasantness that goes along with the bloodletting—the people whose needs are usually ignored are the survivors. Similar to the employees forced to leave, those who remain also encounter feelings of guilt, distrust, fear, and anger (though obviously feeling some relief that they kept their jobs).

The previous chapter dealt with how managers can field painful questions from departing employees. Just as important to a company is how managers respond to employees who remain and are expected to maintain business as usual.

Trouble is, unless an organization finds a way to deal with feelings of insecurity, lack of trust, and sinking morale, they can expect the revolving door to continue; but this time, employees may be leaving both willingly and quickly (and the ones who leave willingly are usually the best—the very ones the company most needs.)

27.1 THE COMPANY SURE PULLED A FAST ONE ON EVERYBODY. IT MAKES ME WONDER IF I'M NEXT?

As happened at thousands of other companies, the unwritten workplace rules have changed. Gone is the implicit paternal relationship that lasted for many decades between your company and its employees. Under this social contract of implied stability, if an employee worked hard the company would take care of him or her—maybe for life.

Today the relationship is more like a revolving door. Loyalty and tenure are out—immediate performance and production are in. So, after your organization has rolled some heads, how do you respond to the remaining employees that they aren't next?

Surviving employees have a strong need to hear that managers genuinely share their pain. What they don't need is for you as a manager to pass off the bad news of layoffs as only good news. It's not just good news, and when you pretend it is, you both insult their intelligence and give them good reason to be suspicious of everything you say afterwards.

In your comments, remind employees that nothing is forever, no matter where they work. Business sometimes means bloodletting. It happens to companies of all sizes, in all industries, and yes, even in companies that are still profitable. Combine the logic of why that person was kept on as part of the overall logic for the entire action. And then bridge to the future, which is where hope lies. Your replies can't give hope, but you can describe a future in which they themselves may see the hope it offers.

"You weren't laid off for the simple reason that you are a highly valued employee. *This company, like thousands of organizations, needed to restructure itself to be more competitive.* We had too many tentacles in too many places, and the company's *bottom line was too close to the bottom.* If we didn't take this action, we would have lost customers and might have had to lay off even more employees. We very much want you to stay and help our company become an industry leader again."

"Our jobs in this company depend, to a large extent, on the future well-being of our company. Doing our jobs to the *best of our ability will be the best insurance* that your employment—and mine, too—will continue in the future."

These responses reflect a more open, collegial tone:

"I won't make empty promises to you. I'm also feeling a little numb over what just happened and a little guilty that I get to stay when other good people lost their jobs. *The fact is that nobody's job is assured these days, anywhere.* This was a wake-up call for all of us, and I for one am eager to be a part of change. It may have been long overdue, and I believe some good things will come of it. After you've worked through your own emotions, *I hope you'll find reasons* to stick around and see what happens."

"I know you are feeling *some sadness over your friends* who had to leave. I'm feeling the same way. It was a painful but unquestionably necessary move. *We very much want you to stay, and we value the work you've done here.* If we can all resolve our feelings and get through this hard time, we have a good chance of making things better for all of us. I hope you'll find reasons for staying."

First and foremost, let them vent. They deserve it and they need it. Probably so do you. No communication is possible when emotions are so high they prevent real listening—they won't hear the message in your reply. Encourage venting, yes—but never, for any reason, should any of this vented frustration and anger be taken personally or used against anyone in any way. This is critical to maintaining trust and a healthy working relationship—and not just in the context of cutbacks.

To get the discussion going, you may need to show some courage and discuss a few of your own feelings. But again, just to get them started talking. Remember that the personal and institutional healing that needs to take place is an ongoing process that could last for years.

27.2 HOW CAN YOU EXPECT US TO PRETEND AS IF NOTHING HAS HAPPENED?

Your employees have heard a great many horror stories about layoffs, some true and most distorted as they were passed from person to person. These stories are mixed with the memories of too many instances where other companies treated employees with callousness—numerous examples of organizations dumping hordes of loyal employees without warning and seemingly without concern.

After a layoff, many companies try to pretend as though it's business as usual. Everybody's supposed to show up for work and ignore the empty desks and missing friends and colleagues. Employees are expected to act thankful they still have a job, keep their noses to the grindstone, and make the clients happy.

Back at your company, you are attempting to be forthright at least within your department. You want to be candid about what the situation really is but not so much so that the department dwells too long in an unpleasant past. The problem is that after spending years convincing employees that longevity and loyalty are what your company is all about, the recent layoffs shattered the old image while rumors and hard feelings are fostering fear and cynicism.

Your duty as a manager to communicate and lead is being put to the test with this question. Your reply shouldn't be so explicit that your comments would get you in trouble with senior management, but you don't want to alienate the employees by merely reciting platitudes. You can acknowledge the concerns behind the question while also leading the employees to your goal of resolving hard feelings and rebuilding work relationships. If you are a manager who understands that, some of these quotes may help you respond.

> *"We don't expect you to pretend* as if nothing has happened. We are all experiencing a whole range of emotions. We're all going through a period of change *and we need to confront our concerns head-on and resolve them.* We want to do everything we can to help you deal with these concerns so they don't intrude on other parts of your life. Why don't you tell me what your thoughts are?"

> "I sincerely apologize if we've given you that impression. I hope none of us pretends anything. I want to be as open as I possibly can. *It's not unusual for companies to restructure.* People lost their jobs because we needed to downsize in order to stay competitive. It happens every day, in every type of organization. *None of us have to feel guilty about that.* We all wish we could have kept them, but that wasn't practical. We also realize it's going to take all of us some time to get over what happened. *We need to deal with it openly, and we need to agree on the best ways to move ahead."*

> "I realize that what we all just went through was pretty tough. The people who were let go aren't the only people who are upset. *Those of us who were fortunate enough to keep our jobs are wounded, too.* But I need to say, though we have to allow some time for healing, I feel good about the fact that the company is on the road to recovery. We were too bloated. Now that we made some painful decisions, *we know what we have to do to survive.* I'm excited about that, and I hope that after time you will be too."

The higher up the organizational ladder, the more managers ignore or altogether deny the rhetorical questions of angry, cynical, or depressed employees. By doing so, the executives don't allow themselves or their employees to experience the emotional release necessary for everyone to get on with their lives. Instead, some senior managers hide behind a facade of rationality and authority even though they experience the same anxious questions.

On the other hand, managers can't go about with a constant aura of overwhelming fear and uncertainty, regardless of what they feel deep inside. They must display assurance and optimism as they help lead the organization.

Don't pretend as if nothing has happened. It's much like losing a family member. Not helping people to grieve, to share their pain and find ways of coping prevents them from healing. Unresolved feelings will last a lifetime at work or at home. It prevents people from being good employees. Unless your responses deal with that, be prepared for low morale, poor productivity, distrust, and high turnover.

27.3 YOU'VE JUST FIRED HALF THE STAFF IN MY UNIT. HOW CAN YOU EXPECT THE REST OF US, WHO ARE ALREADY OVERWORKED, TO TAKE ON THEIR DUTIES?

When an organization expects remaining employees to absorb the duties of departing co-workers, it can lead to extreme overloading and stress. It will take time to sort out what really can be done by the remaining employees. They will be slow at first at doing new processes but will improve as they learn shortcuts and make fewer mistakes. As the manager, you will be surprised how much more will be completed in one area while others fall short of everyone's expectations. Senior management at two levels away from the front-line action will be learning and reevaluating and it's hoped reallocating duties and resources.

Meanwhile, you have to keep your balance amid a roller coaster of emotions and production surprises. When frustrated, overworked employees demand to know how you can expect them to do twice the work with half the people, consider the following responses:

> "You're right. It would be unfair for us to expect that of you. There are some *essential tasks that you will need to take on,* but we will redefine your job at the same time. We'll learn as we go along. Draw up a list of things

you are currently doing that you believe are not terribly crucial. I think it's important that you have some input about what really needs to get done. We'll work together to establish a *realistic workload."*

On the other hand, if your organization's approach is different and you have a traditional management style where everything is organized and decided beforehand this may be more appropriate:

"You're right, this reduction in staffing is going to be tough to handle. *I'm in the final stages of prioritizing the work that must get out.* The remainder—the nonessential aspects of our work—will of course become a priority if we sit on it too long. *I will schedule this as best I can* during regular work hours and what's left might be handled through overtime hours. Just as soon as I can determine what it's going to take in the way of staffing to maintain work flow, I might request the rehire of some of our laid-off workers. I know that management will be anxious to cut costs, and overtime is a very expensive way of doing business."

Tough Questions Worksheet

Create responses to the difficult questions you could face on this chapter's topics, using the formulas below. Use **logic, emotion,** and **ethics** whenever possible. Experiment by answering the same question with different formulas to learn which best fits your natural style. Use pencil so you can erase and refine your answers.

Past, Present, Future:

What happened was:

What's happening now is:

The way we'll prevent it from happening again is by:

Problem to Solution:

*The **problems** we have are:*

*I'd like to go directly to a proposed **solution**:*

Problem - Cause - Solution - Timing (PCST):

*The **problems** we have are:*

*They were **caused** by:*

*The **solutions** we may implement are:*

*Our **timing** is:*

Wrong, Right, and What It Means:

*This is an extremely complex area and our track record has **overall** been very good:*

*We do very difficult things and sometimes we have failures. What **happened** is that:*

*What this **means** for us now is:*

Three-Step Explanation:

I understand what you are asking and why it concerns you so much:

Other people who had your experiences probably would feel the same way:

However, I would like to explain a little about this problem·

Other formulas and responses I want to use for tough questions related to this chapter:

28

Avoiding the Damage of the Blame Game

28.1   *Who's to blame for this?*

28.2   *Didn't they screw up?*

There's a popular adage that's been humorously altered to reveal a contrary though just as legitimate truism: "It doesn't matter if you win or lose, it's how you place the blame."

When things go wrong, many people in our workplaces and throughout society rush to fix the blame instead of fixing the problem. It's almost a national pastime.

Answering the question of who's to blame in the office, in the news media, or anywhere, is a difficult proposition. When you point the proverbial finger at another, there is the unspoken implication that you are not necessarily a nice or innocent person for having done so. It's very similar to the "tattletale" stigma of childhood. Nobody likes a tattletale, especially when the kid is right. Likewise, by directing blame at another, you may become human Velcro—unable to detach yourself from the blame you tried to throw elsewhere.

That doesn't mean that placing deserved blame (accountability) where it belongs has to be a losing proposition. It does mean, however, that responding about who's to blame should be done skillfully and cautiously. Or, as some venerable person once said:

> "When you point the finger at another, beware of the three fingers pointing back at you."

The following examples demonstrate why understatements and indirect comments are exceptionally effective in replies regarding blame. They minimize blame by stressing solutions.

28.1 WHO'S TO BLAME FOR THIS?

In corporate life, employees blame managers, who blame the CEO, who blames the employees. In politics, Republicans blame Democrats and vice versa, and everybody blames the President. The rich blame the poor and the poor blame society. The parents blame the teachers, who blame them back. The union blames. . . .

Every now and then a courageous few come forward and—shock of all shocks—refuse to play the blame game.

Fix the Problem, Not the Blame

If your responses resort to needless blame placing and finger pointing, they will be divisive and counterproductive. Unless it's your duty to assign blame to assure accountability, bypass blame and move forward to concentrate on what can be done to fix the problem.

People are naturally attracted to managers who stress the positive and look for solutions, not others to blame. Blame placing wastes time and scarce moments of attention that could otherwise be used to further your goals.

Understatements and indirect comments are exceptionally effective in blame statements.

> "Blaming one side doesn't advance matters; *it just leads to more mistakes.*"

> "Our intent is not to assign blame. Our intent is to *study what happened and decide what to do about it.*"

> "Constructive criticism is a good thing. I think that it's important *we use the information provided by the audit in a sensible manner. We need to keep our perspective,* rather than attack and berate the university system."

> "There is no clear-cut angel and demon in this case. We aren't working to fix the blame; we're working to fix the problem. *We're focusing on what counts, making sure the problem doesn't happen again.*"

> "It will be harder to deal with the people involved if we get ourselves caught up in a finger-pointing game instead of seeking the right solutions. The bottom line is for people to *stay calm, avoid the blame game, and work through the problem* in a rational and scientific fashion."

28.2 DIDN'T THEY SCREW UP?

It is a signature of human nature that most of us are better experts on the failings of other people than we are of our own shortcomings. As the old saying goes, "Each of us would need a large cemetery in which to bury the faults of our friends and only a small parcel for ourselves." Moreover, saying *he* or *she* screwed up, is much easier to admit than *I* screwed up.

Some people feel better about themselves when they can be right by getting you to agree someone else was wrong. Whom do you know who loves to gloat when he is proven right?

Although there are valid reasons for a manager to concur with group judgments about someone's errors, remember that the grapevine will distort your comments as it conveys them to the person being criticized. So when the office gossip approaches you with a did-he-screw-up question, consider these examples on how to respond with finesse:

"I have a personal rule *not to be critical of* my colleagues."

"Even an act with the best intentions often has *a side effect or consequence that was never intended* and that no one wanted."

"I think that whatever happened was *not done with the intent to do harm.* There were some errors of judgment, but I haven't found anybody who calls them right all the time."

"The mistakes he made the last couple of years overshadowed the *contributions he made during the previous 25 years.*"

"What happened was wrong, but it has come to approach the specter of a Shakespearean tragedy. *They made a big mistake, but they are not evil.*"

"Did he react inappropriately? Absolutely. *But was the reaction understandable? I think it was.*"

"*They've acknowledged their mistakes all along.* They know they've made an error in judgment."

"By and large, *it's been an effective and useful program.* Certainly there have been errors. But I don't think it was malicious."

"The officers admit they should have done more, and they admit they made a mistake. *They are deeply sorry.* They were not harboring any intent to commit a crime. They were, in fact, civil servants *doing what they believed would best serve* the community and the participants."

Not Becoming a Target Yourself

No matter how you respond, you could become a target yourself when re-plying about screw-ups by other managers or employees. For example, if your response fails to acknowledge the harm done, you appear to agree with the criticized action. If your response faults the accusers for pointing fingers, you create a new fight and attract their criticism.

Instead of attracting an attack, keep the focus away from you. As the preceding comments illustrate, respond by directing attention to the intent and context of the faulted action. Aim your comments somewhere be-tween completely exonerating the faulted person and not letting critics to-tally condemn him.

Although the three major elements of effective statements are emo-tion, ethics/standards, and logic/facts, only the first two can do much good when the facts are against the blamed person. So remind critics of honorable intentions, reasonable standards for judgment, and even contri-tion, which may evoke forgiveness and end the criticism.

Tough Questions Worksheet

Create responses to the difficult questions you could face on this chapter's topics, using the formulas below. Use **logic, emotion,** and **ethics** whenever possible. Experiment by answering the same question with different formulas to learn which best fits your natural style. Use pencil so you can erase and refine your answers.

Past, Present, Future:

What happened was:

What's happening now is:

The way we'll prevent it from happening again is by:

Problem to Solution:

*The **problems** we have are:*

*I'd like to go directly to a proposed **solution:***

Problem - Cause - Solution - Timing (PCST):

*The **problems** we have are:*

*They were **caused** by:*

*The **solutions** we may implement are:*

*Our **timing** is:*

Wrong, Right, and What It Means:

*This is an extremely complex area and our track record has **overall** been very good:*

*We do very difficult things and sometimes we have failures. What **happened** is that:*

*What this **means** for us now is:*

Three-Step Explanation:

I understand what you are asking and why it concerns you so much:

Other people who had your experiences probably would feel the same way:

However, I would like to explain a little about this problem:

Other formulas and responses I want to use for tough questions related to this chapter:

29

Shielding Yourself from Questions on Guilt and Lies

29.1   Oh, come on, don't you think it's obvious he's guilty?

29.2   Don't you think she's lying?

Whether it's the company grapevine or the news media, it's hard not to join sound-bite discussions and armchair psychology to reach drive-thru conclusions. What do you say when you're asked to comment on the alleged lies or guilt of co-workers or business colleagues?

Guilt: Despite Western civilization's judicial process where innocence is legally presumed until guilt is proven, most of us don't really judge others that way. A good case in point was the O. J. Simpson trial. Down deep we thought we could generally figure out whether he was guilty or innocent long before the jury rendered its verdict.

Lies: In the old days, calling someone a liar might result in the two of you standing back to back stepping off paces, then at the count of ten whirling around and blowing each other's brains out. Today, that's what attorneys are for.

Nowadays you can call someone a liar, or at least seriously allude to it, without using the unpleasant word itself. Sometimes it is actually better to call a spade an "agricultural implement," an idiot someone who's "intellectually misguided," and a fool "someone who helps prove Charles Darwin's Theory of Evolution: Man really did descend from apes." Here are some suggestions on how to step away from the rush to judgment, without offending important business contacts or co-workers.

29.1 OH, COME ON,
DON'T YOU THINK IT'S OBVIOUS HE'S GUILTY?

When an employee allegedly gets his hand caught in the company's cook- ie jar, the gossip mongers race to conclusions. Because everyone is talking about it, it's hard to avoid being asked for your reaction.

Most of the facts will be locked up tight while the company con- ducts an internal investigation. If the police and local district attorney become involved, then it gets really dicey, adding more spice to the speculation.

With all the rumors swirling around, it's best to respond without slinging mud or coming off as a goody-two-shoes. There is little to be gained but a lot to lose by pronouncing someone guilty prematurely. But it's hard to say nothing when co-workers expect some type of response. Consider a reasonable, middle-of-the-road answer. Remind questioners that there are facts and a valued process to sort them out, and that you want to respect the process. By taking a stand on the process, you can avoid commenting on a person's likely guilt or innocence.

> *"That's too serious a charge to speculate on."*

> "It's easy to sit back and Monday-morning quarterback and say, 'Gee, why did he do it?' I think that's *premature judgment."*

> "It's too early to make such an accusation. It's all based on circumstan- tial evidence. Quite frankly, that kind of evidence is like Lego blocks *that can be constructed into all sorts of explanations.* We need to *respect the person, and the process,* and not jump to hasty conclusions that could cause damage to both."

> "He has been charged and there will be a trial. He is innocent until proven guilty. I think we have to *be careful about people's rights."*

> "It looks funny. But there is nothing we can put our hands on at this point that is clearly improper. The appearance might not be what we like, but *it may be all within the parameters* of what's permissible."

> "They've acknowledged their mistakes all along. They know they've made an error in judgment. *How serious an error is for others to judge who have access to facts,* and not just rumors, guesses, and speculation."

29.2 DON'T YOU THINK SHE'S LYING?

Whenever someone utters false remarks about us, we inevitably question the motivations behind the accuser. "She's lying" can blurt from our mouths before we pause a nanosecond to think. Too late, harm's done.

It's one thing to say the critics' statements are incorrect. It's altogether another matter to say she intentionally said something false, that is, she lied. You have to ask yourself whether it's worth the risk of being blunt if that will trigger additional strife. If the critic is your boss, do you want tell a third party you believe your boss is inaccurate and immoral too (a liar)? If the critic is one of your employees, do want the boss to hear later that your response tagged him a liar, not just inaccurate?

After you have answered those tactical questions, consider these responses:

> *"Knowingly or unknowingly,* people are laying out information that's not accurate."

> "The facts show that she is not correct, but I don't know if her inaccuracy is intentional. *I don't know why she made incorrect statements; they just are.*"

> "They've got an interesting argument, but *they overstate it.*"

> "Both of us, from our own point of view, are going to *see only a part of the truth.*"

> "I think the office has been victimized by some people who are *not exactly neutral* on this subject, who have not looked at this in a serious way, and who are *not dealing* with the information in what I would call *valid terms.*"

> "*It's evasion and finesse* more than lying."

> "Are they lying? Well, it would *not be entirely wrong to say that.*"

> "Asking them about the effects of environmental tobacco smoke is akin to asking the fox about conditions in the chicken coop."

Specificity Is Not Always the Soul of Credibility

Most people don't like acrimony and will tune you out when you create it. Calling someone a "liar," for example, creates a caustic barrier to the positive messages you want to get across. A little finesse can help you make your point and keeps your listeners' minds open.

As the responses above demonstrate, a direct question does not always need to be met with a direct answer. Sometimes the intelligent use of analogies, qualifiers, or similar methods can help you make your point while escaping a sticky situation. And there is nothing wrong with euphemisms. There is nothing cowardly in making your point in a way that causes minimal damage to yourself and the critic who may have knowingly said untrue things. There's nothing brave and heroic in triggering wasteful quarrels by calling someone a liar when it does not serve your purpose.

On the other hand, sometimes you may need to neutralize a false-speaking critic by being very blunt and tagging her a liar. Neutralizing a liar may help maintain your support and sway the undecided in your favor. But don't respond that way unless you identify beforehand strategic reasons for doing so.

Tough Questions Worksheet

Create responses to the difficult questions you could face on this chapter's topics, using the formulas below. Use **logic, emotion,** and **ethics** whenever possible. Experiment by answering the same question with different formulas to learn which best fits your natural style. Use pencil so you can erase and refine your answers.

Past, Present, Future:

What happened was:

What's happening now is:

The way we'll prevent it from happening again is by:

Problem to Solution:

*The **problems** we have are:*

*I'd like to go directly to a proposed **solution:***

Problem - Cause - Solution - Timing (PCST):

*The **problems** we have are:*

*They were **caused** by:*

*The **solutions** we may implement are:*

*Our **timing** is:*

Wrong, Right, and What It Means:

*This is an extremely complex area and our track record has **overall** been very **good:***

*We do very difficult things and sometimes we have failures. What **happened** is that:*

*What this **means** for us now is:*

Three-Step Explanation:

I understand what you are asking and why it concerns you so much:

Other people who had your experiences probably would feel the same way:

However, I would like to explain a little about this problem:

Other formulas and responses I want to use for tough questions related to this chapter:

30

Effective Responses When You're Accused of Hurting People

30.1   Aren't you responsible for harming these people?

30.2   Are you saying your company didn't cause this?

30.3   If you aren't guilty, then why did you settle out of court?

What do Tylenol and Exxon have in common? Both companies suffered a major crisis that threatened their existence. One reacted remarkably; thus it didn't take long to restore public confidence in its products. The other reacted badly and seriously eroded its reputation. Put another way, Exxon's Valdez accident was a major headache that might have gone away more quickly if they had taken Tylenol's powerful medicine for handling tough questions.

After several people died as a result of product tampering, the makers of Tylenol responded with speed, candor, and a convincing commitment to right any wrongs—perceived or real. The company quickly regained the public's respect and trust and averted a much more serious situation.

Exxon's Valdez nightmare is another story. It was a public relations fiasco, made worse each day by the company's perceived refusal to accept responsibility or to deal openly and sincerely with the public and the media. As a result, public trust in Exxon has definitely not been restored.

Granted, these two examples are large-scale catastrophes, but they illustrate an important point that relates to any instance in which you or your organization has been accused of hurting someone. Whether it's the accidental death of an employee, a layoff, or a cruel remark, how you handle issues of blame and responsibility can have major repercussions for years to come, outside and inside the company.

For example, "what" you say reveals what you think about the situation, "how" you say it reveals what kind of organization you are. If you say, "We lost two planes and their pilots," you're saying something quite different about your organization than if you said "Two of our pilots were killed today when their planes crashed." That old lead emphasis sends a subtle message. You stress people first if you want to be viewed internally and externally as an organization that cares about its employees.

There are always the legal considerations. Many companies have learned the hard way that quite often in today's society, the court of public opinion can be more damaging than the court of law. The public is not just outside the company; your employees constitute one of the most important publics you have.

30.1 AREN'T YOU RESPONSIBLE FOR HARMING THESE PEOPLE?

If the answer is yes, you must walk the legal-versus-moral tightrope, a precarious balancing act made more dangerous if the news media get involved.

Organizations and people alike tend to deny any wrongdoing, even when it's glaringly apparent to everyone else that they screwed up royally.

The Court of Public Opinion Is Just as Risky

In most instances, it is in your best interest to accept responsibility if it's rightfully yours. This may include a public apology circulated internally as well. Plain and simple, apologies validate the sufferings of people who feel they've been wronged. People often make a lot of noise simply because they want an apology. It's a very deep-seated human need and demand.

Unfortunately, apologies are as rare as a blue moon. How often have you heard someone say, "I screwed up. It was a stupid mistake and I'm very sorry. I hope they can find a way to forgive me."?

Many lawyers undoubtedly will tell you otherwise, as they are accustomed by training and nature to wage the fight months later, possibly out of sight in a tedious court proceeding. Meanwhile, you may be forced to parry hostile queries while fighting the immediate battle in the court of public opinion.

It may be your employees asking troublesome questions, it may be the media, or both. One thing is certain: The immediate perception could easily cost you more in dollars and goodwill than what you eventually lose in court or in the board room (and that usually goes unreported).

Consider the following "apologies." You may choose to use the shorter responses as effective starting points for your longer replies. (Also refer to section 1.6.)

> "It's a mistake that I made in a tough situation, a very emotional situation, and I used poor judgment. But *I learned from it and I apologize* for the confusion and embarrassment that I've caused."

> "I am deeply sorry. *My initial concern was to protect others.* In hindsight, I realize there were other alternatives that should have been and could have been explored to protect the integrity of the process."

> "At the time, I certainly thought I acted appropriately. Obviously, with 20-20 hindsight, *I wish I had done things differently.*"

> "I really have literally *no excuse and no justification* for using that choice of words. Clearly, I had my mouth in gear before my brain was engaged."

> "In looking back, I can understand how this appears. It looks as if I was stupid, but I certainly did not feel that way at the time. I've torn myself apart over this in the last week. But I honestly believe *it would not have made any difference.*"

> "It was a misunderstanding. If it was a mistake, *it was an innocent mistake.*"

> "It was a mistake and *it is not defensible.*"

For strategic communications, you should recommend that senior management designate one skilled communicator, particularly if the organization is apologizing for its mistakes. If your company doesn't have someone that skilled, get outside professional help immediately (that night, not the next morning) from a reputable public relations firm with crisis management experience.

Getting help immediately is critical because public (including staff) opinion is usually fairly well formed in the first few hours. That means that if you or your company's spokesperson says "no comment" to co-workers and to the outside public as well people will view everything you say thereafter through an entirely different lens than if their first impression of you had been more positive. After that, people are only adding to their initial information, and it's hard to get them to change their basic assumptions about the nature of the players. It has a lot to do with *selective perception and selective retention.*

Admit, Apologize, Bridge to the Positive

These next responses were made by managers confessing to everything from accidentally killing someone to polluting the ocean. They all have one thing in common: They admit to, but don't dwell on the negative.

When you have screwed up on a grand scale and you don't know what to say, it may be a good time to use a perspective formula that explains what you did wrong, what you did right, and what it all means. (Refer to section 2.8.) Follow this four-step example to focus attention on the positive things you are doing to fix the problem and make certain it doesn't happen again:

1. Acknowledge the mistake.

2. Apologize for the situation.

3. Say you'll pay the penalty, if appropriate.

4. Bridge to how you are changing things so it won't happen again.

Here are some masterful responses based on this formula:

"The accidental disconnection was a tragic mistake and *we take responsibility for it.* We have expressed our sincere regret and condolences to the family and *offered any assistance.* We will be *reviewing all of our procedures* to see what changes need to be made so nothing like this can happen again."

"The fine, if there is a fine, is of less importance to us than the actual incident being brought to our attention, because it allows us to *take the appropriate action to ensure this doesn't happen again.*"

"I'm embarrassed by this. We're definitely at fault there. *We're tightening up our procedures as a result of the investigation.*"

"You are not always going to do everything just right. The key is to *recognize mistakes, correct them* to the best of your ability and *move forward.*"

"Consistently, our effort has been to *do the right thing.* Some are saying there are loopholes in our policy, and we've got to look at that. *I'm willing to do what must be done* to make sure this never happens again."

As countless organizations have learned the hard way, you're usually better off if you are the first to admit to the problem. Studies have shown that people tend to rely on the first source of information. Don't make the mistake of thinking you can keep it a secret—bad news travels fast (and office gossips and reporters love nothing better than a cover-up.)

If it's a legal matter, work out with your attorney what you should say. Tell the attorney "no comment" is not acceptable because you're just as concerned about the court of public opinion.

Three-Legged Stool Supports Sturdy Reply

The following responses contain three of the most important legs that support effective one-sentence or one-hour persuasive statements. They contain logic, emotion, and some sort of standard. (Refer to section 1.4.) As you read the sample responses, look for hard facts and logic, then words that express emotion. Last, look for something that tells the listener if the speaker's points are in the range of reasonableness (what people want to hear is this: We know about the problem, we're concerned about the problem, we're doing something about the problem).

To help you see this powerful combination, read this statement from a university administrator who included all three elements:

"While *it's unfortunate* charges would be filed against any of our students, we do have *71,000 students* that include hundreds upon hundreds of athletes. There's no reason to think that our population of people would not be prone to *some of the same things you find in society at large.*"

Logic with facts: "*We have 71,000 students . . . hundreds of athletes . . .*" (shows perspective: enormous number of students involved)

Words of emotion: "*It's unfortunate . . .*" (shows empathy)

Standards or reference: "*No reason . . . our population would not be prone to the same things . . . in society at large.*" (shows they're in the range of normal or typical)

This three-part combination is particularly effective if your company is unable or unwilling to accept responsibility, or is downplaying the problem's significance. Here again are more comments that include these elements:

> "We did the right thing and *acted appropriately* once the problem was discovered. Do we have a *confidence* problem? Of course. But I wouldn't have done anything differently. We acted thoroughly and openly and always with the *public's interest in mind.*"

> "While we *regret* any mistakes and inconveniences to customers that occurred, they were *not intentional.* We are confident the overwhelming majority of the *27 million vehicles* we serviced in 1991 and 1992 were done properly and safely."

> "We probably made *400 decisions* during the incident and some of them *may have been wrong,* but, by and large, we did a *tremendous job.*"

> "I think that whatever happened was *not done with the intent* to do harm. There were *some* errors in judgment, but I haven't found anybody who calls them right *every time.*"

> "We're talking about *less than 1 percent* of the engines that it's happened to. We've *voluntarily* gone to the U.S. Consumer Product Safety Commission with this information. As we speak, we've got crews out in the field fixing these tanks, *dealing with the situation.*"

> "*I can't imagine,* in the retrospect of this, how we could have done it any differently. Usually I'm one to *second-guess* myself, sometimes ad nauseam, but not in this case."

> "While this incident *is a blemish* on our record, it does not reflect the attitudes or actions of the *vast majority* of our police who are *hard-working, sensitive officers.*"

> "We deny these allegations, and we plan to fight this thing vigorously in court. We feel the notion that there is any sort of price signaling in this industry is *absurd.* If there were, one *would assume* the industry would be showing a profit. Over the past two years this industry has *lost $7 billion.*"

> "We *regret* that abuses were committed, but in no country or government can abuses be *totally avoided.* We can only *learn* from our past mistakes and *establish controls* so that they are not repeated."

Most people will accept a sincere apology and forgive someone who admits his or her transgressions and then makes it clear he or she will do better. ("Go and sin no more.") No, not *everyone,* but most people will. Accepting your apology doesn't mean what you did was right or that you won't have to pay damages; it just means you're sorry. That means a lot by itself.

Just make sure your intentions are sincere. It's unwise (and virtually impossible) to fake sincerity for very long. It is also unwise to confuse sincere apologies with weakness. People who express sincere concern for the suffering of others are also showing their strength of character.

30.2 ARE YOU SAYING YOUR COMPANY DIDN'T CAUSE THIS?

Cause and blame are different. Cause is just that: Something causes something else to happen. But blame incorporates cause with badness, wrongdoing, and implied intention or neglect of duty. You can concede being the cause while making the distinction that blame is something else.

Are you to blame? Are you guilty? If you are and will admit it, the process is easy. If you are not, it's almost impossible to prove your innocence within the limits of a short response to a hostile question. Only in a court of law will you get enough time to prove your point—office politics and public opinion aren't so generous. Our office and the rest of the world, too, demand quick capsulized responses so we can move on to the next rumor or allegation.

But you can create a lot of understanding and even favorable doubt by using elements credible to the audience: simple facts, logic, and relative standards (ethics and values).

> "I understand the *temptation* to lash out and lay blame on someone. But pointing fingers and saying I'm a bad person isn't going to solve anything. Yes, I was part of the *cause* of this accident, but I *didn't do it on purpose.* I regret that it happened, and I accept my responsibility to do everything I can to see that it doesn't happen again."

> "I think when a *tragedy* of this magnitude occurs *it's natural for parents to look for answers.* Even when something happens on the school grounds, the school is clearly *not the only force* in that student's life."

The common emotions and values most of us share are the basis for empathy. Look at the preceding responses to see which naturally appeal to you and study them to find out why. Then you'll be equipped with the skills to create your own persuasive responses to tough questions about cause.

30.3 IF YOU AREN'T GUILTY,
THEN WHY DID YOU SETTLE OUT OF COURT?

Question: Why is it that we often think the other person is guilty as hell if he or she settles at the courthouse steps just before the trial?

Answer: Grade school civics class told us that if we fight for what's right we'll be vindicated by justice.

Reality: We carry that myth into adulthood, a Hollywood romantic ideal that good wins out over evil in the end. Sorry. Any experienced lawyer knows it often doesn't work that way. So you settle if the information indicates you might get creamed in court or if the cost of defense will far exceed the settlement cost.

> "We *deeply regret* the tragedy that occurred. Today's decision was not an easy one to make. While the exact cause and reason for the accident remain unresolved, we believe *it is in the best interest of everyone involved*—our employees, the families of miners who died, and our company—to *resolve the charges* and look to the future."

> "We don't think there's anything *wrong* with the product. The product saves lives. But sometimes you have to settle because a *jury verdict can be very high and no one can predict* what a jury will do. We can't afford to take that *chance.*"

> "A settlement often has *nothing to do with innocence or guilt.* In this instance, we felt that to continue to fight this thing would mean spending a great deal of time and money we'd prefer to spend on programs that will *benefit our employees,* not fill the pockets of lawyers."

Tough Questions Worksheet

Create responses to the difficult questions you could face on this chapter's topics, using the formulas below. Use **logic, emotion,** and **ethics** whenever possible. Experiment by answering the same question with different formulas to learn which best fits your natural style. Use pencil so you can erase and refine your answers.

Past, Present, Future:

What happened was:

What's happening now is:

The way we'll prevent it from happening again is by:

Problem to Solution:

*The **problems** we have are:*

*I'd like to go directly to a proposed **solution:***

Problem - Cause - Solution - Timing (PCST):

*The **problems** we have are:*

*They were **caused** by:*

*The **solutions** we may implement are:*

*Our **timing** is:*

Wrong, Right, and What It Means:

*This is an extremely complex area and our track record has **overall** been very good:*

*We do very difficult things and sometimes we have failures. What **happened** is that:*

*What this **means** for us now is:*

Three-Step Explanation:

I understand what you are asking and why it concerns you so much:

Other people who had your experiences probably would feel the same way:

However, I would like to explain a little about this problem:

Other formulas and responses I want to use for tough questions related to this chapter:

31

Prevailing When You Bug People
for Tardy Work

31.1   *Why are you harassing me when you know I'm not done?*

31.2   *Haven't you noticed we've gotten busier? How can I do more
        without reducing quality and making mistakes?*

31.3   *How can I do ten things at once when I'm only one person?*

The more your projects depend on others, the more opinions, styles, delays, and alternative paths there are. Sometimes it seems as if you're herding rabbits through a cabbage patch. Attention is easily drawn away to more interesting subjects as people amble away on their own agendas. Some sit while others scamper along. Half follow you to the garden gate while others eat the veggies. They're not acting as one.

As the manager, your most frustrating part of heading a project is finding that assignments aren't ready when you need them. As with every major project, you have deadlines, and if all the elements don't fall into line, it will cause big trouble for you.

31.1 WHY ARE YOU HARASSING ME WHEN
YOU KNOW I'M NOT DONE?

As you continue to ask for status reports from tardy staff, they react negatively and you wonder if you are intimidating them by your zeal for this project. Do they see you as part of the team, or as the task master? Will you provoke them and thereby slow them down further? And you certainly don't want to sound like your former autocratic administrator, who stifled creativity with her frequent criticisms woven into inquires about status.

Despite your qualms, you venture out to bug people for their work. The first one contends your question amounts to harassment. When does follow up become harassment? The answer is when the employee thinks so, at least for practical purposes. Don't bother telling the employee your inquiry isn't harassment—that would only cause a useless argument over who's right on that point. Until you resolve, or at least address, the emotional issue, you are not likely to obtain information that will be as complete and useful as you need it.

> "I am sorry if it *sounds like harassment to you. What I am trying to do is ask a question* about where you are with an important assignment. *My interpretation* of this is that I am simply asking a question. I know I've asked it several times this week, but I need to keep track of how close you are to the end. I hope it won't irritate you, but I will need to check with you again several more times until it is completed. What can I do to help you get done? What can I clear out of the way?"

> "I don't mean to harass you or cause stress for you. I am under the gun to get this project in on time. The entire project can't go forward without your piece, *so it's very important.* I really am just trying to see where you are in the process so I can dovetail your work with everyone else's. *I need to keep checking with you often because this is so important.* What else is on your agenda, and which tasks could be set aside? *How much more time will you need for this project and how will it fit into your schedule?*"

These responses attempt to remove at least one barrier between you and the employee by apologizing for how your status inquiry may look like harassment to her. Note that the responses do not agree that the status inquiries are harassment, only that you're sorry she sees them that way.

Dwelling on that point for more than a few seconds wastes time and increases the chance that the two of you could fall into an argument about whether your inquiries constitute harassment. By swiftly returning to the original issue—when the work will be done—you can also use the moment to ask about work load and time commitments that may be causing the delay.

The preceding responses also include a standard, which are the sentences about the importance of the assignment. Inserting such a standard in your response creates a frame of reference that provides perspective to the employee. That could offset a possible feeling by the employee that the assignment is boring or worthless. These responses imply that the employee is important to you because you value her expertise.

As demonstrated in the following, sometimes you may decide that you need to reestablish a new, firm deadline while including a small amount of honest flattery to smooth over ruffled feathers.

> "I realize you're a bit away from completion, but I am very grateful for the effort you've made so far. I can give you a little more time, *but I need it on my desk July 1.* My team requested your help because *you are the expert in this area* and my project is incomplete without your input."

> "This assignment seems like busywork, I know, and there is a lot on your plate, but if you can, *please wrap it up by Thursday.* I will not only be off your back but *I'll let your boss know how valuable you are to this project.*"

31.2 HAVEN'T YOU NOTICED WE'VE GOTTEN BUSIER? HOW CAN I DO MORE WITHOUT REDUCING QUALITY AND MAKING MISTAKES?

When many businesses and agencies downsized, the average workload upsized. At the same time, many business leaders jumped on the Quality-movement bandwagon. At the top, it looks really good. Labor expenses have been cut. The company is more competitive at the global and national levels. That's because they are now speaking the same Quality language and conforming to the same Quality procedures adopted by suppliers, vendors, and the competition nationally and globally.

But the worker bees down your corporate ladder are gasping for air. Not only are people now doing the work of two or three former employees, but now the work needs to be error-free, follow all sorts of documentation guidelines, and still meet deadlines!

If you handle this wrong, you could lose other hard-working employees, which would mean even more work for those left behind and wasted hours for you as you search for and train new people. This is another kid-glove situation for delicate handling. You need productivity, and you don't want your comments to slow them up even more.

> "Yes, I know everyone is extremely busy. And we know the work load is not going to slack off any time soon. *But we've still got to maintain*

quality somehow. We can't keep doing things the same way or we will still have the same problems. We all need to sit down and brainstorm on how we are going to handle things around here. How about we hold a short meeting next Tuesday, or all of us go out for pizza next week after work? It'll be easier to look at the work flow when we're away from the phones and more relaxed."

"Let's get some coffee. We're all getting stressed out. Let's take a break for a bit. *It's crazy around here, and you know it won't get better until we make some changes.* This project has to get worked in somewhere and it will be easier to talk about it away from office distractions."

Acknowledge their weariness from being overworked, but reinforce that this hyperpaced new environment is here to stay. Use your reply to lead your staff toward solutions, while conceding these may be only partial solutions for the immediate future. Help them step back and see the big picture again, how they all fit together.

As shown in the following, when your replies make them a part of the solution and improvement process, you can guide them toward more efficiency and help them maintain work quality and morale.

"Let's make a list of everything we need to do and when. If we prioritize, we can *find some less important tasks to push out of this month's schedule. . . .* Are we doing any jobs that we could *either pass to another department or hire temps to do?* Maybe there are *a few steps* we could eliminate, at least for a few months. This could give you more time to devote to the important projects."

"*Error-free work is a realistic and worthwhile goal.* Everything we can do correctly the first time saves hours we waste having to go back to correct mistakes. *We don't need to slow down on everything,* just agree which jobs need our greatest attention. Sometimes we get so close to a job we miss alternative ways of getting to the same end. Any fresh ideas?"

Doing a good job does not have to mean slowing down. We were always told just the opposite as children, so your replies may need to shatter this myth. Tell the staff that the worldwide Quality Improvement movement is proving speed and quality can go together very effectively every day in the largest and smallest organizations. But answering that your staff must do the *same* things faster will not get better results. It boils down to analyzing your tasks and developing new options and ways, tiny or large, to get to the same end by your deadline.

31.3 HOW CAN I DO TEN THINGS AT ONCE WHEN I'M ONLY ONE PERSON?

In contrast to the previous question, where too many assignments threatened the employee's overall work quality, maybe the person who asks this tough question is single-task minded. Maybe she has difficulty juggling more than one thing at a time. Is she one of those individuals who can do one job well as long as there are few distractions? But, as soon as you start adding on other duties, does she shut down? Is she totally overwhelmed?

Before you respond to her tough question, you need to determine what is the problem confronting you: an employee with far too many assignments, or a person who needs to line up her work in a mental row, so she does not see her assignments as a pile of work clutter.

> "I don't need you to do *all of these assignments at once.* Let me put a stick-on memo on each report that says when it's due. Go through them and estimate how much time each will take you. *Let me know if you will or won't have enough time for all of them*—we can make adjustments if we get to that point. Then you can put assignments in order and just do them from top to bottom. *Will that work for you, or do you have another suggestion?"*

> "Maybe I gave you too much at once. I was trying to clear off my desk. Sorry. Let me start over. When you're done with this report, drop by my office and I'll explain the next document."

These replies may relieve some of her anxiety, so she can focus on one task at a time. The reorganized work load probably will be less stressful even though there are the same number of tasks to do. The preceding comments signal that you are open to making adjustments and that great harm isn't going befall her if everything isn't done immediately, as she apparently feels. They also signal that you welcome her checking with you when she feels she has too much to do in the time available.

The single-task-minded employee is easily distracted and so works better in a quiet environment. Into what environment have you put this person? Because you control more of the conditions than the employee does, you are more responsible for the results caused by them. You might want to assign this person a desk away from high-traffic areas, windows, and chatty co-workers.

Since this employee may have trouble focusing, break large jobs down into smaller pieces to make the work seem less intimidating. It gives the overwhelmed worker breaks, helping to keep frustration from affecting performance.

Tough Questions Worksheet

Create responses to the difficult questions you could face on this chapter's topics, using the formulas below. Use **logic, emotion,** and **ethics** whenever possible. Experiment by answering the same question with different formulas to learn which best fits your natural style. Use pencil so you can erase and refine your answers.

Past, Present, Future:

What happened was:

What's happening now is:

The way we'll prevent it from happening again is by:

Problem to Solution:

*The **problems** we have are:*

*I'd like to go directly to a proposed **solution:***

Problem - Cause - Solution - Timing (PCST):

*The **problems** we have are:*

*They were **caused** by:*

*The **solutions** we may implement are:*

*Our **timing** is:*

Wrong, Right, and What It Means:

This is an extremely complex area and our track record has **overall** *been very* **good:**

We do very difficult things and sometimes we have failures. What **happened** *is that:*

What this **means** *for us now is:*

Three-Step Explanation:

I understand what you are asking and why it concerns you so much:

Other people who had your experiences probably would feel the same way:

However, I would like to explain a little about this problem:

Other formulas and responses I want to use for tough questions related to this chapter:

32

Keeping the Lid on Despite Lurid Questions

32.1 *Do you think it's fair to me that my ex-husband is having an affair right here?*

32.2 *We want the dirt! Who started the affair? Do their spouses know?*

32.3 *This is totally against my values and religion. Why do I have to not only accept but work with homosexual lovers?*

32.4 *I'm not having an affair with her! Are you going to find out who's spreading these rumors?*

Given the powerful, deeply embedded sexual drives of the human animal, sexual tension and attraction in the work place is unavoidable, consequently so are the related tough questions. You as the manager are not really facing anything new. You know that your employees fall in love, date, split up, get married, have marital spats, and otherwise ride the emotional roller coaster of adult relations.

But, seeing all this action "up close and personal" in your work environment can be disruptive, and you know you want to manage the inevitable good and bad feelings delicately. You realize it's unrealistic (not to mention illegal) to ban most relationships, but you need the tools to respond to hostile inquires born out of jealousy, curiosity, and vicarious titillation.

32.1 DO YOU THINK IT'S FAIR TO ME THAT MY EX-HUSBAND IS HAVING AN AFFAIR RIGHT HERE?

Your goal at the company is to manage your department well, not play social worker or be Ann Landers. Yet an employee in a ruined relationship may see your control within the organization and subconsciously assume you can affect her personal problems too. Of course, you have no desire to get in the middle of a relationship spat unless it's truly related to work output.

For several years, your shop manager and the secretary in the sales department suffered through a rocky marriage together that ended in divorce. After a year alone, your shop manager has started dating the new receptionist. They have kept the romance out of view and rarely have contact with each other during the day. The former wife, not fully recovered from the end of her marriage, still harbors a lot of anger. Her unresolved feelings are beginning to irritate other members of the sales department, who have grown weary of her tale of woe even though they like her dearly.

Now she wants you to answer whether its fair to her that her ex-husband is involved with another employee. Because of the extreme sensitivity of the situation, you should consider moving away from specific personal replies to general comments. (See section 2.7 for related ideas.) Going from the specific to the general in this situation may create the space your hurt employee needs to turn herself around. However, you might also add some suggestions for her own personal well being, which is a legitimate concern to you.

> "I know you were hurt pretty deeply, and I feel bad for you. I am willing to do whatever I can to help you to get over this. *However, a manager does not have a right to intervene in anyone's personal life* unless the job is affected. I'm not a counselor, but you may find it helpful to see someone to help you *resolve your feelings.* People who are hurt and don't resolve their feelings can't get on with their lives very well. Don't you deserve to hurt less and get past this sooner? Would you want to talk with someone from our Employee Assistance Program?"

If you prefer to be more direct and personal, consider the following response, which addresses the facts of the situation, the limits of company authority, and the general standard of behavior as reflected in the discomfort of other employees. Each of the three factors can add more influence to your comment.

> "*It's not a job-fairness issue.* I realize you might feel embarrassed by their relationship, but Tom and Kim do their jobs here with no problems. I hope you will find something else to talk about with the sales people. They have to work with Tom and Kim too, *and the staff feel uncomfort-*

able when your comments put them in the middle. I know you don't want to be unfair to your friends here, because they'd like to give you support as you work through your feelings."

"Tom and Kim are rarely together here. *They are not flaunting their relationship.* It's more obvious to you probably because you're much more sensitive to it. Maybe it would be better if you stayed away from Tom's shop and Kim's reception area for awhile and aim some of your pent-up energy into your work. However, seeing a counselor might help you get past this faster. Anyone can resolve these feelings by herself, *but a counselor could help you do it sooner and with less pain.* Don't you deserve that?"

As a boss, it's hard to respond to a tough question like this, because you are not just being asked what's fair. You are also being asked to throw the weight of your opinion (influence and judgment) on her side. She subconsciously wants you to validate her belief that she is "right" and he "wrong" or worse. As a manager, you can't separate your authority from your responses so sometimes it's better to suggest she get social advice from a close friend or counselor, instead of the boss.

32.2 WE WANT THE DIRT!
WHO STARTED THE AFFAIR? DO THEIR SPOUSES KNOW?

There is no communications medium more powerful and demanding than the office gossip machine, always crying to be fed. Now it's trying to find out what you know. Anyone with a good piece of gossip holds others' rapt attention. Yet you know it's just a bit cruel discussing people behind their backs, not to mention invading their privacy. As the boss, you don't want to be involved in spreading the gossip further, so you want to avoid divulging what you know, which would make matters worse.

You and your husband decided to get out of town for the weekend. While relaxing by the hotel pool, he points out a couple publicly displaying their affection. As they walked by arm in arm, you realized they were two of your marketers, both married to other people, both with small children at home. You spent most of the weekend avoiding them, but even the hotel bartender was cracking jokes about the "midlife" teenagers.

Back at work, one of your fellow managers confides that he, too, has seen them out on the town. Your department is hot for new information, now that the grapevine has informed them you were all at the same hotel together.

Although you don't want to slight the rumor mongers, you also don't want to participate in encouraging their gossip. If you choose to shrug off the gossipy inquiry while also attempting to dampen their enthusiasm, you could use a veiled screen like this:

> "*I was too busy to notice* what other people were or weren't doing. I can hardly handle what's going on in my own life much less pay attention to what's going on elsewhere. I haven't heard anything, *but if I had, I wouldn't pay attention to it anyway.*"

> "A lot of people were at the same hotel, eating and talking for hours. I would guess *quite a few rumors got started from that, but that doesn't make them true.* It's none of my business, and I'm too busy with important things."

These responses attempt to steer the listeners to a subtle hint on fair standards of behavior (good people don't gossip much). Sometimes, however, we need stronger reminders about good behavior, so you might add another persuasive element to increase the power of your responses. The following rejoinders add an emotion factor (don't hurt people). If the rumor is solidly believed and you determine that your tactic is to cool down the hot talk directly, you might say something like this:

> "I hate to add fuel to the fire, so I don't have much to say. We didn't see much worth talking about, and I don't want to hurt their families. *Everyone should think twice* before spreading this rumor; *a lot of people will get hurt for no reason.*"

> "*These kinds of things can end up very explosive,* and good people can get hurt. I don't want to have to testify at a divorce hearing, so I'd better keep quiet. *That might be useful advice for a lot of people here today.*"

> "I can get caught up in gossip just like the next person, *so I don't want to sound like a hypocrite.* It's just that I try not to repeat stuff like that when I remind myself of the consequences. *I think we'd all feel pretty bad if people were talking about us like this,* so I don't want to do that to either of these people, or to anyone else."

As the manager, everything you say takes on the power of your position. A slightly critical remark can come across as a sharp rebuke to a less

KEEPING THE LID ON DESPITE LURID QUESTIONS

powerful subordinate. So, too, does repeated gossip; when the manager contributes to it, the ugly rumors build speed and force, increasing the damage to the victim's reputation.

If you don't want to get caught up in the seamy mess of gossip, you can sidestep the questions by bridging to ethics—you don't want to participate in harming these people or their families. Although your responses won't stop the gossip—no one can—your replies can speed up or slow it down, depending on whether you give it a push with more juicy tidbits or slow it down by bridging to ethics.

32.3 THIS IS TOTALLY AGAINST MY VALUES AND RELIGION. WHY DO I HAVE TO NOT ONLY ACCEPT BUT WORK WITH HOMOSEXUAL LOVERS?

Despite laws and court rulings regarding discrimination based on sex—gender and sexuality—placing a homosexual or lesbian employee among some co-workers may nevertheless trigger fear and anger. You realize you must still manage to keep the employees working together even when their religious and social views push them apart. But you know as well that all the laws and business practices in the world can mean nothing when you are faced with deep-seated attitudes and emotions.

Your restaurant is facing a very busy two-week period. Situated on the city's main square, a major musical and dance festival downtown area will mean your walk-in traffic will triple as you are the only sit-down eating establishment in the area.

Two of your four chefs are gay and have been in a monogamous relationship for years. They do stand out in the crowd, but are some of your fastest and most reliable employees. You found that one of your waitresses has two years' experience cooking in a hospital. You need this woman in the kitchen. You've just now discovered her feelings, but your back is against the wall, and you need to convince her that you cannot change the work schedule for the next two weeks. She wants to know why she has to work with "homosexuals."

> "The restaurant is facing its heaviest traffic ever. That means we have to all pull together and put our feelings aside, *or the next two weeks will be hell for us all.* Without your talents in the kitchen, there is no way we

can meet the rush next week. I am not asking you *to like these guys* or approve of them, just be more cordial. *Letting your feelings direct your behavior drags you down,* and it's not worth it. Please set aside your feelings and pitch in. Will you do that?"

Can you identify the three persuasive elements in the above response: logic, emotion, and ethics? The preceding response uses logic in three places:

❒ To produce maximum results, the restaurant's staff team must have efficient teamwork.

❒ It costs her too much to let her feelings run her behavior.

❒ The kitchen can't produce enough food without her talents.

That ethics factor is revealed in the phrases "more cordial" and "to like these guys or approve of them." The emotion factor is there but less obvious. The choice of words, particularly "please" and "hell for us all," would evoke emotional reactions in almost any person. (Refer to section 1.4 for related advice.)

Try to select words that present one or more of these persuasive elements (logic, emotion, and ethic/standard) in the following responses. Not all responses need or have all three elements.

"I understand now how you feel, *but you'll be working so hard there won't be much time for those feelings.* This might be an opportunity for you to learn more about them. *They're not aliens, they're people,* and the other chefs really enjoy cooking with them."

"I know your beliefs are very much against homosexuality. You have your religious views, and other people hold different views. *Our restaurant isn't going to pick sides one way or the other.* These two men are allowed *by law* to work here, just as any of our employees are. No one is asking you to approve of their lifestyle, but we do ask that *you work as well with them as they do with you.*"

"I view these men as good chefs—period. I appreciate that you have made efforts to accept them, but I am asking you to try again. Maybe you can look at them as just members of your work group and *ignore what their lifestyle is outside of this restaurant.*"

32.4 I'M NOT HAVING AN AFFAIR WITH HER! ARE YOU GOING TO FIND OUT WHO'S SPREADING THESE RUMORS?

Gossip that implies an affair is going on when there really isn't one ruins careers, marriages, friendships, and work teams. Even if the basic gossip starts out as accurate, it'll become distorted and overblown quickly as it races through the office grapevine.

As the manager of an accounting firm, you're extremely busy during the current tax season. Gaining a new major account last month meant you had to assign two of your top people to the project. They had to dedicate long hours and weekends together to work through the new data and make the filing deadlines. Most of the time you were there right beside them. Keeping the client happy meant additional time entertaining them and their spouses, and when the job was completed successfully the two employees and you tossed the client a party at the country club.

You couldn't have been happier—until you got a tearful call from the male employee's wife. She received an unsigned note elaborating on the details of the two employees' "affair," claiming to be the reason he wasn't home much these past weeks. You know from firsthand experience this is not true. You've been so busy that you ignored a lot of the office gab, but now you remember an increasing number of teasing comments from various employees. Because the gossips threaten to split your firm down the middle, you know you need to get involved because of that. But you don't want to conduct an inquisition accusing innocent employees and destroying morale.

> "I know you're not having an affair, and I reminded your wife that I was with you two during this assignment. I am very upset about these rumors, too, and I want to stop them. *However, I can't go around accusing everyone. At minimum, I am going to speak personally to each staff member.* I will keep at this until the rumors are stopped. I promise you that."

> "These rumors caused unnecessary family problems for you, *and they are interfering with the operation of this firm.* I do intend to do some discreet asking around. *It would be better if you didn't pursue this yourself.* I want to find who is spreading the rumors and put a stop to them, without hurting other innocent employees."

> "I am sorry about what happened, and I will do whatever it takes to reassure your wife that these rumors are not true. I know you are

---

Tip: Interrupting the big lie is important to morale.

Why should you interfere with the big lie? This is why: If we hear something bad once about a person, we begin **to wonder** about that person. Hear something bad a second time, and we think he **might be** that bad. Hear something bad a third time, and we start to believe it. That's why it's important to include in your responses that you intend to **interrupt the flow** of such rumors, so they don't become the big lie that is repeated so often it's believed and then damages morale.

---

angry, but you know I can't stand up at the next office meeting and demand that the guilty party raise his or her hand. *The inquiry has to be done privately,* if I'm to find out how something innocent was twisted into an alleged affair. *If the rumor was intentional, I will severely reprimand the culprit."*

When responding to pleading inquiries on what you are going to do about upsetting gossip, don't dismiss rumors as worthless information that the victim should just ignore. His reputation has been damaged and he's worried about it, so that makes it very real, not just an imagined concern.

Tough Questions Worksheet

Create responses to the difficult questions you could face on this chapter's topics, using the formulas below. Use **logic, emotion,** and **ethics** whenever possible. Experiment by answering the same question with different formulas to learn which best fits your natural style. Use pencil so you can erase and refine your answers.

Past, Present, Future:

What happened was:

What's happening now is:

The way we'll prevent it from happening again is by:

Problem to Solution:

*The **problems** we have are:*

*I'd like to go directly to a proposed **solution**:*

Problem - Cause - Solution - Timing (PCST):

*The **problems** we have are:*

*They were **caused** by:*

*The **solutions** we may implement are:*

*Our **timing** is:*

Wrong, Right, and What It Means:

*This is an extremely complex area and our track record has **overall** been very **good:***

*We do very difficult things and sometimes we have failures. What **happened** is that:*

*What this **means** for us now is:*

Three-Step Explanation:

I understand what you are asking and why it concerns you so much:

Other people who had your experiences probably would feel the same way:

However, I would like to explain a little about this problem:

Other formulas and responses I want to use for tough questions related to this chapter:

33

Why in My Back Yard?
Great Responses to NIMBYism

33.1   *Why is the company putting that thing in my back yard?*

33.2   *How come you guys never build these things where the rich big shots live? Why do you always avoid those areas?*

33.3   *How do we know this project is really needed?*

33.4   *Won't this pollute the environment?*

33.5   *Why should we trust what you are saying? Aren't they paying you to say whatever they want?*

Wouldn't it be lovely if you and I could be neighbors and our hilltop houses overlooked a lush meadow where deer prance and birds flutter, singing happily ever after? Wouldn't it be nice if you and I had all of that and everyone else lived in those apartments on the other side of the freeway next to the waste-treatment plant, the unsightly transmission lines, the gaudy shopping mall, and the steel-building industrial park? *But Not In My Back Yard (NIMBY)!*

As citizens of our communities and our workplaces, we demand countless services and accommodations while screaming bloody murder if the equipment or byproducts of those services are located near our office desks or our little corner of the world. Whether it's the community or the office, the rule is the same: Put it anywhere but not near me—not in my back yard.

Picture yourself a midlevel technical manager with your vice president in front of a citizen's group at the neighborhood library at 7:30 P.M.

Wednesday. You're there with municipal officials to explain why your recycling company has picked a nearby vacant site on which to build a small plant that will require some truck traffic and larger power lines.

33.1 WHY IS THE COMPANY PUTTING THAT THING IN MY BACK YARD?

This is the granddaddy of them all—"Why put it here?" Don't be misled. The questioner isn't really asking "Why here?" He's getting ready to tell you the answer, but politeness and good tactics require you to start with his supposed question.

Tell them the major reasons while you weave in how this plant and its work force will be good neighbors. You'll accommodate the residents in any reasonable way. If all you do is answer the question but don't also get across the other positive information you have, you'll not succeed. It's a lot like any competitive sport or military action: All defense and no offense means a guaranteed lose.

Use the three persuasive elements: logic, emotion, and standard/ethics. (Refer to section 1.4.) The first of the following replies gives the factual, technical reasons why the site was chosen. But that is not enough. The reply further includes the emotional appeal of ensuring a good appearance and the promise of being a good neighbor. The good-neighbor promise incorporates a good feeling as well as an implicit agreement to behave according to the unwritten neighborhood standard of conduct. Telling people you will be a good neighbor means you promise you won't do anything to offend or threaten them.

> *"There are many reasons* why this site was picked as the best overall. We looked at quite a few *before* this one was selected. One of the most important reasons is that this site fits the city's *strict criteria* for light industrial zoning. The site is big enough so that the building and vehicles will fit in neatly and orderly. *It will have a good appearance.* I understand you may be concerned about some stranger building something near your homes. *But I promise you we will be good neighbors,* we definitely will work with you to find what *we need to do to fit in here."*

> "Let me try to respond to two questions I think I hear. One is why did we pick this site and the other is *how does this plant fit the general area,* including your adjacent neighborhood. If I don't answer your question

---

Tip: Make mistakes in practice to increase success later.

Practice responses to the likely tough questions **before** you go to the meeting. Even if you know the answers inside and out, you don't know that you can **summarize them and weave in your persuasive points** unless you've tried a few times aloud. Consider hiring a public relations firm skilled in this area to help you prepare. (Refer to sections 1.10 and 1.11.)

---

when I'm done, let me know and I'll try again. There are many reasons why this site was picked . . ." (go to response above).

The next quote demonstrates an old but effective sales technique: a "feel, felt, found" answer. If you really have had a similar experience, use this formula to build rapport and encourage them to identify with you.

"I know how you feel. I felt the same way when a similar situation faced my neighborhood. But you know what I found? It was not what I expected. It turned out okay. What we learned was that . . ."

Most people expect you'll try to hoodwink them with fancy talk and hollow words. Surprise them by being straightforward and direct—politely meet the questions head-on. That will win points for you, because you will be talking with them, not at them. The direct approach removes a potential listening barrier in their minds, because they know they don't have to shout to get your attention.

You really don't have a choice when facing these questions—if they've got the intestinal fortitude to ask the questions, they won't accept fancy words in lieu of straight answers. And don't go to the obvious blue-collar neighborhood wearing Gucci shoes. That is not to say that you should go in jeans either. The point is to be sensitive to the audience intellectually, physically, and emotionally.

33.2 HOW COME YOU GUYS NEVER BUILD THESE THINGS WHERE THE RICH BIG SHOTS LIVE? WHY DO YOU ALWAYS AVOID THOSE AREAS?

This question stems from the grand conspiracy myth that the rich and powerful are always above the law and control all the big institutions—

yes, it happens sometimes, but not as much as the movies portray. Your questioner has noticed that the expensive subdivisions filled with doctors, lawyers, and CEOs don't have many commercial and industrial sites nearby. It seems logical to him that the rich folks have some special control behind the scenes.

When NIMBYism arises, build your responses to win acceptance instead of satisfaction. Certainly satisfaction is much more desirable, and go for it if you can do it. However, be prepared to settle for acceptance of whatever it is you are attempting to place near someone's home.

No one wants to live next door to a landfill or similar site, so it is not practical that you will be able to truly satisfy all the NIMBYites. Just think of how you'd feel in their position. If you pin all your hopes on satisfying them no matter what, you may create your own downfall by frustrating yourself while raising the opponents' expectations too high. The only thing they'll be satisfied with is for you to locate it elsewhere.

Therefore, your responses and strategy should be targeted to win acceptance: What do I have to say and do that will cause the opponents to accept the proposed facility? It might be educating them on what is really going in there and how it will operate. It might be listening to what their objections are and adjusting the plans where feasible. Responses that offer compromises might lead to acceptance even though the opponents still won't be satisfied.

> "*I don't know about all the other commercial and industrial sites* in town, but I can talk about *why we picked this site* and why other sites were not selected. We picked this site because . . . (and repeat the criteria and reasons).

If you judge that the hostile questioner and his neighbors may truly be listening, consider this comment. It says that lots of people over a long period of time made many independent decisions, including well-off people who buy the more desirable (and more costly) land farther away from areas zoned for commercial and industrial purposes. This comment would be the beginning of a longer explanation, which should be attempted only if the audience has calmed and is ready to listen.

> "This city, like most cities, was built over a hundred years, and many people made thousands of decisions on where to put what. What I've noticed is that the most desirable *and most expensive* residential areas are usually *built pretty far from commercial and industrial areas, not the other way around*."

33.3 HOW DO WE KNOW THIS PROJECT IS REALLY NEEDED?

Here the questioner is actually asking two questions. Is the facility actually needed? And the more important but hidden question is: Where's your proof that it is really needed?

This is a watershed question. It will determine whether support will flow to you or away from you. The audience, possibly the news media too, will be listening. They might have video cameras or tape recorders going, so your answer may live on for a long time.

Use the question as an opportunity to educate listeners by bridging to information that supports your claim that the facility is imperative. If you are prepared, you could effectively employ the SIA formula (Simplify, Illuminate, Advance; see section 2.6 for related information).

You can clear up a lot of misunderstanding by simplifying what exactly is being planned. That may offset the ever-present rumors. Educate listeners on how the facility will operate safely. Advance your cause by adding your commitment to the future and the process you will follow to fulfill your promises.

To employ the SIA formula for a complex issue, you must know more than the who-what-where-why-and-how of your project. You must also be ready with specific, concise responses to these opposites:

- ❒ Why *not* later?

- ❒ Why *not* a different type?

- ❒ Why *not* somewhere else?

- ❒ Why *not* by someone else?

- ❒ Why *not* a different method?

This response effectively weaves in all five considerations, directly or indirectly.

> "We need this facility built as *soon as possible,* otherwise the cost will double. We have the *most experienced* project team available. The team considered every *practical alternative,* including not building anything. This is the *most cost-effective and least disruptive* option of all our choices. All the other sites *lack* adequate road access or sufficient parking. The recycling method proposed for this plant will have the *least effect* on the environment. I can offer details on that if you'd like."

33.4 WON'T THIS POLLUTE THE ENVIRONMENT?

Conventional wisdom holds that we are poisoning planet Earth and all of us on it. We all have heard about the scientific evidence supporting that view. Consequently, every additional construction site and new product can be seen as another assault against the Earth and a step closer to our demise. Hence you not only have to deal with local NIMBYism but with worldwide impacts, too.

The days of the ruthless robber barons and uncontrolled environmental irresponsibility are long gone, but the polluted legacy remains, reflected daily in news accounts and suppertime discussions. Responding to questions about whether your proposal will hurt the environment requires the most sincere and thorough comments about your stewardship of the piece of Earth you want to use.

Tell them that as a responsible corporate citizen (emotional appeal), you recognize your duty (standard/ethic) to join in with the rest of humanity to protect the local and world environment, which we will hand over to our children someday. Stewardship requires careful planning and self-discipline, unlike the daring and careless exploiters who conquered the wilds but left a legacy of pollution and hazardous wastes.

If your responses demonstrate your true commitment to stewardship, you will have a better chance of winning a housewarming instead of a lawsuit from your new neighbors. First, consider asking them diplomatically to open their minds, which probably closed tight when they heard of the proposed construction.

> "I would like to make a special request of each of you here today. I ask that—for at least a couple of minutes—you turn off your perception of me—whatever it may be. *Please hold back your judgment of what I will say until you've heard my short explanation.* Please listen as though what I am saying might be true; then judge it afterwards—you can always throw it out of your mind. *But you may not really hear me if you let your perceptions shape my words. . . .*"

If you don't think you should or need to ask for their unbiased attention, you could go directly to this type of response:

> "While we may wish it weren't true, we need to realize *that there is no environmentally benign way to build anything.* Anytime you cut a tree, open the ground for a building, release something into the air, or dis-

turb the water, you affect the environment. I don't suggest for a moment that our proposal won't change the environment somewhat, but I do believe *the changes will be extremely small.* I could elaborate on that if you'd like. . . ."

"Although you may have good reason to doubt the motives of anyone proposing a new building near your neighborhood, I know our *organization is committed to having a clean and healthy community.* We realize also that if our communities are going to have jobs, products, and services, we must find ways to do that without polluting the environment. Our proposed plant will use the best environmental technology available. *We've learned from the mistakes other people have made, and we aren't going to repeat them.* We will be monitored, and the information will be public, so you can help us keep our word."

"We have studied every environmental aspect regarding this site. We have consulted the best experts available and continue to seek input from anyone who wishes to comment. If you think our team may have missed something, let us know, and we'll check it out. *We will continuously review environmental information and improve our methods even more.* We'd welcome your involvement to help us make this the *cleanest operation possible.*"

33.5 WHY SHOULD WE TRUST WHAT YOU ARE SAYING? AREN'T THEY PAYING YOU TO SAY WHATEVER THEY WANT?

About the time that you have completed a masterful job establishing the need and irrefutable logic for the recycling plant at the disputed site, someone pulls the rug out from under you. They ask what nearly everyone readily believes—that everyone's integrity can be bought. The corollary is that all experts lie if the price is high enough.

Since you can't physically open your soul so they can read the inscripted message saying you aren't lying to them, how do you land on your feet with this question? How do you retain credibility when the questioner is trying to yank away the integrity on which you stand?

Integrity, like beauty, lies in the eye of the beholders. If the beholders believe you share the same values and generally act like them, they are more likely to believe your integrity. You can add that you share common concerns, such as your concern for your own family, but then bridge to something more tangible. Bridge to the facts on which the decisions are based. If you are properly prepared, you should be able to clearly explain the key facts so that any lay person can understand the fundamentals.

> "I can answer your question *but only you can determine if you should trust me*. Yes, I am paid for doing my job, *just like all of you have been paid in your jobs*. Like all of you, I strive to be an honest person, someone I can look at in the mirror and feel good. And like you, I value the important things in life such as my family, my integrity, and certainly my job and paycheck. Yes, there are a few people who will say anything for a buck. *But I'm not one of them*. We determine honesty by a person's track record. You can check any of the projects I have worked on and you will find I have been honest and straightforward with everyone I've dealt with. *All of my recommendations are based on facts* we have gathered, and that's where you can check me out. *The facts speak for themselves, so you won't have to rely just on what I say*."

That being done, your credibility should naturally rise. Remember that no matter how much you protest the insinuation regarding your honesty, no amount of bluster will ever force them to believe you. Indeed, just the opposite happens (Shakespeare: Me thinks thou dost protest too much . . ."). Reinforce your integrity by bridging back to the facts every time.

Tough Questions Worksheet

Create responses to the difficult questions you could face on this chapter's topics, using the formulas below. Use **logic, emotion,** and **ethics** whenever possible. Experiment by answering the same question with different formulas to learn which best fits your natural style. Use pencil so you can erase and refine your answers.

Past, Present, Future:

What happened was:

What's happening now is:

The way we'll prevent it from happening again is by:

Problem to Solution:

*The **problems** we have are:*

*I'd like to go directly to a proposed **solution:***

Problem - Cause - Solution - Timing (PCST):

*The **problems** we have are:*

*They were **caused** by:*

*The **solutions** we may implement are:*

*Our **timing** is:*

Wrong, Right, and What It Means:

*This is an extremely complex area and our track record has **overall** been very **good:***

*We do very difficult things and sometimes we have failures. What **happened** is that:*

*What this **means** for us now is:*

Three-Step Explanation:

I understand what you are asking and why it concerns you so much:

Other people who had your experiences probably would feel the same way:

However, I would like to explain a little about this problem:

Other formulas and responses I want to use for tough questions related to this chapter: